"Protective Custody"

"Protective Custody"

A Family Imprisoned by the Japanese
1942 - 1945

Thomas P. Lewis

PHP

Personal History Press
Lincoln, Massachusetts

A Note from the Publisher

Personal History Press is proud to publish Thomas Lewis's *"Protective Custody."* The riveting text was written by Mr. Lewis soon after he returned to the United States, from notes he made while imprisoned. Twenty-first century readers will notice a few allusions concerning ethnicity that would be expressed differently today, but are artifacts of the time and circumstances. We know the author's true perspective, because late in the book he writes, "Will the lessons of this World War II, the war that should end all wars, teach us values in tolerance and brotherhood that will make Peace on Earth available to all mankind?"

Copyright 2020 Donald Lewis

ISBN: 978-0-9983619-8-7

Library of Congress Control Number: 2020905892

PHP

Personal History Press
Lincoln, Massachusetts

*To the soldiers of the 1st Cavalry Division
flying column of February 3, 1945.
Their courage and sacrifice
saved the prisoners at Santo Tomas.*

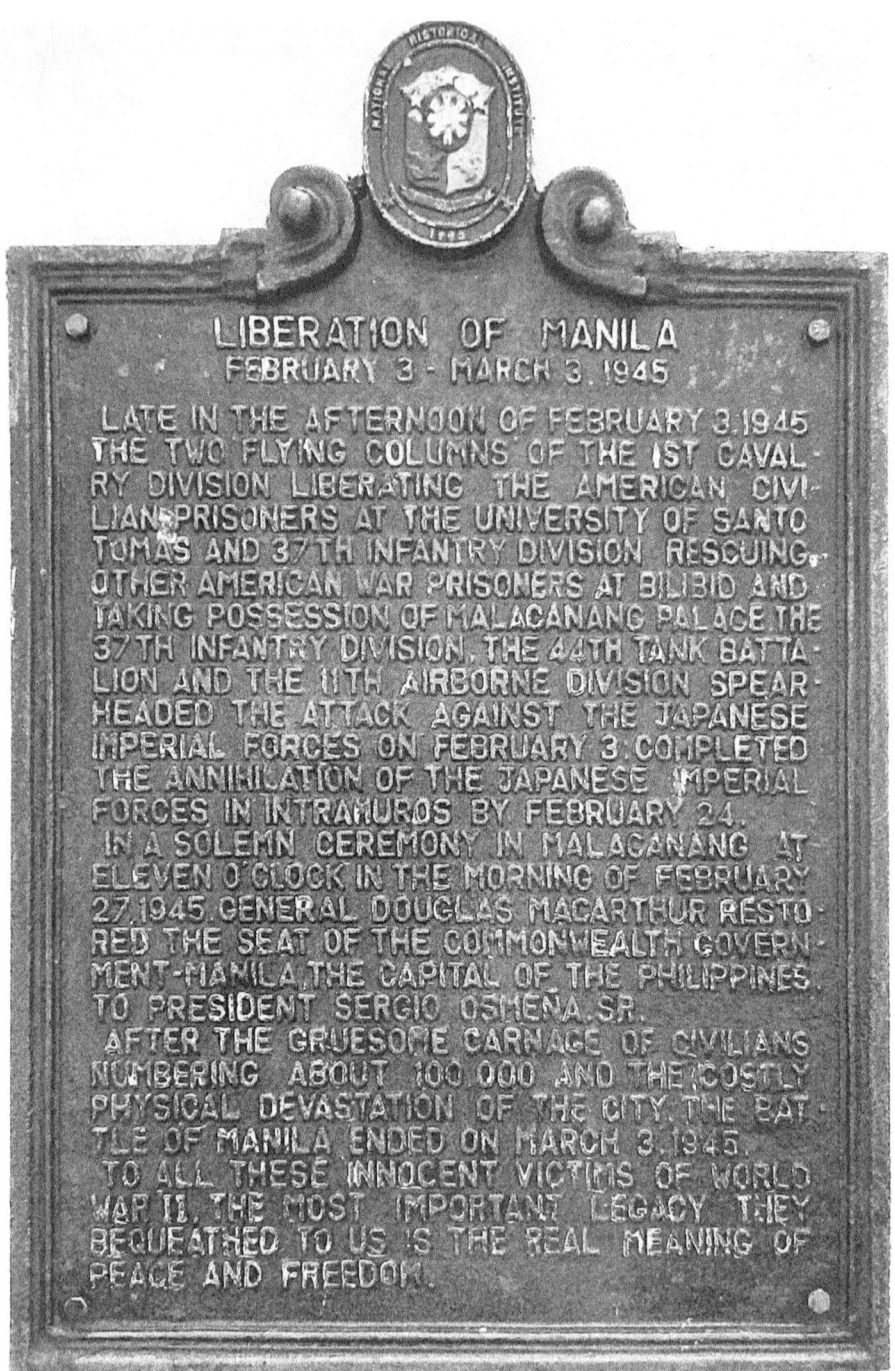

Historical marker in Manila

Foreword

    This is a true story of an American family's survival during World War II that should be heard and remembered.

    These are the words of my father, Tom Lewis who with my mother, Eleanor fought bravely through the suffering and deprivation of over three years of internment in Santo Tomas civilian concentration camp. They labored and sacrificed in order that we could survive our incarceration—no easy task with two little boys to care for. At the time we entered Santo Tomas, my brother Roger was three years old. I was an infant of seven months.

    This book was completed after the war using copious notes written during our imprisoned years and kept safe by stuffing them into the bamboo that framed our shanty. "Protective Custody" is the term used by the Japanese military establishment to mask the activities behind the walls of War Prisoner Camp No. 1, Manila, Philippine Islands.

    It is a tribute to the bravery and perseverance of not only my family, but the more than 3,000 other internees in this camp attempting to survive behind barbed wire. Many did not make the long journey and died from tropical diseases, malnutrition or Japanese brutality.

    Fortunately, Mom, Dad, Roger and I, after three long years, were able to outlast the Japanese and were finally liberated and returned to the USA in 1945 via military transport ship. We were the lucky ones. The four of us plus my four younger sisters, Diane, Claire, Lori and Irene were reminded frequently that our life in America should not be taken for granted and always appreciated.

We went on to spend a lifetime of thanks and happiness for all we have. Dad passed away in 1985 at the age seventy-one and Mom lived to the ripe old age of ninety-two, leaving a legacy of six children, nineteen grand-children, twenty-three great-grand-children and one great-great-grand-child. We lost Roger recently at the age of seventy-nine and little sister Lori way too early at sixty-three. Although I was very young during those years in the camp, I will always remember and be grateful for their courage, strength and everlasting love.

Don (Donny)
February 2020

Thomas Lewis holding baby Donny in 1941

I

Guatemala, "Land of Eternal Spring" had been our home for most of the last three years. The capital, where our rented chalet was located, nestled on a plain some 5000 feet above sea level with the Sierras on one side and the Pacific slope on the other. The climate was ideal with constant sunshine, warm days and cool nights, interrupted only by the seasonal rains, which came, as they said, "by appointment."

My territory was all of Central America with the major portion of my time divided between Guatemala and El Salvador, our biggest markets. We had arrived in the early months of Eleanor's first pregnancy and our son Roger was born at the Hospital Rosales in San Salvador in September 1938.

To date we had thoroughly enjoyed our living experience in both of the latter countries, having visited the colorful mountain villages of the Quiche and Cakchiquel Indians. We spent a glorious weekend at Tzanjuyu on the shores of Lake Atitlan whose still deep blue waters reflect the surrounding peaks, some of which rose to a height of more than 13,000 feet. Only thirty miles from Guatemala City is located the historic headquarters of the Conquistadores, Antigua. The town, which is located at the foot of the 12,000-foot volcano, Agua, contains many of the buildings constructed in the sixteenth century, still in good condition and, as in the case of the Palacio de los Capitanes, in use today.

On the road to Antigua one could see at a distance the still active cones of Fuego and Acatenango, the latter rising over 13,500 feet, and occasionally belching smoke and ash. Guatemala's rugged highlands stretched north-westerly some five hundred miles to the Mexican border and along the way, from vantage points along the so-called "Carretera Internacional" or the Pan-American Highway, all seven of Guatemala's volcanoes, live and extinct, could be seen in a single line, cresting the broad slopes to the Pacific.

Guatemala's and El Salvador's lush lowlands on the Pacific, or wet side of the Sierras, produced bananas, sugar cane and some rice, while higher up on the slopes, some of the world's finest coffee grew. Sparse rainfall to the east of the mountains resulted in a vast desert area where cactus, sisal, and maguey were the only greenery to be seen. In the mountains, the Indians produced corn but only as their own staple while their women busied themselves with dyeing, weaving, and patterning the cloth which has become world-famous for its color and beauty of design. Like all resident foreigners, Eleanor spent a good deal of time collecting Mayan artifacts and cloth.

Guatemala City was extraordinarily clean and modern and boasted an elegant cinema patterned after New York's renowned Roxy Theatre. We saw *Gone with the Wind* in what turned out to be the social event of the year at the Lux!

Is it any wonder then, that October 2nd, 1940 became one of the most fateful days of our young lives when my boss, Walter Partrick, paid us a short visit, all the way from the home office, to ask us if we would give all this up? This was to be the chance of a lifetime for us, a new assignment which would mean moving to the Orient where I would manage their Philippine business and eventually, if all turned out as planned, to be responsible for all of their interest in Southeast Asia. An added carrot was the chance to visit Japan and China en route to Manila, which would be our home base.

Walter pointed out that Parke Davis's third largest export market was at that time the Philippine Commonwealth and I would carry with me plans to establish a manufacturing plant and expand sales into Malaya, Java, Sumatra Borneo, and New Guinea. The exoticism of lands far distant whetted our imagination but Eleanor's willingness to travel turned out to be the deciding factor. With the added responsibility came financial incentives that finally tipped the scales in my boss's favor. We also felt that, as is common with some employers, an opportunity, once offered and turned down, would not be quickly repeated.

The affirmative answer given to Mr. Partrick the next day initiated a series of complicating factors. Eleanor was now pregnant with our second child and delivery was scheduled for April. She would be forced to go on to New York ahead of me since neither Pan-American Airways nor the United Fruit Company Steamship Line would carry her later than the start of her eighth month. I would have to stay on until my replacement was on the scene and appropriately introduced to all of our market in Central America. To cover the five republics would take until mid-March at least.

As a result of our new plans, Christmas and New Year's were a bit hectic as much preliminary running around would be necessary to obtain passage, get exit visas and go through the usual red-tape of leaving a foreign country and returning to the United States. We booked passage for Eleanor and Roger on the February 5th sailing of the S.S. *Antigua* out of Puerto Barrios, Guatemala's only Caribbean port. We gave up the chalet and I rented an old room at the Hotel Palace, a quiet residential place away from the tourist trade, I hoped! I had stayed there during my first brief, introductory tour of Guatemala, before Eleanor had joined me on my return trip to what had then become a "permanent assignment."

By the time the sailing date had rolled around, Eleanor had become nervous and uncomfortable with a seven-month bulge under her belt! I would miss my family, and to prolong our parting I arranged a business trip to Puerto Barrios with customer calls along the return trip. We were able to enjoy the spectacular trip down the eastern slope of the Sierra by train, together. Leaving Guatemala City at 5000 feet, early in the morning, the old narrow-gauge railroad wound its way with the help of switchbacks and hair-raising trestle-crossings down into the desert country below. After many stops and a jolting, tiring ride of some nine hours, the train reached the port terminus where Eleanor's ship awaited.

The train trip was always interesting despite its length. Its reason for being was primarily the transport of bananas which were picked up in the lush wetlands of both the west and east coastal areas of the country. The United Fruit Company maintained large plantations at Tiquisate in the western lowlands and at Bananera and Quirigua in the east. The latter settlement was noted for the discovery of Mayan stelae, stone monuments whose carved inscriptions told much of the early Mayan civilization, dating back to as early as 500 A.D. Naturally the train stopped at these settlements and also at towns which hugged the banks of the shallow river which meandered along near the railroad right-of-way for many miles. At each stop, the passenger cars were besieged by vendors of all sorts of unidentifiable foodstuffs, eagerly gobbled up by most of the coach passengers. Our car was euphemistically called an "Observation Parlor Car" and we were its only occupants for most of the trip. It did have some mohair-upholstered settees which were far more comfortable than the wooden benches of the third-class section.

As soon as we disembarked from the train, we were rushed through Customs and Immigration so that Eleanor and Roger could board the Antigua, due to sail almost at once. I hugged my curly-haired two-and-a-half-year-old and told him to take care of his mommy until I could be with them once again. I wished Eleanor a smooth and safe passage remembering the bout of seasickness with which she was laid low for most of the trip from New York to Guatemala.

Loneliness overwhelmed me as I stood on the dock, waving the departing flagship of the "Great White Fleet" out of sight. Eleanor and Roger would not lack attention as the ship carried merrymaking tourists en route home from other Caribbean ports. I now faced seven or eight weeks of tedious, unending work, relieved only by the training and travel incidental to producing my qualified successor. As it turned out, my assignment was finished by the end of March, too close to the arrival of our new baby to be comfortable. Furthermore I was now scheduled to participate in the training of several Latin Americans, recruits for Argentina, Cuba, and Mexico, starting the week of April 7th, in Detroit. The baby was due April 1st and I would dock in New York on March 28th!

We had never heard of "Murphy's Law" but here was a classic example. Everything that could go wrong did! It started with the baby being late—and neither Eleanor nor I would tolerate being apart at the time the birth would occur. This and subsequent events created a real "pressure cooker" for me during the next two weeks. The company was most considerate and the new men awaiting my arrival in Detroit were given a few extra sightseeing holidays which they surely appreciated, but even these favors had their limits. So I was told finally that on Monday April 14th, the training sessions would begin with me, or without me!

As the days moved rapidly on to my deadline, nature held back for a showdown. Now well past the forecast delivery date, I was forced to make the decision to go on to Detroit the night of Sunday, April 13th, in order to be on hand for opening training session. I left Grand Central Station at 8:30 p.m. on the "Wolverine" and after a sleepless night reached Detroit the following morning, taxiing to the Book-Cadillac where reservations had been made for my stay. I was greeted at the desk by our Vice-President for Foreign Marketing and a reception clerk with an urgent message that Eleanor was in labor at Christ Hospital in Jersey City, New Jersey!

My dismay would have touched a heart of stone and Dick Jeeves was only human after all. He said, "Tom, I'll help you get a flight back to Newark and, don't worry, I'll handle your duties until you get back here…but no later than tomorrow, I hope!"

I did everything but kiss his hand and within the hour I was in the air on an American Airlines DC-3. Thanks to fast taxi service from the airport, I was at Christ Hospital by 1:30 p.m. but in spite of everyone's efforts our baby boy, to be called Donald Edward, arrived minutes before I did! I was able to see my wife and determine that all was well. She was still groggy but sufficiently alert to say, "Isn't it wonderful! A beautiful boy. Where were you?"

My joy was dampened when I told her what had happened and that I had to fly right out again. My remark that she was in good hands didn't do much to cheer her up but I had to leave her now and I knew that she would eventually understand.

II

The next two weeks dragged along but once completed I was back home and ready to comply with Company's instruction to reach Manila no later than mid-June. My first approach to the Passport Agency in Washington was met with the cruel categoric refusal to permit my wife and children to go further than Honolulu. After traveling so far together in the Western World, I was not about to wander off to the Orient all by myself. I presented my problem to the Home Office and they in turn contacted their distinguished Washington attorney who arranged for a personal interview with the Passport Bureau chief; a Mrs. Shipley. En route to the meeting, I put my best possible presentation together, anticipating strong opposition from an unsympathetic female bureaucrat. I was depressed by the rumor that our ship, the S.S. *President Coolidge*, flagship of the American President Lines, would probably carry no women passengers beyond Honolulu, her first port of call out of San Francisco, and that she was to become a military transport possibly by the time we would be scheduled for sailing. I also heard that orders had been issued to various Far Eastern Commands to return all military wives and children to mainland U.S. by earliest transportation available. This was the most disturbing news of all.

I reached Washington and was told by our attorney that I would have to go unaccompanied to lay my plea before Mrs. Shipley herself. The appointment had been made and I approached it with little confidence, realizing now that I was asking my wife and two young children to share an entirely new risk, the grave possibility of our entry into the war against the Axis powers. Although the Far East seemed a long way from the European hostilities, Japan was flirting with Germany and Italy, probably in order to gain important trade concessions with the United States. I knew that I had to go. My job was at stake and I really never believed that the war would escalate to the Pacific.

As I trudged up the wide marble staircase leading to the Passport Office, I realized that the woman I was about to face could have little sympathy for our cause. She would be protective and unyielding in her attitude that our women and children had no business in a war-endangered area and that would be the official State Department position to which she was subject.

At first, after being ushered into her presence, I was nervous and ill at-ease but her surprisingly warm and friendly personality quickly made me feel quite comfortable. Mrs. Shipley wanted to know all about our travels together in the West Indies and Central America and seemed impressed with our abilities with languages, and our easy assimilation into the Latin-American community to the extent of having our first child born in San Salvador. She was well informed as to the quality of life in the Philippines and said that we could handle that change without difficulty.

Her final decision came as a result of two things. I quoted Eleanor's final admonition that she would rather be with me than to have me go alone, and wherever we went, the children would have to go too! Mrs. Shipley confessed to having her final reservations put to rest by the U. S. press reaction to the joint declaration by General MacArthur and President Manuel Quezon yesterday reiterating the impregnability of Corregidor and other defenses on Luzon, plus the size and effectiveness of the half-million-man Philippine army.

The issuance of our passports with permission to travel to Japan, China, and the Philippines was not granted without many admonishments from Mrs. Shipley, especially, in the event of the slightest suggestion of hostilities, Eleanor and the children would be sent home immediately. Since that would have been my intention, I easily assured her that I would carry out such a promise.

So, one day, early in May just three weeks after Donald's entry into the world, we gathered together our sons, dog, thirty-six pieces of baggage, including the wedding gifts we had stored during our stay in Latin-America, in one confusing mob scene at Grand Central Station. Both of our families were there to see us off since we would not be returning for four years according to my contract. We had been able to book not only ourselves and luggage on the "Advance Commodore Vanderbilt" which would take us to Chicago where we would transfer to the "City of San Francisco," Southern Pacific's crack train to the coast, but our new car and such necessities as baby carriage, bathinet, and other hard to-come-by necessities would also accompany us on the same trains.

We pulled out of the station at 8:30 p.m. full of excitement over the dreams of new worlds to conquer. The four-day train trip, with all of its inconveniences, was a huge adventure highlighted by meeting newlyweds Robert Taylor and Barbara Stanwyck on the platform at Cheyenne. They were friendly and a most handsome couple, tanned and radiant after a honeymoon in the mountains of Wyoming. That was another note for our book of mementos.

Reno, the "biggest little city in the world" gave us material for personal jokes about divorce, being the famous spa for such "splits" in that era. At this time nothing was more remote to us than the dissolution of our marriage which had endured the many trials and tribulations of "living abroad"!

The High Sierras were still deep in snow drifts and Lake Tahoe was a jewel in the setting of pine-forested mountains. Our train negotiated the hairpin curves which made possible a difficult passage over the series of rugged mountains between Nevada and California. The final night aboard brought early darkness and we tucked away all hands soon after dinner, happy with the thought of an early arrival in Oakland the next day.

The venerable Palace Hotel was our address for the next week, pending the departure of the S.S. *President Coolidge*. Our new car had been delivered to us without delay so that we had the advantage of our own transportation during our stay. Some wonderful cousins of mine made our stay most enjoyable through sightseeing tours of the majestic redwoods, Sausalito, the Coit Tower and other stops too numerous to mention. For generations, this branch of my family had populated and developed the lush San Joaquin Valley, raising apricots and other produce to the extent that my father's first cousin had been known as "The 'Cot King" in his time. I was proud of this heritage even though I was a "distant" relative in terms of geography.

Donny, like all good babies, slept most of the time while Roger amused himself being "Sniffy's" trainer and guardian. "Sniffy" of the undistinguished name was a pedigreed toy Boston Terrier, black and white and cute as any eight-month-old puppy could be. We had carried him from his birthplace, San Salvador, to Guatemala, to New York, and now onward to the Far East. He was healthy and seemed to thrive on our kind of travel.

Eleanor had regained her figure, to her delight, and was in the best possible mental as well as physical condition. My mind was weighted down with the vital decision I had made and which would certainly affect our lives and future happiness. Once on board ship, there was no turning back and we stood quietly side by side, on deck, as we watched Alcatraz, the Presidio, and, finally, the Golden Gate, slide by. Suddenly, or so it seemed, we were out in the broad Pacific watching the California shoreline disappear in the misty distance until finally there was just the endless horizon and the immense sea and our momentary loneliness.

This ship was huge to us, who had only several trips in banana boats to compare. Activities began almost immediately, and we were soon aware that very few passengers had been booked beyond Honolulu and of these only two were women! The remaining males were military in the majority and once we had cleared Hawaii we found some wonderful new friends. Ray Spivey and Mary Berry were to be married upon their arrival in Manila and we all looked forward to getting together once we were settled. Mary had a cute Pekingese with the unlikely name of "Tin Pu" who in turn became "Sniffy's" best friend. They shared the kennel area on the top deck all to themselves and being its only occupants received more than their share of attention throughout the entire trip.

The many passengers who disembarked at Honolulu were identified either as servicemen or their returning wives. We heard "Pearl Harbor" mentioned over and over and the various branches of service in that area were getting a good share of those departing passengers. Our first visit to the Territory was short but memorable. We had time for an afternoon swim at the Royal Hawaiian Hotel as well as a short tour of Waikiki and the city of Honolulu.

As we again sailed from the harbor, the remaining passengers gathered along the rails to cast their leis into the sea, a tradition signifying that someday they would return.

Once at sea our lives became fairly routine. Roger no longer waited for Mother or Daddy to take him up to the game room after breakfast. He was sought out regularly by a friendly marine, Major Jensen, also Manila bound, or, if he got there first, an Army captain who was bound for Tientsin in northern China. Both had left their own young sons back home with their mothers intending to bring them out at a later date. One morning Eleanor and I could not locate Roger in his usual haunts and after checking with a couple of friends were told that he was last seen on his way to the cocktail lounge with a couple of young Navy Lieutenants in tow. We got there just in time to see him draining a shot glass apparently filled with beer! He was perched on top of the bar with the bartender enjoying the scene and Mother was about to light into all three of them when they quickly assured her that the glass contained nothing more than ginger-ale.

Several days out of Honolulu we were informed that the noted explorer/author, Richard Halliburton, was crossing the Pacific from west to east in a Chinese junk and that he and his crew would be in sight off the starboard bow shortly thereafter. All hands were there to see the strange craft as it passed us nearby, all sails set and slowly proceeding over the vastness of the ocean toward its distant destination. The forward part of its hull was nose down in the water and the stern so high it seemed that the captain must look down from the heights equal to a six or seven story building. The hull was gaily painted and the sails were decorated with oriental figures which we could not identify because of the distance between us.

This sighting was the last contact known to be made by the Halliburton vessel in his ill-starred adventure. Long overdue later, it had to be assumed that their frail craft perished with all hands, probably in a sudden Pacific storm, somewhere to the east of our position.

During the latter part of our twenty-one day journey our thoughts turned to the folks we had left behind, both at home and in California. We talked of our plans for the immediate future. We thought of the people we would meet, their language, customs and how we would adjust. Eleanor had been a staunch and ready partner when it came to severing home ties, despite the close relationships she had always experienced with her mother, father and brothers. For a girl who had previously traveled no further from home than Washington or Albany or Atlantic City, she had never expressed any reservation about living in the West Indies or Central America, certainly drastic changes from the quiet sedate home life to which she had been accustomed. Not only had she survived the new environment, but also had two babies en route and was now about to enter a third and even more unusual environment than that of her past four and a half years. I was proud of her and of myself for choosing such a wonderful mate. Not only was she beautiful, but also a perfect, in my book, wife and mother. She may have had uneasy thoughts at various points along the way of our lives, but if she did, she never let me know them.

Originally scheduled to stop at Kobe, Japan, the ship sailed on by as deteriorating diplomatic relations between the U.S. and Japan made the call inadvisable. En route to our next scheduled stop, Shanghai, we entered the East China Sea with a sudden and dramatic change in the color of the water around us. The clear blue Pacific gave way to the silty yellow of the waters deposited by the Yangtze at her delta. This, one of the great rivers of the world, traverses China in navigable condition from the far western province of Yunnan across more than a thousand miles of rugged mainland to its mouth thirty or so miles east of Shanghai. Its name changes from province to province but to the outside world it is always the Yangtse Kiang.

We were well within the mouth of the river before land actually came in view. The delta area was so flat and treeless that its land was suitable only for the cultivation of rice. The paddies seemed to melt into the river making it seem as though flood conditions existed all over the land. We learned later that most of the seemingly flooded terrain was in its natural state, as dikes, hidden from our eyes, controlled the entry of water into the rice paddies. We left the Yangtze at the confluence of the Huangpu, a small tributary which would bring us upstream to Shanghai. As the ship turned ponderously into the narrow river, we saw the fortified city of Woosung to our right. Sampans and junks in increasing numbers could be seen along the river banks and as our ship began to penetrate their ranks, they passed us without breaking stride. To us the faces were indistinguishable, one from the other. Nowhere did we see a smile or any sign of recognition. It was as though our great ship and its curious passengers were just part of the usual scenery.

The sampans were uniformly propelled by sweeps backed by rag-tag sails. They carried whole families with each member seemingly available for the arduous task of moving their domicile up or downstream. Their faces echoed a hopelessness that made clear to us their poverty. Their clothes were drab, tattered and dirty.

Obviously, the sampan saw their life begin, struggle, and end as most of the families consisted of babies and elders along with the mid-aged adults.

Our nostrils were assailed with unfamiliar odors, pungent, combining wood smoke with spices and strange cooking. There must have been considerable vegetable decay as well as human waste as the muddy river was turgid with clumps and unidentifiable masses. We remarked to one another that we wouldn't want to fall overboard here!

As we proceeded up the river slowly and into the greatly overpopulated metropolitan area of the city of Shanghai, the very atmosphere seemed to be charged with misery and death. In the now-twilight, we noticed shapeless forms in the dark polluted waters through which we slowly moved. Some whispers said that they must be the dead bodies of the starving refugees who had perished and been thrown into the river. We wondered if the ancient practice of the poor was still carried out, that of drowning unwanted girl babies!

In mid-river we dropped anchor, just beyond the city limits. A motley assortment of boats, "water-taxis," came at us from all sides, most of them under human propulsion. Crescent-shaped sampans, with the women dressed in typical chino pants and black cotton shirt, standing high in the stern, pushing slowly and patiently their long poles to move their sampans into the ship's lights. As they came close to the vessel, the rest of the family adopted various attitudes of supplication, hoping that some coins would be thrown down to them by the rich "foreign devils" now lining the ship's rails. Their sing-song voices provided a new kind of musical background to this scene. We were moved to pity at the overwhelming poverty of these countless boatloads of people which quickly surrounded the *President Coolidge*. The conflicts which pitted Chinese against Chinese plus the invasion of the Japanese to the north of Shanghai were driving hordes of refugees to this now overflowing metropolis. The result had to be wholesale starvation for these hopeless masses.

The fighting between the Nationalists and the Mao-led Communists was indecisive and destructive to most of the civilian population and the added threat of a Japanese invasion caused the responsible parties to agree upon an "open city" status for Shanghai. So we were safe for our short visit, even though we were warned of risks in the event that we strayed from the downtown shopping area. This was fine with us as it included the night clubs, gambling casinos and stores.

Our friend, Frank Jensen, Major, U.S.M.C. offered to baby-sit for our boys while Eleanor and I went ashore for a night club tour. He assured us that knowing Shanghai from a previous tour of duty, he had no great desire to see it again. Most of all he simply missed his own kids and would have a great deal of fun taking care of ours for a short time. Concern over bottles, feeding schedules and diaper changes were banished by the nurse who promised to look in at the appropriate times and do the necessary. I suspected that she also might have had some designs on the good-looking Major Jensen, but I knew he could defend himself if called upon. So we joyfully proceeded on our first date since Don's birth.

After dressing for dinner and the scheduled casino and night club tour we joined Mary Berry and Ray Spivey and the rest of the party on deck and found to our dismay that the only way ashore would have to be by water-taxi. Those sorry fragile and very un-seaworthy-appearing vessels shoved and muscled each other in getting to the ship's ladder where eventually we would all disembark. Mary and Eleanor being young and attractive and the only females on board forced Ray and I into competition to see who would provide the most assistance in getting the nervous ladies into the winning water-taxi. Ray didn't even make the first one and I was only lucky enough to scramble aboard by jumping and hanging on for dear life to the canopy which was meant to provide cover in case of rain. My foothold was at best, precarious and I shuddered at the prospect of losing my grip and falling off into the black cesspool of a river. Nevertheless we made the short voyage successfully and I shepherded both women away from the eager military escort and awaited Ray's arrival on the next water-taxi.

The boulevard fronting the river was the Bund showing its British influence with numerous imposing banks and other ponderous financial institutions lining the side of the road opposite the river. It was neat and clean and far from the menacing parts of the city about which we had been warned.

There were more odors from this port area, mostly the strange and exotic smells which came from cargoes being brought in from other foreign ports. But to us the enchantment of setting our feet on land, for the first time, in the Far East, filled us with wonderment and joy. Again we realized how far we were from home and country and how utterly foreign to us would be the people, language and customs. China! The very magic of the word called to mind the maps we had studied and the vastness of the land with its teeming millions of human beings. The streets were crowded, even now after dark. Confusion and noise soon overcame us like a damp blanket. "Let's get away from the port area and get to the Cathay Hotel where dinner awaits our group," someone said, and he hailed a line of rickshaws waiting at the curb.

The four of us preempted two of the leading rickshaws and said "Cathay Hotel!" An unintelligible grunt probably meant "Okay! Let's go!" And so we did, with our trotting driver swinging into the "wrong" side of the street, joining the traffic flow, unconcerned, it seemed, with the motor vehicles on either side.

We were cases of shattered nerves with the unaccustomed "wrong" side of the street traffic, the noisy pedestrians seemingly oblivious to the moving vehicles and the cars and trucks which constantly threatened us with annihilation. Nevertheless we stretched our necks so as not to miss a single sight along the Nanking Road which led away from the Bund to the downtown area. For the first time we saw narrow double-decker twin-trolleys edging their way among the other traffic and out of this chaos there slowly emerged a strange sort of order reassuring us that maybe life wasn't so cheap here after all. Rickshaws were everywhere, lining the curbs, drivers awaiting their fares, either dozing in the reclining carriage seat or engaged in animated conversation with their fellow coolies. Our rickshaw was pulled along at a steady pace by our loping, lightly dressed, durable though apparently undernourished driver.

Most of the world's colored neon lights were here in Shanghai tonight, or so it seemed to us. Night life was the bright life and all of the shops were open and doing a brisk business. We arrived at the old Cathay Hotel, a European oasis in this oriental setting. Our dinner was served without delay and our touring group made haste to get finished and on its way to the first casino stop. We went by taxi to DiDi's, alighted from our cab with the unneeded assistance of a White Russian Field Marshal-turned-doorman. If ever was sought an opulent atmosphere, inside we found it!

DiDi's, owned and operated by former members of the Czar's household, we were told, was a transplanted palace complete with crystal chandeliers, lush carpeting, period furniture and beautiful white Russian hostesses who guided us up the broad staircase to the gaming rooms. If we were to gamble, the drinks were free. We chose to go on to the "ballroom" where an orchestra played and a crowd jostled itself around the dance floor. A former cossack heaved a small table onto the dance floor cutting into its few remaining inches of free space, found four uncomfortable chairs, accepted his tip, and left us to our own devices.

There was an interesting show, featuring scantily clad girls and Ray and I constantly expected one of them to land in our laps. However disappointed in our luck we may have been, we finally left to try the roulette tables. There we fared no better and it became time to move on to our next tour stop.

Bromfield's adventure stories dealing largely with British Colonials were never flattering. They were depicted as arrogant, living and working in an environment of "white supremacy," referring to all peoples whose skin was any shade darker than their own as "wogs." All of these unpleasant associations seemed embodied in the person of one individual who chose the moment of our departure from Didi's to plant himself in front of our cab, driven by a Sikh, to coolly and deliberately light a cigarette, then to continue puffing so that our cab could not move. When he turned away toward his companions to carry on some conversation, I asked our driver to toot his horn, which he did. This was absolutely ignored and in a bit of anger I stuck my head out of the window and asked this fading symbol of the white man's supremacy abroad if he "would mind getting the hell out of the way!"

Even though he must have recognized that we were Caucasians, it now became a matter of "saving face." It was obvious that the fellow had a bit too much to drink, so rather than prolong the stalemate, I got out of the cab in order to persuade this character that he was making an ass of himself. I suggested to him that someone might think that he was an American and that was my chief concern. "We would also like to get on our way, if he didn't mind!" His friends got the point and each one taking him by an arm, coaxed him to get back on the sidewalk before there might be a "bit of a row"!

We all breathed a sigh of relief as we pulled away for our next stop and Eleanor reminded me that there should be many things to consider before looking to spend the night in a Shanghai jail! Joe Farren's cabaret looked as though it had been transported from Las Vegas without the loss of a single electric bulb. It was located in the British Concession and did a remarkable business as a world-famous gambling casino. The bright lights sparkled from moving ceiling reflectors and games of every kind were in full and noisy swing. One-armed bandits lined the walls and no one paid much attention to anything else until show-time was announced. Once again we were favored with good seats and were entertained royally by some of our best known show people.

Twelve o'clock slipped by and the champagne lost a bit of its glow. We realized that we were running out of gas and so decided to find our way back to the ship. There were no taxis to be seen and as we felt a bit of fresh air could help, we decided to walk a ways along the now deserted street. Bubbling Well Road intersected Nanking Road not far from the casino and that, we new, would take us to the Bund and the water-taxis and eventually our ship! Somewhere along the way we would surely find an empty cab.

The British Concession was well guarded by Sikh policemen—tall, tanned, and with their long hair tied in a top-knot beneath their helmets. Their frequent presence allayed any apprehension we may have felt at this late hour. As we strolled along our way a large sanitation truck slowly rumbled past carrying what was unmistakably a jumble of human bodies. We were shocked almost to nausea as we identified these as the mortal remains of those pitiful refugees who, arriving in the sanctity of the big city, wound up dying of starvation in the doorways and alleys of their rich brothers, many of whom acquiring their riches through collaboration with enemies who bought their arms and ammunition. These were the bundles of rags, human beings we had seen huddled along the route from the hotel to the night clubs.

"China Relief" was a euphemism for the frustrating attempts the United States had made at helping these unfortunates, while the rest of the Western World was engaged in a mortal struggle for victory in war-torn Europe. The situation was hopeless with such relief supplies as we could produce winding up in the pockets of the Nationalist leaders, or private war-lording individuals who cared little or nothing of the fate which was destroying their peoples. We continued silently and sadly on our way, thinking of the injustice which comes with the selfishness of many of the world's rulers.

Mary Berry said, "Ray, I just can't walk another step!" Which was about the way we all felt. But we had not seen a cab since leaving Farren's. The rickshaw was always available to us so I suggested that we hail one. At least they would get us off our feet. Everyone agreed!

We finally reached the quay and rented a water-taxi for the trip back to the ship. It took ten damp minutes of passage through the murky waters where this time every dark shadow just had to be the body of an unfortunate refugee. By the time we were back on board, we were stone-cold sober with our reflections of the night's events. The boys were sound asleep with Major Jensen fully clothed and in his own land of dreams on the day bed. We met Betty the nurse in the hall and we learned that Donny had been fed his bottle at 11:00 p.m, so it was dreamland for us, too.

The ship was not due to weigh anchor until late that evening so we decided to go ashore for some shopping in the afternoon. The nurse generously offered to take the boys in tow for the few hours we would be ashore and we became more and more indebted for the excellent babysitting services provided by her and Frank Jensen, who was a bit embarrassed by not being awakened when we finally got back to the cabin.

Nanking Road by day was noisier and even more crowded than it had appeared to be last evening. Except for the omnipresent rickshaws and the oriental faces, we could have been crossing Herald Square in New York City on its busiest shopping day. We changed some dollars for Shanghai currency at the rate of one for eighteen. This made the Shanghai dollar worth about five and a half U.S. cents each. Our objective primarily was the famous Wing-On department store which we reached by rickshaw. We quickly lost our self-consciousness and fear of being whisked off to some never-never land by a wicked coolie rickshaw driver as we marveled at his skill in dodging traffic, people, buses, cars, and trucks alike! We then had to agree that this was probably the safest mode of travel in town.

The confusion at the Wing-On Department Store beggars description. Crowds of multi-nationals pushing at counters piled high with merchandise, all in apparent disorder and with no regard as to size or price. We were simply engulfed, surging forward with the mass of humanity until we were able to break loose at a department which seemed to feature lady's lingerie. Eleanor squealed with delight and dove into a mound of embroidered silk slips and nighties. Two or three salesgirls materialized from the crowd and helped her with the unfamiliar sizes and prices. Meanwhile I edged over to a counter loaded with men's khaki shorts and sport shirts. Shoes were arranged on an adjacent counter, also in helter-skelter fashion, tied together by their laces to prevent the breaking up of pairs, I suppose. I needed a pair of shorts and spotted a nicely tailored West Point drill in medium size. The salesgirl, like those busy with Eleanor, spoke rudimentary English and used the abacus to calculate my bill.

Twenty Shanghai dollars was the price! This was an unbelievable U.S. $1.10 and I was happy to have them wrapped and handed to me before she could change her mind over my apparent bargain. We made a few more small purchases and left the store like two kids, so pleased with our bargains were we! Among our purchases was a silk brocaded pajama set for Eleanor, size "40" -oriental, but which turned out to be too small for her, but would probably wind up as a gift for some lucky person back home.

Shanghai was simply too fascinating to rush back to the ship so we walked among the by-ways and alleys off Bubbling Well Road, reveling in the many curio shops with their stocks of exquisitely carved ivory and jade. Ornamental silver and brass were sold in open bazaars run mainly by East Indians, some wearing caste marks, and all of the women dressed in gracious saris. They would walk up to anyone who was not moving by at a fast trot, grab them by the arm and urge them to have "just one small look at this supremely fashioned brass Buddha."

Our cash situation limited our ability to purchase and so also we were restrained from being cheated. One had to be expert to distinguish between ivory and bone or, for that matter, between glass and jade. Sterling carried its own mark of identification and substitution was made difficult. We limited our purchases to a few brass artifacts as souvenirs and one beautifully carved elephant bridge which just had to be a "steal" if it was truly ivory.

Our return to ship was still in broad daylight and we saw life as lived by the "boat people" for the first time in all its crowded ugliness. Nanking Road ended at the Bund along whose waterfront the water-taxis had found their milieu. The competition for fares was spirited and we finally selected one of the sturdier craft, bargained for the price of the short trip to the *Coolidge* in midstream.

Without benefit of sleep other than our short nap this morning, we decided to unpack our "goodies" before doing anything else. Our first surprise came with the opening of my package of shorts only to find that I had carried back not one pair but two! The sales slip was plainly marked $20 Shanghai but because I had asked for a "pair" of walking shorts the friendly clerk translated that as "two." The second surprise was a set of bronze bells sold to us as East Indian handicraft, only to find a tiny legend inside of each, "made in Italy." We had a good laugh for we were now bona fide tourists!

The ship weighed anchor at 5:00 p.m. and slowly picked its way downstream among the clusters of sampans. They floated together in groups with narrow canals of free water between each group. There was an absence of color save for the dark brown sampans and the gray, black and browns of the almost uniform clothing worn by men, women and children alike. Most of the tired, drawn faces of the adult women were framed by long hair, black or gray according to age, tied neatly in a knot at the nape of the neck. The men wore their hair short, many having shaved their heads, probably as a matter of convenience.

We looked and marveled over the fact that teeming millions of Chinese lived their entire existence right here in the river. They cooked on tiny braziers lighted by only a few pieces of charcoal. The odors of evening meals reached us as we moved downstream and we visualized steaming rice, enhanced perhaps by a small piece of duck or fish, spiced with garlic and ginger. They would be lucky to have a green vegetable such as broccoli or kang-kong, a leafy spinach-type, to help them stay alive. Our own Western world was a long, long way from this!

III

Continuing to watch the receding land as daylight faded, we soon lost sight of the people, either busy with their life in the sampan city or tilling the rice beds on the river banks. The scene became one of desolation whose solitude was broken only by the frigate birds and gulls following the ship. Flat, empty land as far as the eye could reach, marked the rice paddies in the Yangtze delta. Our ship was well out in the broad channel and with the sounding of the "second sitting" gong, we left the twilight and went below.

Just before going to bed, now at sea, we sighted an active volcanic island not too far off the port bow. The cone was belching smoke and fire intermittently and was a wondrous sight to behold at this safe distance. The seas were calm and remained so for the entire trip down the China coast to Hong Kong. The next couple of days were bright and clear and next morning-we were treated to the sight of a school of sharks following our wake to pick up the garbage which was periodically dumped over the side.

We were out of sight of land until we sighted Formosa to the east of us. The northern tip of the large island ran into the sea in a series of rocky promontories, one of which had claimed the S.S. *President Hoover*, sister ship to the *Coolidge*, only a couple of years back. We were glad to be passing the place in the clear daylight.

The Straits of Formosa are known for their sudden storms and squalls in season and we were glad that this was not the season. Typhoons, like their Caribbean counter-parts, were most notable from October to December and their paths brought them over the Philippines, across Formosa and the Straits until their energy was spent in the China Sea, somewhere off the coast of the mainland.

Eleanor and I had studied travel information and had learned of the beauty which is the port of Hong Kong. Nevertheless, we were unprepared for the breathless beauty of the misty sunrise which slowly lifted its curtain and revealed the fabulous port. The roads which constituted the entrance to the main harbor were dotted with islets with a backdrop of the ramparts of Victoria Peak on Hong Kong Island. Moving slowly among the harbor islands was the now familiar boat traffic, Chinese-style. High fan-tailed junks with crazily shaped and colored slatted sails came close enough for us to see the gargoyles painted on the bow and stern. Good spirits vied with evil, their relative power measuring the eventual harvest of that particular voyage. Gaily painted demons drove away any threatened bad weather and various unidentifiable objects, swinging in tempo to the pulse of the waves, each had their purpose to carry out. On every craft all visible hands were busy at one kind of labor or another. Nets were being dried or mended, sails repaired, decks scrubbed and laundry either washed or hung up to dry.

These families may have been poor according to the standards of the western world, but they were happy, industriously working for the common good, absolutely the ultimate experience in togetherness. Seeing three and even four generations of one family sharing their entire lives on one tiny sampan or junk gave all of us plenty of food for thought!

During my training period with the company, I had become quite friendly with Reg Owens whose eventual assignment was a post in Hong Kong. He subsequently married a very sweet local girl of Australian antecedents and we now looked forward to renewing an old acquaintance. Our Marine Major and Nurse Betty came again to our aid as baby-sitters and we anticipated a couple of exciting day trips ashore. Our ship docked at Kowloon, across the bay from the Hong Kong island and we quickly readied ourselves for the "All Ashore" signal. It was the mid-morning of a hot humid day, bright sunshine in a cloudless sky. Eleanor and I dressed lightly, anticipating the heat but we found no discomfort as the commuter ferry plowed its way across the breezy bay. Again we experienced the wonderment of being in strange land, among crowds of Orientals, whose language, dress and customs were so alien to us. We were again the tourists, camera strung around my neck and a guidebook in hand.

We had arranged to meet Reg and his wife at the Hong Kong Hotel one hour after the ship docked. After a quick walk through Customs for a day's pass, we took a short taxi ride to the hotel and there they were! My old bachelor buddy had not only taken unto himself a beautiful wife but also had added quite a few pounds. He promptly returned the "compliment" and off we went to have some fun.

Hong Kong thoroughfares were narrow as Shanghai's. Again the police were Sikhs, tall and competent and with their characteristic long hair neatly rolled and tucked away under their turbans. Having resided in Hong Kong for four years, Reg and his wife were "old China hands." As a matter of fact they were scheduled for periodic leave the following spring, 1942. We were so anxious to see the city that we put off lunch in favor of a window-shopping stroll along some of the city's principal streets. We were impressed by the difference in shops. Whereas in Shanghai all was confusion and disorder; here, strict convention prevailed. The window displays were professional and the merchandise was neatly stored and priced. In the curio shops we were assured that the merchandise was bona fide. Jade was jade and ivory was ivory! We began to catalog in our minds the things we would seek out and buy on our return trip to the United States four years away. We did break down and use almost all of our remaining money supply to buy several pieces of hand-carved ivories, the "Eight Immortals" and "Kwan Yen," the Goddess of Mercy with her beads and crown so resembling the statues of the Virgin Mary. We also bought a beautiful mahjong set. We bought all we could carry and far more than we could afford and returned with our friends to the hotel where we were invited to a long overdue lunch. We were taken up to the penthouse where a former cook of the old Imperial household now owned and operated one of the best restaurants in the Far East, according to Reg.

Our experience with Chinese cuisine had been limited to the chop suey and chow mein bistros in Manhattan and

Tom and Eleanor purchased these carvings in China on their way to the Philippines. Prior to their internment, Tom buried them near their house in Manila. After the family was liberated they were able to find their souvenirs and bring them home.

we were now to enjoy a delightful service that would be long remembered. We were ushered into a partitioned room overlooking the lovely harbor. Slippered female Chinese came in with perfumed steaming towels and one gently loosened my collar and wiped my face, neck and forehead. Not so the ladies, in deference to their makeup, I suppose. A fragrant jasmine tea was served throughout the meal. The dishes with minute delectable morsels of food followed one after the other in interminable procession and surprisingly enough never seemed to fill us. Sharkfin soup, Szechuan duck, pungent ribs, pork and beef built my recollection of this fabulous meal for months and years thereafter. Alcohol in its usual highball or cocktail was simply not part of such a feast but we did enjoy tiny cups of warmed rice wine which were never allowed to stand empty.

    We parted reluctantly with a promise to see them again on our way home in four years.

IV

Our long and pleasant Hong Kong weekend over, we sailed for our next and final port of call. Eleanor and I were on deck bright and early the morning of June 10th, 1941, to catch our first glimpse of "The Pearl of the Orient." We had crossed the China Sea from northwest to southeast to enter Manila Harbor, which is located on the west coast of Luzon about midway between the northern and southern tips of this island. The port itself was protected at its entrance by Corregidor, a fortified rock some twenty miles west, across the bay, from the city. This small island, Corregidor, sat at the apex of a semi-circular peninsula of land just across the strait from Mariveles, a city of the Bataan province.

As we approached the port area, Corregidor was seen on our left and along about ten miles further into the bay, we could make out the naval base, Cavite on our right. Eleanor said that she was not reassured by Corregidor which was no Gibraltar on close inspection. Perhaps its hidden fortifications were far mightier than the lump of rock promised.

In somewhat less than an hour we tied up at Pier 7, alleged to be the largest and most modern in the Orient. By this time the temperature had risen to ninety-four degrees and the air was still and humid. Our first impressions gathered through passage of customs and immigration were not pleasing. My new associate who had been asked to ease our entry showed up only as we were struggling to find our baggage, a taxi and a place to stay. His terse greeting was limited to, "You're late, you know. I expected you here last month!"

Since he was to be relieved of his contract shortly, I did not permit myself to be either surprised or disappointed by his attitude. He had arranged for a suite at the Bayview Hotel on Dewey Boulevard, a choice location as it turned out. We would stay there until I could work out more permanent accommodations. We were left on our own as soon as we departed from the area of Pier 7 and I arranged for our baggage and car to be cleared and transported as soon as the family was comfortably settled at the hotel.

There was not the slightest sign of the dreamy, somnolent atmosphere of the tropics. Manila seemed to be a rather un-homogenized mixture of east and west and Dewey Boulevard that resembled Collins Avenue, in Miami, in the number and character of hotels and residences along the bay-front.

Three weeks later we were still enjoying our hotel accommodations although just about ready to move into our newly-rented house in Quezon City. On this particular day our weather consisted of gale force winds, a deluge of rain and as we looked out of our fourteenth story window, no sunshine in sight. We did see a panorama of flame trees in full bloom and the imposing Luneta where many new and beautiful government buildings had recently been completed.

Our new quarters were very temporary since the owners would be returning in a little more than a month from their state-side vacation. The bungalow was located in a compound with an iron gate. Our neighbors were a Chinese female doctor and her husband, and a Swiss couple who welcomed us with the warning that there had been a number of burglaries even though our compound was surrounded by a stone wall, and that it would be wise to sleep with a gun within easy reach. Needless to say we were anxious to find something of a safer and more permanent nature.

Manila proved to be a city of wide contrasts. The north side of the city was separated from the south by the winding Pasig River. Here was located the business and commercial life of the city and along the Escolta and Avenida Rizal banks and offices nestled cheek to cheek with rambling wooden structures housing an assortment of oriental shops. Horse drawn carromatas, calesas, and caretelas possibly outnumbered automobiles. The former were preferred by the Filipinos because of economy. Trolleys, jitneys and buses tried to take care of the remaining problems of transportation but the mixture of all of the foregoing forms resulted in traffic jams galore in the downtown area.

Further north, beyond the business area was Tondo, a settlement populated largely by Chinese refugees and the poorest of the poor immigrants who found their way to Manila from other Southeast Asian countries. The poverty was reminiscent of what we had seen in Shanghai with several families occupying a single dwelling, on stilts over open water in many cases. Manila's population was swelling fast with this current influx of refugees.

Across the Pasig to the south was the Luneta, a spacious park-like area designed to house government buildings. The newer hotels and the spectacular Jai-Alai sports palace gave this area a look of the future. Modern architecture had encouraged the upgrading of the southside residential section of the city and the structures along Dewey Boulevard, including the American High Commissioner's Office which made the waterfront the place to live.

We had been most fortunate in obtaining a lovely house in San Juan, Rizal on a rent-purchase arrangement. The house was small, with two bedrooms, a living-dining area and kitchen on one floor, and a set of rooms and laundry downstairs, constituting the servants' quarters and a garage and playroom on the same level. The property was walled-in and for sentries we inherited a set of five geese who belligerently protected the property from all comers, including us.

The back of the property looked out upon the famous Wack-Wack golf course beyond which was Zablan Field, an airfield, part of a five mile long Nichols Field air defense installation. At times we found the noise of the military planes disturbing, yet comforting in the sense of security it gave us.

We faced the usual problems of getting settled and were finally in a comfortable groove of daily life. We had some problems in securing reliable servants but lucked out on a cook, Ricardo Abengana, who had worked for several Americans before us. He became majordomo and was responsible for securing a houseboy, amah, and laundress, all of whom were probably related in some fashion to him. Honesty was a matter of degree and our servants would be highly regarded since their pilferage was of minor things like soap and rice. We found our houseboy Peter to be rather not-so-bright but obedient and a hard worker. He got up each morning before sunrise and by 6:00 a.m. was busy with our hardwood floors which were kept immaculately shined by tying dry coconut husks to his feet and then scuffing the boards as though he were skating. Actually, he did it with so much gusto that the children were awakened and so were we, within the first hour of his performance. The oil from the husks penetrated the hard wood floors and gave them a beautiful gloss.

Sunday mornings became a special occasion as we were usually awakened by the delectable aroma of freshly baked coffeecake or sweet rolls. Ricardo turned out to be a great number-one boy! One of those mornings we awoke to the crash of what seemed to be an entire china closet. Throwing our robes about us we went out to see the damage. All four servants were lined up, Ricardo to the left, then Peter, Flor, and Teresa. There was a mess of broken crockery and much concern on the part of the guilty one, I'm sure. However, in true Filipino fashion Ricardo looked at me and said,"T'weren't me, mum!" Peter, expecting more sympathy from the lady of the house, shook his head and said,"Nor me, sir!" (This to Eleanor.)

The girls giggled a bit and, shaking their heads negatively said in unison, "We are not the one, mum." This last was directed at me since the decision to place the blame would fall on my shoulders. I guessed that the whole incident was an unavoidable accident and told them simply to clean up and forget it. I was thinking more about the crossover use of "sir" and "mum" and chuckling a bit at the incongruity.

Although we lived in comparative security with housebound servants and five honking geese, burglaries were rampant around us. Friends who had their windows protected by bars suffered an elaborate break-in with the bars removed from the windows, both husband and wife chloroformed in their beds before they could raise an outcry, a gun stolen from beneath the pillow on which the husband slept, only to marvel at the loss of some laundry which turned out to be the sum total of things taken. Who will understand? Who can tell you why?

We enjoyed sitting in our backyard swing with the children, to watch the sunsets in late evening. They were extraordinarily beautiful across the bay and out over the China Sea. Eleanor and I had little difficulty in acclimating ourselves to the new surroundings and we felt at peace with the world. We had written home to our families to reassure them against the constant talk of war in the news. People around us said that Manila was too well-protected to be menaced by the sea-born invasion of an enemy force. Even practice blackouts which had been instituted some few months ago were now discontinued.

Business had taken a healthy upward turn and it looked like all was right with the world. I was twenty-nine years old and approaching my thirtieth birthday and when I reminded Eleanor of the painful goodbye I would be saying to the youthful twenties, she laughed, refusing to give me her sympathy. Further, she reminded me that she was, at this time, actually three years younger than me. That, of course, was temporary since her birthday came before mine, by four months.

Both of us spoke fluent Spanish and I found this to be a great help in travelling throughout the islands. I managed to pick up a smattering of Tagalog and Visayan, the dialects of the northern and southern islands, respectively. I learned that there were variations in the dialects to the extent that a native of one province could find difficulty in communicating with a native of a neighboring province. Certainly Tagalog, which had a wealth of Spanish and English derivations, could not easily be understood by the native of Mindinao who spoke only Visayan. A further potential conflict existed because of religious differences, the northern islands being predominantly Christian and the southern, Moslem.

My business was with ten distributors, seven of whom were Chinese. We had one Filipino, one German, and one American wholesale distributor to round out our system and my future objective was to eliminate these in favor of a manufacturing operation and assume the responsibility for distribution on a direct sale base. Of interest is the fact that the Chinese, most of whom came from the Southeast of China, dominated the wholesale and retail pharmaceutical business. They were adept at manufacturing and packaging imitations of the best-known over-the-counter brands.

We found the Filipinos friendly and courteous but not inclined to clasp an American to the family bosom. The Chinese who were there in great numbers were most friendly and anxious to be befriended. They were the merchants, the real force behind retail business. While the Filipino was often content to sit back and grumble at his secondary role, he was loathe to make any effort to better his lot. The Chinese merchant found no opportunity too insignificant to exploit.

In early December we had a delightful surprise by way of a visit from Major Frank Jensen, the Marine officer who had befriended our children on our trip from San Francisco. He expressed some misgivings about U.S.-Japanese relations and the current talks being held in Washington between our Secretary of State Hull and their ambassador Nomura. He also mentioned that service families had been returned to the States in large numbers. We knew that some of our friends, planning to return home for their periodic leave, had been able to reserve passage with a delay of as much as three months. There was an exodus in progress and until now not even a hint had reached us. Being just recently arrived, we had no thought anytime of maybe playing it safe and turning right around, as it were, and going back home. We had a circle of new-found friends, some pharmaceutical associates and others from various American enterprises, all of whom felt as secure as we did. Life went on and we settled into a pleasant routine of business lightly mixed with pleasure.

V

Sunday evening, December 7th, was unusual in that several couples including ourselves, having seen the Jai-Alai matches, lost our money and had a few drinks at the "Tap Room," decided to "make a real night of it!" This entailed a mass movement to the roof-top restaurant of the Great Eastern Hotel where the finest Chinese meal was obtainable. There were more drinks and much gaiety and a promise of several beautiful hangovers the following morning. The party atmosphere was enhanced by the decor of Chinese lanterns and balmy weather, making the night one to be long remembered. Since I had to face a working Monday as well as very early Mass on the holy day of The Immaculate Conception, we left the party at midnight. It was still going on full blast.

The next morning I struggled out of bed at the earlier hour in order to have breakfast, attend Mass with Eleanor and get to work by 8:30 as usual. My hangover was a bit unusual but the rest of the early morning passed as sort of a blur until I resumed consciousness during Mass. I dropped Eleanor off at the Brothers' house where she planned to call for a taxi to get her the rest of the way home. Stan was employed by Pan-American Airways as Airport Manager and Thelma, his pretty young wife made their home not far from the church in San Juan. The girls played mahjong once every two weeks. They had two children, Susan, a year older than Roger, and John who was a year younger.

Eleanor told me later that she rang their bell and when the door was opened looked in upon an incredible sight. Everyone seemed to be running, carrying blankets, struggling with mattresses and with Eleanor's entrance, Thelma looked at her in amazement and said, "What on earth are you doing here? Haven't you heard the news?"

Stan, who was heaving a large mattress against the picture window of their home added, "The radio says that Pearl Harbor has been bombed and strafed by Japanese planes and Camp

John Hay near Baguio is right now under attack. They expect the Jap planes to be headed this way!"

Eleanor's reaction was shock. She could not grasp the portent of Stan's words. He said, "Look, I'd better drive you home right away. Tom will undoubtedly hear the news on his car radio and be heading for your house so let's go right now!"

Stan was in something of a state of shock, too, and on the way to 41 Guevara all he could say was, "I don't believe it! It can't possibly be!"

Meanwhile I had driven toward my office on the Escolta with no intimation of the dreadful news now in the making. I did not have my car radio on but I did notice the heavy flow of traffic outward bound from the city. Busy with my own thoughts of the week's work ahead, I paid not too much attention to the excitement around me. Until I reached the office door I knew nothing but there a distraught secretary greeted me with, "Isn't it terrible, Mr. Lewis! What are we going to do? They will be coming here any moment and drop bombs on the city!"

Seeing my bewilderment, one of the salesmen, handed me a copy of the Manila Bulletin, an "Extra" with the screaming headlines that Pearl Harbor had been attacked, strafed, and bombed early this morning, Sunday, December 7th. Because of the International Date Line the identical moment in the Philippines was Monday, December 8th, 1941. All of our employees were waiting for some reaction from me and to prod me to action they reminded me that the enemy had already been busy only two hundred miles to the north and were expected to attack Manila at any moment! My thoughts were confused and all I could think of was the safety of my family. I sent them all off to their homes telling them that we would be in touch as soon as things became clearer. I really don't know what prompted that sterile advice but it was all that I could get out at the time. I closed up and got in my car and joined the general panic departure from downtown.

I can't remember the actual circumstances of that drive back to the house, but it was interminable! It did give me some time to take stock of our particular situation and I concluded that we would probably be as safe at home as anywhere else. Of course I would have Peter and Ricardo help me build some sort of protection around the house against stray damage from shrapnel and gunfire. We would check with neighbors and friends and see what they planned to do.

As I pulled into the driveway, Eleanor and the two children were waiting in the garage doorway, wide-eyed with the panic that gripped us all. I took them in my arms and said, "We will probably be safe as bugs in a rug here under the house if we can build reinforcements of the floor above us and the windows and doors opening into the garage. All four servants stayed with us as their families lived quite a distance away in the provinces to the north. They figured that the relative safety of the known outweighed the possibilities of the unknown.

We kept watching the sky over the port area for the expected arrival of the Japanese planes and gradually day moved toward night without their appearance. Throughout the afternoon we exchanged fruitless conferences with our friends, the Red Cross, and the High Commissioner's office which all added up to the same unsatisfying conclusion, "Sit tight and remain calm!" Meanwhile we continued to watch the sky with constant dread and the approaching nightfall with even more panic.

The first bombing, when it came, was a terrific shock. The eight of us had munched on some cold food, fed the children and sat huddled together in the garage, having bundled the boys into the car for greater security. The city was blacked out and the radio was silenced. The heat was oppressive and the night clear and ideal for an air-raid. Sometime before midnight, in desperation bred from the awful discomfort of our cramped quarters, I said "The hell with this. Let's get upstairs and into bed so we can at least get some rest for whatever we have to face tomorrow!!"

Eleanor reluctantly agreed and we each took one sleeping child under our arms and headed for the bedrooms. It seemed as though we were just tucked in when the air raid sirens started screaming their warning, almost simultaneously with the screech and crump of falling bombs. It was one o'clock in the morning and the attack was over the port area and the airfield no more than three miles away! We snatched the children from their beds and dashed again for the dubious shelter of the garage. We caught glimpse of a bright moon overhead as the streaking flash of tracer bullets revealed the center of the attack. The noise was terrifying, mixing the sound of diving bombers, anti-aircraft fire, machine guns and falling bombs!

Each of the servants as well as the four of us had sought the most protected spot in the garage, in the car, under the car and beneath blankets behind boxes or whatever shelter was available.

We prayed, and we cried but during each pause in the bedlam we smiled at each other with the reassurance that we were still there. Meanwhile the operators of the air raid sirens kept sounding confused signals, an "all clear" during one moment of intense bombing and an alert when the action had finally ceased. All in all, the raid took less than an hour and although we stayed huddled together in our shelter, there was no further action that night.

Ricardo and I had found some burlap bags and in desperation we got a couple of shovels and broke our backs filling them with dirt. It helped deaden the panic of our minds and served to provide some shelter against the windows of the lower floor. The house was on a slight rise and had some natural protection from the trees and the wall, but the upper floor was vulnerable. When we saw the sun come up and realized that if there was further action in the air, we would now have visual warning. We straggled upstairs to try to put some breakfast together.

The children were surprisingly unconcerned with the hectic events, too young to realize how upset we were. We tried not to show our own fear and with panic-stricken servants it was not easy.

The radio was busy with instructions as to what course to pursue but really helpful only in keeping everyone where they were. We were slightly cheered by the news that eleven of the Allied Nations had joined in declaring war against Japan. Beyond this, there was an obvious absence of hopeful tones in every speech and every news update. The latter was full of the devastation wrought at Pearl Harbor and there was obvious censorship of local news as to what damage had been inflicted on Cavite, Clark Field, and John Hay, the military camp near Baguio. As I walked into our bedroom with the idea of changing clothes, I passed Eleanor's vanity and saw a strange jagged piece of metal lying next to her comb and brush set. My natural inclination was to look up, and there in the ceiling was a gaping hole, through which this nasty piece of metal must have passed. Shrapnel! And it had narrowly missed getting one of us! Our mattresses were strewn across the living room floor hopefully to add to the flimsy protection we had in the area beneath.

Only now, when we had a chance to calm down and reflect on last night's excitement did we realize that the car itself inadvertently added to our danger with the gasoline tank as a potential home-made bomb! Jack Magda, a close-by neighbor and employee of one of our distributors came over early to check and see how we had survived the night. He told us that he had a friend who was custodian of a closed-up mine in nearby Bampanga province. He had been in touch and if we would be interested we could all seek safety away from the port area which would presumably be the focal point of any continuing attacks. We could drive there in our cars in about two hours and the living quarters would be at our disposal as long as we wanted.

Entrusting the house and all of our possessions to the servants, we packed the children in the car and took along linen, blankets and food for a few days, hoping that all would quickly resolve itself and we could return. We followed the dirt road route set by Jack and his wife and finally arrived in a closed-end valley which promised seclusion if not safety. Night fell quickly and the crusty old caretaker, an ex-miner, Mr. "Tetch" Wood, left us to our own devices. It turned out to be more like camping out and Jack and I agreed to share an all-night watch.

Somewhere we had come into possession of two rather rusty pistols and a dozen or so bullets which fit their barrels. They were more for moral rather than physical aid in the event of an attack.

Jack told me that this was an area where there had been some "Hukbalahip" activity. These were the communist guerrillas more commonly known as the "Huks" and noted for their bloody raids on unarmed citizenry. That shredded my thin reassurance and I started my watch as fearful as I had been during the air raid of the night before. Along about midnight I saw flashes of fire in the hills across from the mine. They must have been ten miles away and the sound of gunshots never materialized. In this blackest of black outs, for the night was overcast, my excitement caused me to call Jack and the two of us spent the remainder of the night vowing that the unknown wasn't worth the effort and we would return to San Juan first thing in the morning.

A long-to-be-remembered zero point in our morale came at 11:00 o'clock the next morning, Wednesday, December 10th, as we drove toward home and away from the Ipoh mine. We were listening to the car radio when a flash announcement came across that a large convoy of Japanese ships had been sighted off the northwestern coast of Luzon. With that announcement, somehow we knew we were doomed. If Corregidor and Cavite were not to be factors in resisting an enemy invasion, there remained little or no other defense.

Our worst fears were confirmed later when the United States American Forces in the Far East issued a communique confirming that elements of the Japanese invading force were engaged in landing operations on the northwestern coast of Luzon between Vigan and Aparri. Subsequent reports referred to combat on land, and with the little knowledge I had of the island's geography, I knew that our forces were being pushed back.

Back home again and in constant contact with friends, we all concluded that escape would be impossible. The port area was thoroughly destroyed in the first daylight raid which took place at noon this same Wednesday after we got back. The planes came in waves with the sun at their back and from our vantage point in San Juan, we could see the rain of bombs on the port area, Cavite, and at times, on what we just knew to be non-military targets. The city was covered by a pall of smoke and fire belched through when some hit was on an explosive target. The formations were of threes and the anti-aircraft fire was pitifully grouped hundreds of feet below its targets. We could see the disintegration of the docks and harbor buildings and the occasional whine of a bullet sent us scurrying to the relative safety of the shelter below the first floor of the house.

As we watched in horror, the planes turned toward us. They were after Zablan Field directly beyond the Wack-Wack golf course and we scrambled, children under our arms, the servants now panicky and of little help to us. We reached the shelter of the car-less garage and piled ourselves into a small target in the corner, with one mattress serving as our protection.

The bombs fell, the house trembled and dust arose from the grounds around us. We huddled and prayed. The drone of the motors seemed to be fixed just overhead and we felt quite close to death in those unforgettable moments.

The raid paused in about a half hour and we dared to come out into the open to find a few pieces of wicked-looking shrapnel on the cement walk in front of the house. There was one spent machine-gun bullet sitting on the top step as if to say, "Good thing *you* weren't standing here!"

This was War!

The news that night was more discouraging than ever. The residential section of Manila had been hit with considerable loss of life and property. We were stunned to learn in the same broadcast that the mighty British super-warships, the *Prince of Wales* and the *Repulse* had been sunk in the South China Sea!

Our whole world was collapsing around us. The unbelievable was happening and we, as well as our close friends, were completely bewildered as to which way to turn. The Japanese invaders looked to be unstoppable and our vaunted defenses crumbled while we watched. Survival, a word found only in books, now became our greatest concern.

There was a mad rush to the food stores for supplies and I had to fight for a share of what was left. Prices suddenly soared and our cash dwindled. I was able to wheedle a couple of cases of canned milk for the children from a small shopkeeper, a Chinese who, like me, was almost ready to collapse at the idea of being caught downtown in the business district in a possible air raid.

The next two weeks were holocaustal with the Japanese planes systematically destroying anything of military significance. Fires, not only from bombed-out oil dumps but also from areas of wooden shacks, barrios hit by stray bombs, burned brightly day and night. The sky over the city was a constant pall of acrid smoke and from our house which commanded a view of the city and port area, we could see most of the devastation. This, plus the continuing bad news over the radio reduced us to a state of shocked hopelessness.

Because of the apparent disregard for civilian safety on the part of the Japanese invaders, General MacArthur, who was preparing to leave the country with his family, issued a declaration that Manila would be an "Open City." This meant that there would be no military defense of the area and under the terms of civilized warfare, it would serve to stop all military action, except possible occupation, by the invading forces. This was to become effective Christmas Day.

By now we were fairly inured to the bombing and since our residential area had not been touched save for falling shrapnel or spent bullets, we decided to carry out our original Christmas plans which meant setting up the children's electric trains, cooking a large meal, and even having a few friends in for cocktails. They brought their children and it started out to be a fun affair, momentarily removed from the worries over the future.

The air raid sirens started wailing their warnings toward late afternoon and shortly thereafter the "Open City" was under the usual frightening attack. The raid kept us in the cellar and garage until darkness fell. We drank, and the more we drank the more depressed we became. The blackout and the 6:00 p.m. radio news just about killed any interest in further social amenities and our friends left us in the dark for the security of their own homes shortly after. We were told to be ready for an important message to be broadcast by President Roosevelt, the morning of December 27th, directly beamed to the Philippines. This was some comfort since we speculated that it might be the long expected announcement of a large convoy already on its way to rescue us.

At 11:00 a.m. the morning of December 27th (7:00 p.m, December 26th, in Washington, D. C.) the inimitable voice of our President introduced his customary "fireside chat" with "My friends!" In my recollection, never had the chief executive of a state promised so much, including a seventeen-mile-long convoy presently being assembled, and here we held our breaths, and he went on to reveal its destination as New Zealand and Australia. At this point our spirits began to sink for there was nothing in his speech which indicated a quick rescue for us. The final blow came when he brought his talk to a dramatic conclusion with the statement, "and I promise you that we will redeem the Philippine Commonwealth no matter how long it takes, no matter what the cost!"

That was it! That was the final word which would seal our fate as hostages to guarantee the return of General Douglas MacArthur. We would become prisoners of the enemy with no plan for rescue in the near future, to prove to the Filipino people that MacArthur, who proclaimed on leaving Corregidor for Australia, "I will return," would indeed. Furthermore, President Roosevelt promised and guaranteed the independence of the Philippines once we would have been rescued and order restored to the islands. With these commitments, America hoped to win the loyalty of these people.

As the year drew to a close, a few of our friends, those without children particularly, chose to follow the army in retreat to Bataan. We immediately lost contact with them for these last few days were devoted to preparing for the occupation of Manila by the Imperial Japanese Army. We moved from our house in San Juan and joined two other couples, Mary and Ray Spivey and Kitty and Fred Goldmann, the latter two being at least twice our ages. Our next temporary home was a large three-story brick house in a nice residential area of the city. It was surrounded by a wall and had a rather substantial gate of solid wood. En route we lost the two female servants who decided to go and join their relatives in a nearby province. Peter and Ricardo stuck with us and Peter became as good a substitute amah as the real thing. He was the one now in charge of washing diapers. Ricardo volunteered to cook for everybody and we truly would have been lost without him.

When we learned that the house belonged to the man who owned the largest liquor distributing firm in Manila and who was a friend of the Goldmanns', we did our best to drink up his household private stock rather than pour it down the toilet as the High Commissioner's office had advised us. And that was all the advice, official or otherwise that we received since Commissioner Sayre had joined the MacArthurs on Corregidor and had long since departed for safer shores. With the Commissioner and his family gone, the office was left in charge of First Secretary Claude Buss who surely had his hands full in these last few days. He could not be blamed for any failure to communicate with each and every one of the two or three thousand Americans still in the Manila area.

There was no New Year's Celebration! I took Ricardo and Peter out to the house to get more clothes for the four of us.

VI

Today, January 2nd, 1942, the Imperial Japanese Army entered Manila as per an accord reached with the remaining Philippine government officials. An area including the environs of the city had been designated Greater Manila and a temporary government was constituted to deal with the Japanese Commander Lt. General Homma. President Quezon had designated Jorge Vargas, former Executive Secretary, as Mayor of Greater Manila hoping that he would be an acceptable negotiator with the Japanese. On Saturday, January 3rd, the Rising Sun flag was seen flying over the High Commissioner's residence on Dewey Boulevard and a roundup of "enemy aliens" had begun.

Back in our "hideout" we huddled together remembering some of the horror stories we had heard about the "Rape of Nanking." Would the soldiers burn the city? Would there be looting and maltreatment of our women? No one knew, and like anyone stricken with a crippling disease, the worse terror came from not knowing than from facing up to reality. As it turned out our fears were groundless as the process of occupation had so far been orderly. Americans, British and Dutch nationals were being rounded up systematically and detained in various centers. By telephone, the Red Cross had warned us to be ready at any time as we would be asked to take along a small bag of necessities for each person for temporary detention while we were to be registered. Naturally our greatest concern was for our two small children as bedding and proper food could not be carried by hand.

Toward evening of the sixth, Tuesday, we were startled by a loud banging at the gate, Peter came calmly along the driveway to the gate and with great deliberation removed various chains and bolts which we had secured for safety. We watched through the venetian blinds and as the last chain fell away, the gate was shoved open and three rough-looking Japanese, one only in uniform, strode boldly up the drive toward the house.

We had to undo the latch and open the door. The ugly fellow in front, in uniform, must have been a private for there were no signs of rate or rank on him. He spoke loudly and with a belligerence that probably masked his fear in a strange situation like this. One of the civilians who turned out to be the Japanese-mestizo owner of a bicycle factory not far from the house, intervened in spite of the soldier's obvious impatience and explained that we were being ordered to leave the house immediately. The soldier again took up where the interpreter had left off and shouted insultingly in our faces that the house immediately became the property of the Imperial Japanese Army, or so the translation came out. No question about who was giving the orders. The private soldier outranked the civilians.

Our fury and humiliation at this treatment was kept under control only by the futility of our situation. My one thought was to get permission for Eleanor to stay with the children and servants, in the house, if possible. I had to make a stab at being hospitable so I asked the interpreter if they would like to use the nearby bathroom. After a short consultation, the soldier decided to accept my invitation. He exclaimed with delight when he saw what must have been unfamiliar chrome fixtures and with the help of the interpreter proceeded to bathe himself while partially disrobed. He amused himself for a full fifteen minutes while his audience just stood around watching. He used the guest linen like a Turkish towel and finally turned around to us, dry and reasonably clean. He smiled a very toothy grin and said, "aregato!"

As his humor seemed to be improved, I ventured to make my plea that Eleanor be allowed to remain. A vigorous discussion among the three Japanese ensued. I was suddenly informed that he (the soldier) had agreed to let them stay. The interpreter, who was not unfriendly, suggested that the rest of us waste no time as any further delay might trigger a change of heart on the part of the soldier.

Eleanor, who now was holding the awakened Donny, was horrified by the sudden snatching of the baby from her arms by the soldier who may have only wanted to play with him in Japanese fashion. The baby was still sleepy from his nap and raised no outcry but Eleanor, with mother's protective instinct unceremoniously grabbed the baby out of the surprised soldier's arms, saying "Give me back my baby, you animal!"

Fortunately the soldier did not understand English and the interpreter either missed what she said or purposely ignored it. The soldier, strangely enough, showed no offense at the sudden act. We all started moving to the door in order to get out while the going was good. There was an open truck in the street with a couple of other people like ourselves and we helped load the Goldmanns, Mary Spivey, our belongings and ourselves into the open bed.

Eleanor had been told that we would be taken to Rizal Stadium for a couple of days in order to be registered. Our parting was full of misgivings and we wondered when we would next see each other.

In fact we were taken to Rizal Stadium where we were registered but that incident was followed by loading us into some other trucks which transported us to the old University of Santo Tomas.

Our pity went out to the elderly and helpless who were treated with the same lack of courtesy and consideration that was our lot. We arrived in late afternoon to be dumped in the parking area in front of the main building where we joined hundreds of other prisoners who had already arrived. Old and young alike, women and children had been herded into this open space with no further immediate orders or instructions. Friends greeted each other with attempts at rueful humor.

We all felt some release from the tension of the last few days. No longer were we threatened by the unknown, the possible mad destruction of an invading horde. Rumors were already blossoming, some having us readied for shipment to Japan, but no one had any information of any real substance.

The University of Santo Tomas, founded in the 17th century, was located across the Pasig River from downtown Manila and some three or four miles out along Erbaña to the north. The campus was a rectangle covering some sixty acres, surrounded by a high wall on three sides and an iron fence along the boulevard area. There were several buildings on the campus including a seminary where priests and seminarians attached to the university resided. There was a large quonset-type corrugated metal building which served as a part-time gymnasium and a smaller building which we knew as the "Education Building," plus a miscellany of smaller buildings, annexes and garden houses, all of the foregoing surrounding the main school. This was a concrete and stone edifice five stories high and housing sixty large classrooms and various offices, all look inward on a patio. It was a formidable mass of masonry and had been put together in 1927. The remaining campus grounds were used for athletic events and gardening.

Meanwhile we all sought space in which to bed down for the night. There was an effort to organize and a central committee had been appointed by the Japanese. Their efforts were encumbered by the Japanese as well as the stream of new prisoners who kept coming through the gates. These people were "enemy aliens" to the Japanese and the number of nationalities represented were many.

Our small group had split up to fend for ourselves and I finally found a spot beneath one of the rear stairways which promised shelter and a minimum of privacy. My bed was the cement pavement itself but I had had the happy thought to bring along a blanket in which I now wrapped myself. My dinner consisted of one can of evaporated milk, part of the possessions which constituted "food and clothing for two days," so our instructions went. I was tired and I am now living proof that one can indeed sleep on a cement floor, being given these or similar circumstances.

If I had expected to awaken back in the old normal world, this was no dream! These were the same miserable people I had seen, looking for some place to sleep last night, toting their pitiful belongings and wondering what it was all about. To add to my troubles was the ever-present worry over what might have been happening to Eleanor and the children. After satisfying my hunger with some crackers and milk, I made my way toward the iron fence bordering España and to my great relief saw Ricardo out in the crowd. Somehow we communicated and he told me not to worry, that all was quiet at the house. We arranged for future over-the-fence communications and he returned to tell Eleanor, I guess, that I was still alive and in good shape.

I joined some friends and we began the organization of what appeared to be our residence for the uncertain future. The Central Committee, under the watchful eyes of the Jap military, began its task of utilizing the talents of the 2000 men and women who now occupied Santo Tomas University. The unused and dust-filled schoolrooms were converted in to sleeping quarters, separated for men and for women. Our industriousness quieted nerves and kept our minds off the threat to our future. Realizing that our stay was already beyond the two days for which we had been told to prepare, we made jokes about picking the best spot to be safe from the fury of the wet season, yet some eight months away.

Food became the most immediate and acute problem and the Japanese captors recognized that they needed outside help. The Philippine Red Cross was permitted to come in and provide what services they could. We were happy to see burlap sacks of "cracked wheat" brought in and as soon as it could be rounded up on the "outside," there were fresh vegetables, some meat and other essentials. A kitchen was organized, using some of the university's facilities and a group of volunteers became cooks, servers and clean up people. Life became livable with stomachs that were no longer empty and growling for sustenance.

A system was finally devised at the insistence of the Central Committee whereby, under the watchful eyes of the Japanese guard, a package line was made available for families and servants of the prisoners to bring in and, in some instances take out, packages of food and laundry. Everything had to be taken out and examined on the long tables set up for that purpose and only then permitted to enter or leave as the case might have been. I was among those assigned to this "package line" and had the good fortune not only to see Ricardo and Peter now and then, but was treated to one glimpse of Eleanor and the children as they kept out of sight in a Calesa which Ricardo had hired. The horse-drawn vehicle did not draw the attention of the guards as might have an automobile. Anyhow, such was no longer available since I did as much dismantling of our new Dodge as was possible in the pre-invasion panic.

VII

January 1942 was a month of transition, a change of life and a change of attitude. The superiority of nation and race was completely reversed in less than sixty days in the case of the people who now found themselves deprived of their authority, their conveniences, their privacy, all held so dearly as rights inviolable. It was difficult for many to overcome the embarrassment of loss of the comforts of home but we did! We adapted to our new surroundings and their attendant miseries in very short order, perhaps because we were among so many others in the same situation. It became a challenge. If they can do it, so surely, can I! Since the establishment of regular work details, I see ex-millionaires, politicians and professionals working shoulder to shoulder with beachcombers, ex-bums and tramps, all with a single purpose, survival!

Conditions outside the camp were going from bad to worse. Although Eleanor and the children had escaped any harm so far, they were in constant fear. The nearby bicycle factory down the street from the house had turned into a center of nightly revelry and there had been a few nights where sleep was impossible with the noise. There were also incidents of banging on the gates at the house but no forcible entry was attempted. Her mind was never at ease because of the memory of the Nanking, stories she had heard.

She felt a network of trouble slowly closing around her life on "the outside" and food was fast disappearing from the market shelves. So we agreed that she would probably be better off in what was now known as "Santo Tomas Internment Camp" with me, where we would face whatever the danger together.

There was a smaller building behind the main school and it had been used either for a day school or laboratory. As women with children began to come into the camp, it was converted for their particular use since it was one story with about ten classrooms, adequate toilet facilities and a couple of offices where a first-aid room was established. With a lot of help from a couple of mothers who knew Eleanor, I was able to secure a spot in one of the classrooms. I sent word as to what should be sent in during the next few days and when I finally met Eleanor and the boys at the front gate, courtesy of the Japanese sergeant on duty at the time she was weighed down by the balance of the things I had requested. She was a Spartan woman that day as she begged and borrowed from Filipino friends, food for the children and transportation to the camp.

Mattresses, pillows, blankets and mosquito nets had preceded her entry and thanks to the houseboys and the cooperative efforts of my fellows on the package line, all had been set out for my family's arrival in what was now called the "Annex." At first the Japanese guards were reluctant to pass these "comforts" through but the magic password became "bebbies" and I used it whenever anything that would be used by the children came in. Eleanor again showed her fortitude when she had her first view of where she would be living, a six-foot square corner of dusty floorboards that I had managed to lay claim to.

There was an unusual spirit of cooperation among all of the prisoners where mothers and children were concerned. Life and its particular transition at this time was made bearable by help of adults and the many children who were now in custody with us providing playmates of all ages.

One of the most famous phrases made famous by the Santo Tomas rumor mill was "strong help is on the way." But as the days lengthened into weeks, we realized that no one ever mentioned a date when the "strong help" would materialize. We had plenty of news via the Manila Tribune, now under Japanese management. It was allowed to circulate freely and why not? The Japanese military were advancing, almost without meeting resistance, on all fronts. Corregidor was being bombed frequently and we were being slaughtered along the Bataan peninsula. The Marshalls and the Gilberts had been occupied and we had just about given up Wake and Guam. We were cheered by the absence of news about Midway where some kind of naval battle was being fought, and to us, no news was good news.

I had been transferred to new quarters in the Education Building, three floors of ex-classrooms used solely for male prisoners. I was on the second floor in a room with thirty or so others, including a few Englishmen with whom we all became fast friends. Our daily routine was a monotonous series of standing in line for this or that, but primarily food. It did provide a camaraderie that went far to shorten the interminable waiting. The queues, as the British called them, became the market place of news and general information.

By now the Japanese had cut out of the campus rectangle the building used by priests and seminarians simply by constructing a barbed-wire fence which kept us in tighter reign and excluded the seminary and its surrounding grounds. They were also busy constructing small sentry boxes atop the wall, not only at the corners but also at strategic intervals along what might have been an escape route. The front fence was closed off to España Boulevard by the expedient of inserting palm-thatch mats, known as sawali, among, the iron pickets. Only the iron gates themselves left a discreet area for the outsiders to look in or for us to look out on life in the city.

During the lovely January evenings, after curfew and separation of the sexes, as decreed by our captors, a group of the men would sit out on a small rear balcony and exchange rumors, opinions, and mostly lies. Distant lightning flashes gave rise to much speculation, none of which was reasonable, but in some strange way sustaining of our lowly spirits. We were permitted to have subdued lights until 9:00 p.m. and this gave rise to many card games. I loved bridge and we soon found a compatible foursome who went at it regularly each night for an hour or so. Morale was at a low ebb. As we sat one of those nights, a sudden series of distant explosions and machine gun fire froze us to attention. Shouts of "black out!" and "air raid!" caused an immediate scramble and great confusion. Jap guards came around to lock us inside the building, but there was one door which would not close. Two or three dozen of us crowded around to see if we could learn what was going on. We finally caught a glimpse of what appeared to be two sets of tracers in the distant sky, but that was all except pitch black night.

There was a drone of motors and we guessed wildly that there must have been anywhere from ten to a hundred (there was only one). We did hear the unmistakable crump of a bomb here and there but they were small and produced nothing that we could see. It all passed too quickly. In fifteen minutes the night was again black and quiet.

Although we never did learn the facts, our morale improved mightily and we speculated that this could be the start of something big! The date was January 26th, 1942, and no mention was made in the next day's paper or in any subsequent edition. So that was that!

As the days went on, ingenuity became the watchword of our living comfort. Our plumbers used bamboo for pipes and constructed much-needed additional toilet and shower facilities. Our water was good and sweet and apparently in endless supply, thanks to the excellent system built by the U.S. Army Engineers many years before. Through the efforts of several ex-newspapermen a camp newssheet was created and although limited to camp news and gossip, it was tolerated by our captors since they too could communicate with the prisoners through its pages. We had electricians, radio specialists and some entertainers, notably one David Harvey McTurk who with his troupe had been on tour of the Far East when they were caught in Manila and taken into custody with the rest of us. Dave Harvey as he was known professionally, rallied a lot of support for a camp show and permission was granted to construct a stage in the patio space of the Main Building. Floodlights were made out of empty powdered milk cans and ordinary electric bulbs shaded with odd bits of colored cellophane. Volunteer talent was plentiful for the cause was morale building, a must for everyone.

As dusk was gathering, everyone who was able to walk came for this unusual event. The arrival of the Commandant and his staff signaled the start of the entertainment. They were given reserved seats in the front row and even though they were not familiar with some of our slang, they seemed to enjoy the vaudeville, laughing and applauding at the right places. It was here that our parody-camp theme song was introduced. "Cheer Up Everything's Gonna Be Lousey" seemed to sum up our situation so well!

Eleanor and I faced our new life with more resignation than anything else. We treated each day as though it might be our last. There really was no way to prepare for tomorrow except to maintain our faith that rescue would soon be at hand. Early in February we were dealt another blow with a note from Ricardo which reached us through the package line. It read,

> I am very sorry to report, sir, that today many trucks back up to the house and Japanese take everything from the house and put them in trucks. I am hiding in back and they do not see me. I can do nothing. I have try to save a few little things which I keep for you safe.

Although we were depressed by this latest news, we read Ricardo's note with detachment, as though what had happened was not only inevitable but really a part of another existence.

"Protective Custody"

The following are a couple of notes sent from Ricard and Peter. Tom and Eleanor were grateful for the loyalty and helpfulness of the household staff they employed before the war.

> Mr & Mrs Lewis,
>
> Ricardo and I are very sorry to let you know that our house was visited by the Japanese soldiers and they got everything they want. We refused and never give the key to them but they open the door by themselves. As soon as they got in the house they select the things that seems to be worthy. When they leave we phone Mrs Inpeebili and she said she can't do anything because that is what they are doing to all Americans.

Ricardo & his family are living in the house.

As to me, I am suffering to much of hunger. I decided to look for another job. Well that's all and glad to say Dany is healthy.

Peter

Our houseboy — (before war)

III

Mrs Lewis,

You thought saved was keep in our house. But the only question I didn't yet paid rent of my house. So if you please help me to pay the rent so that there is a place to keep my things left there.

Last Sunday and Monday Japanese and some Filipinos came trying to get the ice box and the drawer which you keep the table clothes spoons, fork, napkins and fork. Also the piano. We trying to get the things in the drawer but we don't have the key. I am afraid when they will come and get the drawer they will also get things on it.

Waiting for your decision

Ready

The following notice was read to us at roll-call the evening of February 12th, Lincoln's birthday:

> We regret to report that three men escaped from Santo Tomas last night at eight o'clock. They were apprehended today by Japanese soldiers and returned to Santo Tomas where they were severely punished. Fortunately for them they were brought back to camp instead of being given the supreme penalty of death, the usual punishment for escapees. They will be transferred to some other place. Representatives of the Central Committee visited them before their departure and they asked that this message be sent to the Internees (as we were now known).
>
> 'We deeply regret our actions. We know we made a big mistake and we urge that no one ever attempt it again!'
>
> The Commandant is very angry that his cooperation should have been requited in such a manner and has stated that any recurrence will result in death for the escapees and very stringent restrictions for the Internees. It is therefore, very important that each person interned here take every possible precaution to prevent another escape. (signed) The Central Committee.

The notice bore the imprint of the Commandant's office even though ostensibly authored by the Central Committee, but the final chapter to the incident was horrible. Eyewitnesses later revealed that the three men were taken to a nearby cemetery, provided with pick and shovel and ordered to dig what would become their own graves. They were beaten as their work lagged until they were barely able to stand up and when finished were made to stand in front of their handiwork. A firing squad came forward and, using small arms, fired at the men. Without determining whether they had actually died, the remaining soldiers pushed them into the shallow graves and shoveled the dirt over them until they were covered.

VIII

Our sense of humor, submerged these many weeks by the trauma of change, began to emerge with such signs as appeared in the ladies' bathrooms, where the cubicles had been dismantled for sanitary reasons, "If you desire privacy...close your eyes!"

We chuckled at the incongruous mimeographed forms given us to fill out for the Commandant with such questions as:

Length of residence in P. I.
Amount of money I have with me in camp
Liquid assets
Deposits in local banks and at home?

Undoubtedly this information is destined for the over flowing Ministry of Information in Tokyo, but I would not bet on the accuracy of any we supplied.

We laughed at some of Manila's "fat society" now slimmed down by the restricted diet and hard work. Thousands of pounds had been lost and I really believe that we all were better off for it. I weighed very close to 200 pounds early in December and by March I was down to 160. The time went faster if one worked and played instead of sitting around bemoaning the circumstances. Young mothers like Eleanor had her hands full just caring for two small children, but she found time to have a sewing circle and to monitor the bathroom in the annex. In the latter capacity she was responsible for doling out toilet paper which, of course became scarcer as the days went on. The watchword was "Five sheets today, ladies " and then four and then three and then there was none! Even the substitutes such as the good old Sears Catalogue were carefully rationed and it became quite a burden for the monitor to handle all the gripes.

The camp was now organized to the point where an Executive Committee, headed by an insurance company's branch manager, Earl Carroll, replaced the old Central Committee. Prominent Manilans, Americans as well as British, were appointed to this body and the proliferation of sub-committees began. Many volunteers with expertise in areas which would help create a livable environment were pressed into service. Communication with the outside was preserved through the medium of the package line where I worked and the apparent philosophy of our captors was to keep us reasonably happy by such privileges as this and the camp shows.

The camp was now operating a central kitchen serving some 3300 meals twice a day. The food was simple but there seemed to be a sufficiency of cracked wheat cereal, prunes, duck eggs, pechai and talinum (leafy greens not unlike spinach) to go with whatever food supplies we might have saved to date. Variations in our diet came about whenever the Red Cross uncovered supplies of camotes, bananas, beans, and tea. Once every so often a small supply of chickens showed up and it became a festive meal.

The Annex had its own kitchen and some 600 women and children were fed three light meals each day. Powdered milk was used as long as it lasted but with imports and manufacturing cut off by the war, coconut milk was substituted to preserve the dry milk supply.

At first the camp was ruled by an army lieutenant but in February he gave way to a civilian, a Mr. R. Tsurumi. He had been in the Japanese Consular service and spoke English although not fluently. He made no changes in our own administration and I think we all felt a bit of relief, believing that a civilian would be more understanding, if not sympathetic to our plight. However, we soon found out that he enjoyed no influence with the military who remained our captors over all else. His attitude was to avoid embarrassment over any of the Internees' actions.

By April there had been a substantial increase in the camp population with the capture of most of those who had taken the evidently bad decision to flee Manila in late December. The U.S. forces in Bataan had been badly beaten and the civilians who were in their vicinity had all they could do to avoid the subsequent death march of the military prisoners. As other islands in the Philippine archipelago fell into Japanese hands, more civilian prisoners were taken and shipped to Santo Tomas which was now designated as "War Prisoner Camp #1" on Luzon. These stragglers arrived in pitiful condition, half-starved, beaten, and in tatters. We did everything we could to make livable space for them but our limited resources were strained to the utmost.

I have chalked up to American and British ingenuity some of the engineering marvels produced from bamboo, palm thatch and rattan (bejuca). Much-needed structures were built, structures of bamboo and sawali (palm thatch) with the convenience of running water brought in through bamboo pipes. But equaling ingenuity was the optimism which prevailed to give us recreation in the form outdoor sports. We became avid readers and my supply of books created a demand that benefited us as barter material.

Having some 500 young children and teenagers along with us gave rise to the care of their educational needs. Many of these young people had attended the American School before the war and the staff of teachers who were in camp showed a willingness to organize classes. Teachers were needed to back up and replace those who had not been interned. I was asked to join the Spanish Department by my good friend Prof. Ernesto Joli and was assigned second and third year grades. This put me to work with the textbooks as my fluency was derived from our life in Latin America and not from teaching.

We no longer discussed the progress of the war as the topic of the day. Our new, somewhat regimented social order kept our minds and bodies busy while we passed the time. The *Manila Tribune*, now a four-page daily paper edited under Japanese direction, replaced the old reliable sources of daily news, being circulated in limited numbers in camp with the sanction of the Commandant.

We did our best reading between the lines, ridiculing some of the claims of the Domei News Service. (We identified "Domei" as "Department of Military Erroneous Information.") But they told the truth about their military gains such as the fall of Singapore, the surrender of our forces in Bataan and finally, the fall of Corregidor. Their less credible news items included the daily destruction of the United States Navy and hundreds of aircraft which, if totaled up would amount to more than were ever produced since the Wright Brothers.

Before the fall of Bataan and Corregidor, we shared the belief that our forces would never give up until they could turn the situation around and win the battle. Never did our spirits sink to a lower ebb when the news of Bataan and Corregidor was verified.

Several of our women were wives of men who took part in these actions. They were inconsolable. God only knew what would happen to the prisoners now that they had fallen into the hands of the Japs. The general atmosphere of the camp was one of deep gloom because the war had now moved away from our area and any possible rescue would have to involve the recapture of so much territory before it came to Luzon. Our faith was still there but we had to accept the fact that we would not be rescued tomorrow or next week or next month. We gave up looking forward or backward and simply took each day as it came. There was no planning by anyone for any reason beyond tomorrow. Oh yes, we dreamed of the day of liberation, but in view of our negative circumstances that was only a hazy fantasy.

Among our chuckles was a notice circulated to the Internees by the Commandant in the form of an opinion poll. These are some of the questions:

> Express your frank opinion on the following items:
>
> Which is more responsible for the outbreak of the present war among Japan, America and Britain? America or Britain? Ans. _
>
> What about your forecast of the war situation, will it be protracted or short? Ans. _
>
> Which treatment is more humane, that given local Japanese by the American Army or the one we give to Americans and British here? Ans. _

We were expected to sign and give our age, nationality and sex! Our answers did not please the Commandant and we lived a few days in fear of some loss of privileges, but nothing happened. We managed to get by with an occasional act of defiance but I felt that such behavior as calling a guard a bastard or some equally offensive name when you knew he did not understand you, was like playing Russian Roulette. You could not win! Eleanor and I had agreed that we would stifle our frustrations, keep a low profile especially on behalf of our two small children who had to survive. We would often sit with friends and take stock of where we were and those parents of small children were unanimous in their agreement that there was no escape possible and that the best chance of survival depended upon taking each day as it came, hoping for the best and sticking together.

Beards of all sizes and shapes were making their appearance, some of them due to lack of shaving supplies and some allegedly a defiance "not to come off until the day we are rescued." Because I had a good supply of razor blades and a determined wife as well, I did not succumb to the new fashion. Our clothing became more practical since there were no replacements in the offing. Shorts, T-shirts, halters, and other scanty coverings were acceptable and the sewing groups became extremely busy taking in those many articles of wear that no longer fit because of the weight loss.

Eleanor made clothing by hand for her sons.
Don still has the shirt she made for him.

Eleven babies have been born through April but no new pregnancies are evident. From my wife I learned that women were having irregular menstrual periods and a few had stopped completely and were positive that they were not pregnant. This phenomena had to be blamed on dietary deficiency.

A rather delicate situation occurred one night when a Japanese guard entered one of the ladies' bathrooms. Whatever were his intentions can only be surmised, but the few women present, with great poise and courage imperiously ordered him out. There was some hesitancy about how such a complaint might be brought to the attention of the Commandant, but it was done and resulted in Japanese language signs being placed outside of bathrooms according to sex. As a result of this disturbance, permission was granted for the husbands of Annex residents to stand guard duty whereas no man had previously been permitted to spend the night in that building.

The Executive Committee tried to get permission, according to the Geneva Convention, to send messages home through the Red Cross. The Japanese military, through the civilian Commandant, informed us that neither did they recognize the Geneva Convention, nor the American Red Cross and at some future date a representative of the International Red Cross would be permitted to contact us, maybe!

With the help of a few nurses, four interned physicians and six representatives of American pharmaceutical houses, including myself, some control and maintenance of hygiene and sanitation has been established. There has been a widespread epidemic of enteritis and possibly dysentery, but without lab facilities, medication, and hospital beds, most of the affected had to rely on self-cures. We must have a hospital! That became an obsession with the health team. And we must have medicines!

The Commandant has permitted the construction of a public address system with the stipulation that it is to be used for the publication of his official notices. One of the first was that couples would be permitted to occupy a space 30' x 30' out on the campus and to construct a shelter so that it could be occupied during the day.

The shelters were to be constructed so that a clear view of the interior could be maintained at all times. There would be no physical contact between people of the opposite sex, at any time!

The shelter areas were to be vacated at sundown. Couples with children would be given first choice of location. Many of the families domiciled in the annex chose the campus area behind the building as being away from most general daily activity. We went along with the idea and selected a plot behind the seminary which was now separated from us by barbed wire fences, layered so as to allow the Japanese guards to patrol between us and the building. Our plot was about fifty feet from the wall which bordered a quiet street on the west side of camp.

Supplies of bamboo, rattan, palm thatch and other building materials came into camp through the front gate with the tacit approval of the Commandant since this was one answer to the unhealthy overcrowded conditions of the buildings now open for Internee use. More enterprising of our fellow prisoners set themselves up as contractors, arranging to have these shelters pre-fabricated outside and brought into camp where the buyer would set them up on his 30' x 30' domain. I chose to obtain the parts and attempt to build mine by myself, with of course, much direction and assistance from Eleanor and the boys. The end result was a typical native house, 15' x 12', built about three feet off the ground (in case of flood), with a split bamboo floor (for ventilation and sanitation) and a high conical roof of nipa palm thatch. The supports were bamboo poles, cross-braced to withstand the bad weather. There was not a single nail in the entire structure, everything being tied with rattan (bejuca) or pegged with bamboo spikes. It was cool, and it served us well during the hot summer days as a relief from the humid smelly buildings.

The Lewis Shanty

Our next neighbors in the shanty area, as it now came to be called, were a couple of engineers, one of whom was married. Their structure had been pre-fabricated and sat precisely in the middle of their plot, flat on the ground, with only a plywood floor between them and the earth below. They looked upon my handiwork with some scorn since it did lean a bit to one side and the ridge pole, secure though it was, seemed bent in the middle, much like a sway-back horse.

To cap a series of experiences since Christmas, that would have tested the fortitude of any of us, we were treated to an earthquake which literally shook me out of bed. It happened at one o'clock the morning of April 8th, 1942 and I woke up on the floor in the second floor room of the Education Building to see the night light swing and strange noises of cracking plaster and metal roofs scraping against support beams. We all realized quickly that this was an earthquake. There was a scramble for the outdoors and the confused babel of voices was suddenly stilled by a great white flash of light which must have the circuit-breaker at the main electric plant.

For a while we tried to relate what had happened to the possibility of a rescue attempt and although there was little sleep left for any of us that night we slowly returned in defeat to the reality of the present. Apparently the Annex had not suffered to the extent that the three- and five- story buildings did and the women and children passed the night without ever leaving their quarters.

IX

April 16, 1942, the one hundredth day of internment for most of us, was no different from yesterday or the day before. My little family and I had entered the routine of monotonous prison camp life and so far had weathered it well. Through the medium of the package line we had received food, clothing, and money and with these essentials we existed with a moderate amount of comfort. Food was utilized sparingly and we set aside the non-perishables for the uncertain future, our only concession to planning. Luckily there remained considerable supplies of canned food and it made its way into Santo Tomas, for that was a sure source of money.

The Japanese were wisely retiring foreign currency from the market, issuing in exchange their military pesos at face value.

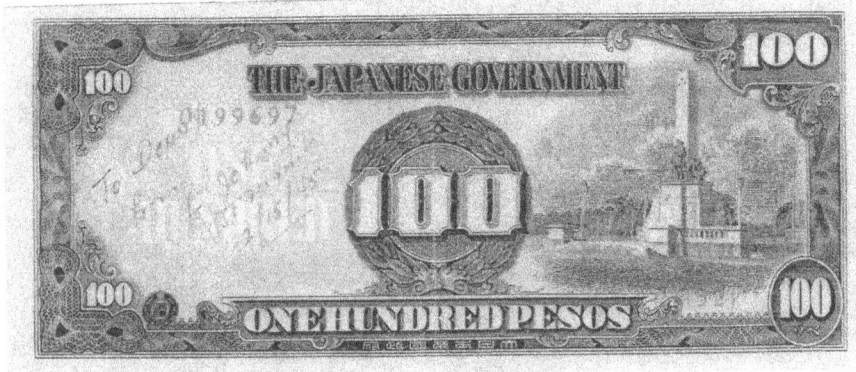

Scrip issued by the Japanese.

To preserve their "Mickey Mouse" money as well as economic stabilization, they pegged the military peso as equal to the Philippine peso formerly equal to $0.50 US. That would work as long as the people would accept the military peso at its stated value. The merchants in Manila who had an eye to big wartime profits decided to insure their permanence by lending large sums of money to the Santo Tomas Internment Camp and to any of the individuals therein who would be willing to sign this or a similar agreement:

> For the loan of one thousand military pesos, within 30 days after the cessation of hostilities, I promise to pay one thousand United States Dollars, in exchange for value received.

The borrowers were either known to the lenders or recommended by business associates such as was my case, making it possible to borrow money to buy the bare necessities for wife and children. The poor Filipino who had been coming in to the package line to offer services or merchandise was bewildered by the rapid deterioration of the paper money issued by the Japanese and soon had to push up his prices beyond our reach. A sort of flea market sprang up in camp and for awhile everything that might have been available on the outside found its way to this impromptu market. The sellers were trying, like everyone else, to survive and their prices reflected the inflationary forces that were causing such havoc outside the camp. The Japanese tacitly permitted the influx of money since they knew we represented affluence to the Filipinos. If we accepted and traded in the Mickey Mouse money, it just had to be good.

Realizing that the future held no promise of financial security based on the military notes, I borrowed and spent for non-perishable foods, every cent I could lay my hands on. These food stuffs were stored in suitcases and trunks which we had Ricardo bring us somewhere along the way. They really came in handy since ordinary storage space was simply non-existent. We had to turn away from the package line as a source of supply because the situation for the Filipinos became almost as bad as ours. The military confiscated everything and the poor Filipino began to see the city as it was, a military encampment where the civilian did not count.

Many of our neighbors tried to start small gardens and with little success. We were approximately six feet above sea level and in a flood plain which had in years past lost its fertility because of salt water flooding. Some of us snickered at the labors of the men, sweating and cursing with inadequate tools under a broiling sun. We were even given seeds by our captors, radishes and other tubers which might have been nourishing if they grew. But I couldn't believe that we would be there long enough for such a crop to mature so when I finally got the message that I'd better try and fail rather than try not at all, I went to our one botanist, a former professor at the agricultural college in Los Banos, to ask his advice. It wasn't all that helpful as he had been wrung dry by others who realized that he was knowledgeable and might help their garden plans. He did give me a few gabi tubers and instructions as to how to plant and nurture them. They were of the tapioca family and would provide some carbohydrate and mineral sustenance if we were able to remove the heavy content of oxalic acid that made them a low-level agricultural preference among the natives. At maturity, the plant root system consisted of a number of tubers shaped like hand-grenades. Above ground the plant was sizeable with leaves known as "elephant ears" since they were at least that large, but unfortunately, not edible. We did find them a fair substitute for tobacco after drying in the sun.

We were now living by the new order and proved it with our diminished waistlines. We all felt more fit than we had in years, physically that is. Our life became so regimented for us that even our original objection to the early curfew changed to tolerance and then acceptance of the joys of a longer daylight. We set aside time for working, a time for playing and a time for reading or otherwise improving our minds. We refused to stagnate! In addition to my teaching assignment, I became co-chairman with Rev. Bob Sheridan, a Maryknoll Missioner, of the camp library. Many books were donated to the cause and we had plenty of customers. In order to preserve our fruitful arrangements for reading, we acted as our own censors to a certain extent. Books which might have compromised us with the Commandant were circulated judiciously and with as little identification as possible. The library was a tremendous support for morale.

June brought the beginning of the seasonal rains. We ruefully recalled the jokes about choosing bed space away from the windows, especially those facing south from whence the weather came. In the early part of the season the rains came heavily and sporadically. The evenings, when dry, were delightful because of the cooling breeze which foretold of more rain the next day. Just before curfew Eleanor, the boys and I would stroll along the few unrestricted paths of the campus, greeting friends, comparing notes and just talking with each other mostly about the good times we had enjoyed together before the war. The moon was still beautiful, especially when full and shining through the huge acacia trees which dotted the campus. In a word, it was romantic, but romance as we practiced it was an almost extinct art-form. We had been forbidden body contact in the more public places where it might offend the Nipponese sensibilities on sight. But the concert music, the full moon and American ingenuity was not to be denied. In the gathering twilight, men and women, before the curfew sounded and they would be forced to separate, could be found in the more secluded spots, acting like any normal couple might back in the privacy of their stateside love nests. Love will (and did) find a way!

Despite these lighter moments there always remained that insurmountable wall between us and "the outside" or freedom. Liberty never was more meaningful to us, the deprived!

The heroic Army nurses who stood beside Lt. Gen. "Skinny" Wainwright at Corregidor were brought to Santo Tomas rather than to any military prison where men only had been kept. We were careful in our manner of greeting, but they were oh! so welcome. They had the background and training to help us organize a hospital, so badly needed and the Japanese gave us permission to use the Santa Catalina convent, now empty, for this purpose. This meant expanding the campsite across Calle Forbes, the street just west of the wall.

A passage had to be constructed so that escapes via that route would not occur. We all worked at some phase of the hospital's development, doctors, nurses and the pharmaceutical representatives who still had some outside connections for the purpose of securing much-needed supplies.

Stu Barnett, John Blair and I were selected to obtain any available drug supplies from the market in Manila under an arrangement with the Commandant office whereby we would make weekly trips to town in the company of an armed guard, identified by an arm band which would testify that we were enemy aliens and prisoners at Santo Tomas. We were permitted to collect money and shopping lists from any source in the camp, arrange for a departure and return trip by hired calesa and then travel to downtown Manila to shock our former wholesalers with this surprise visit.

Before the war we had each been employed by a different pharmaceutical manufacturer and as a result had better connections with those with whom we had done business. We traveled on successive weeks so that there was rarely, if ever, more than one of us out at a time. I can remember the trepidation I felt as I passed through the slowly opening gates out into the "free" world. My Jap guard spoke not a word of English and we did not communicate other than an exchange of his grunted order and my acquiescence. The sight which greeted my eye along Calle España was not too different than the same confusion of traffic which had existed before occupation except that few cars were to be seen and some of these were propelled by a large alcohol burner mounted where the rear seat and gas tank had been. Horse drawn calesas and the larger carromatas were everywhere and bicycles had multiplied like ants. To my relief I was ignored even when we reached our first stop on Avenida Rizal. I had wondered whether the Filipinos had felt any resentment over our abandonment of the defense of Manila and if they would perhaps look at me with anger, but

I felt that their reaction was one of pity, unbelief, perhaps, but understanding of what my position must have been.

Our first stop was a Chinese wholesaler who had a retail drugstore or two as a side line. My guardian seemed to lose interest in exactly what I was doing in favor of an attempt at conversation with a pretty cashier in the outer store. I was fairly free to discuss with my dear old friend Luis what our problems were and he pledged his unreserved help. I had money and I needed everything and anything that could be carried. He loaded me down with vitamins, tonics, and all of the specific items that had been ordered by the Internees. We called the guard in and we all had a bite to eat by way of lunch. As guilty as were my feelings, I knew that this kind of privilege could help my fellow prisoners particularly in the prevention and treatment of the sickness which now struck so many of us so easily.

I was back in camp by 4:00 p.m, passing through the gate and stopping only long enough to drop off my guard. None of the many bundles drew more than a cursory glance from the Sergeant of the Guard and I breathed a mighty sigh of relief.

I met with the representatives of the various areas in camp in a pre-selected spot, away from the watchful eye of the Commandant's office and distributed the goods I had brought with me. There was much excitement and a furious desire for news of the outside world. Unfortunately, on this trip there was nothing I could relate other than a re-hash of the deteriorating economic situation in Manila. Summing up my first trip outside, it was discreet. The greatest sigh of relief came from Eleanor as soon as she knew I had returned safely.

The nurses came to fill an urgent need, staffing the hospital we created. With organization provided by these same nurses, the doctors were able to transfer their field of operations to the hospital and suddenly the real camp sick list became evident. At this time the most common complaints were dysentery, mostly bacillary, dengue fever, a virus infection transmitted by the mosquito and resembling influenza in its symptoms, and an assortment of ailments brought on by our questionable diet.

Our camp population had reached the 3500 mark and included people from all walks of life, beachcombers and criminals to millionaires and saints. Among the former were gamblers and prostitutes who found their respective trades inhibited but not completely wiped out. It was rumored that a few shanties on the other side of camp were quietly used to practice the world's "oldest" profession. I was never able to determine when, where, or how this action was achieved but my wonderment was directed much more at why, in view of the physical condition in which most of us found ourselves. Naively perhaps, I thought that stress and our dietary limitations would have suppressed normal sexual activity and just about have eliminated cohabitation for profit or for other illicit purposes. If I had been right, our morality rating on a scale of ten would have been *nine*, whereas, it apparently was much less.

Gambling flourished, surreptitiously, of course, but poker, bridge, and other card games were played for high stakes either for cash or on post-war credit. While living in the Education Building I became part of a regular bridge foursome, played for small stakes within my limits. One of our players was a complete stranger to all of us until he introduced himself as so and so, convicted of murder and sentenced to life imprisonment just before the holidays, in 1941. I remembered the case from the newspaper accounts at the time. It involved a gambling syndicate in Manila and he was sent out from the States as an "executioner" just about the time we arrived. He did his job, was caught, convicted, and sentenced. The Japanese military cleaned out the prisons and all enemy aliens were eventually locked up together in Santo Tomas. Otherwise he was a quiet fellow with the coldest blue eyes I had ever seen, played a good game of bridge and generally kept to himself.

Our millionaires perhaps enjoyed a little better life in camp than we did, but they were there and they worked shoulder to shoulder with the best and worst of us. Generally they admitted to more happiness and better health as a result of freedom from responsibility and weight loss, now, in contrast to their life before the war. The saints, and there were many, assumed the dangerous authority of the Executive Committee or the most arduous tasks in camp. They were the cooks, the garbage men (a diminishing chore), the internal policemen, and those who had the task of maintaining camp health and sanitation.

Considering the diversity of life styles, language and nationality, Santo Tomas Internment Camp made history in its own evolution into a single community where the entire population worked together in harmony, unselfishly toward the single goal of survival. We had a major complaint but we kept it to ourselves. All of us suffered the complete absence of privacy, day or night, in silent embarrassment. We lived with it only because of its inevitability.

X

Birthdays came and went. Eleanor had her twenty-seventh on March 7th, Donny was a year old on April 14th, and I celebrated my thirtieth on June 19th. Roger would be four September 21st and on all of these occasions Eleanor, with her kitchen magic, managed to produce a cake. She used precious supplies of either cassava or rice flour, brown sugar, baking soda and other ingredients, begged or borrowed. The cooking was done in a covered earthenware pot over a charcoal fire in a home-made hibachi-like stove. I had bartered for a good supply of charcoal which I stored in a large basket beneath the three-foot high floor of our shanty. In case of rain, the basket always had to be lugged indoors. Our kitchen consisted of a galvanized metal sheet on which stood my "stove," a rudimentary sink of the same material with a hole in the bottom for a drain onto the ground below and some old wicker furniture which had come in through the package line, thanks to Ricardo. The prize item of all these furnishings was a Beauty Rest mattress from our house which was placed on a wooden frame and which now served all of us for naps during the hot afternoons.

Since we were required to have the interior completely open to the public eye, we did not have too much protection from the heavy rains which began in mid-year. We did fashion "drops" which for propriety's sake and the Commandant's orders were propped open with a bamboo stick, but could be closed like a shutter when and if we could get away with it. Since we were permitted to use the shanties only in the daytime, the inference was that in case of bad and wet weather we would return to the protection of the buildings where we lived at night.

Thanks to our store of baby foods, Donny was maintaining his scheduled growth pattern according to the book and could even be called "chubby." As a result he utilized more than the usual number of diapers and guess who handled the laundry chores. I became an object of some reverence when I would hang out the family wash on the lines behind the Annex. With eighteen to twenty-four diapers daily, it wasn't long before I earned the title of the "Diaper King." Eleanor had developed a severe infection of her hands, probably due in part to the caustic soap which was all that was available for the laundry. Her hands became so bad that they were in bandages for long periods of time while one or another topical medication was tried with varying but not lasting success. She was more concerned with keeping the children in healthy condition than with her own problems and never uttered a word of complaint despite the pain and inconvenience she suffered.

Some contaminated food was brought into camp in July and both Roger and I became the victims of acute amoebic dysentery. Fortunately for us I knew the symptoms and wasted no time getting to the hospital and obtaining a supply of Lillys Carbasone from John Blair. The promptness of our treatment kept us in bed for only a week when we were pronounced free of infection as well as symptoms. Both of us had lost more weight than we could afford and we had to take it easy for a while. Prof. Joli had taken my classes and Father Sheridan had filled in for me at the library, so I spent my waking hours reading and writing for another week until I felt well enough to get back into the swing of camp life.

Meanwhile the number of people reporting to the hospital with amoebic dysentery, presumably from this same source of infection, increased to epidemic proportions. A flood of new regulations concerning the handling of food came out of the Executive Committee's meetings with the Commandant and for awhile our outside source of food was simply cut off. It seemed that while the effect of bacillary dysentery was more severe on the patient, it responded to treatment immediately and left no lasting symptoms. Amoebic was more difficult to diagnose, treat and get rid of because, even symptom-free, an infected person could remain a carrier. This meant recurrent lab tests to see if the organism remained viable in the stool. Roger and I were lucky since we remained negative on six bi-monthly checkups.

In late September as we were involved in a game of softball not too far from the gate, the players and some few spectators were startled to see an open truck coming in through the gate with a couple of dozen raggedy-looking men who were clearly not Japanese. The truck stopped not far from where we were and, since the Jap guards seemed not to mind, we asked them where they had come from. Their answer, was Davao, Mindanao. During the exchange one of them said, "If you guys are willing, as soon as we get located here, we'll bring out a softball team and show you a thing or two."

The truck soon pulled onto the plaza in front of the Main Building and we watched them pile out and move toward their new quarters, as they were evidently expected. Our brief look at these men was enough to tell us that they must have been through a torturous trip as they looked starved, unkempt and badly the worse for wear.

They would have had to come by boat, probably in the hold of some ancient transport and we were eager to meet and talk with them. We continued our game and just about an hour later we watched about a dozen of this same group of men approaching our game, so we stopped playing, and waited for them to come over and speak.

One tough-looking red-headed individual seemed to be their spokesman and he said, "I hope you don't think we were kidding! We'd really like to play you some softball."

We looked at each other questioningly and I said, "We've just finished our game, what do you all think? How about ten volunteers?"

I guess that most of us realized that this would not be the best moment to ask them to recount their odyssey and so we got together enough men to field a team. The redhead apologized for not having any gear and asked if we would mind their using ours. We agreed and we started to work out our line-ups. A light dawned when I heard the redhead say "Father Quinn, you play first base and Father Sheean, short top."

And so it went. The redhead turned out to be Father McSorley, their Assistant Superior, and the rest of them were Roman Catholic priests, Oblate Missionaries stationed in and around the southern island of Mindanao. Eventually we found out that they played a very good game of softball. They were interned in Davao and about two weeks before their arrival in Santo Tomas they were put on a transport and headed for Manila. Their description of that trip helped us to live a little better despite all of the usual daily complaints of camp life.

Despite the continuing admonitions we received from the Executive Committee regarding the privilege of the "package line" it was abused more and more by the increasing number of notes in and out of Santo Tomas, the entry of alcoholic beverages despite the categoric prohibition of same and it became merely a matter of time before someone became drunk and disorderly or before a cursory search by a Jap guard would turn up a note with some forbidden message in it.

Reflecting the dissatisfaction of the Commandant with the continuing evidence of drunkenness in camp, a series of restrictions regarding the use of the package line were published. The Executive Committee tried to control these transgressions before the Military got into the act by imposing sentences of confinement in the camp jail on a couple of the most flagrant violators. Nevertheless, the Commandant closed the package line for a week and then reopened it with a restriction on the passage through of anything except food. To Eleanor and I this mattered very little because our contacts on the outside were no better off than we were.

The minutes of the Executive Committee for September 28th reflect the diminishing patience of the Japanese military at this point.

> The Chairman reported on a conversation with Mr. A. Kodaki in which he was advised that as a result of inspection by the Military Police this morning, evidences of drinking in camp were discovered, and the Military Police were demanding an immediate answer as to how liquor was coming into camp...

Mr. Kodaki was Chief, Department of External Affairs, a civilian and obviously subject to the Military and therefore sensitive to any embarrassment we might cause him. If the Military saw fit to step in and take over the policing of the camp, the punishments available under their code would be extremely harsh.

In a supposed attempt to keep matters in status quo, Mr. Kodaki had the Executive Committee post a notice of new regulations which follow:

1. No internee shall leave the camp without a written pass from the Commandant's office. While outside of the camp internees must confine their activities strictly to the purpose for which their passes are granted, and refrain from visiting in public places. Discussions of subjects pertaining to the war are prohibited.

2. Unless properly authorized, no internee shall attempt to communicate with any person outside of the camp or passing through the package line, by writing or signaling in any manner whatsoever.

3. The possession of radios, cameras, flashlights or weapons of any kind is prohibited—provided that monitors or patrols may use flashlights in the line of duty.

4. No intoxicating liquor shall be brought into camp, nor shall any internee produce, possess, consume, sell, give away or otherwise handle the same.

5. All outside shanties and campgrounds must be vacated at 7:15 p.m. and from this hour until curfew at 9:00 p.m. all internees shall be restricted to that certain designated area in front of the Education Building, restaurant, and Main and the space under the dining sheds.

6. Each internee shall report in person to his room monitor at 9 p.m. unless he has previously so reported and is in bed or actually engaged in camp duty at such hour. No gambling shall permitted and all games must cease by 10:45 p.m.

7. Internees must conduct themselves in an orderly manner at all times, and each shall perform his or her camp duties as assigned to them.

8. Internees shall be responsible for maintaining and preserving proper order as well as sanitation and health conditions; also for the regulation of internal activities in strict accordance with all

the rules and regulations of the camp...

It is further ordered that all violations, other than petty infractions, of the internal rules and regulations of this camp be reported to the Commandant's office, such reports to include a statement of the facts in each case. The form and degree of the punishment will be determined by the military authorities.
A. Kodaki

The weather pattern changed for the worse in October and severe storms hit us about once a week. They had not yet reached the intensity of a full-blown typhoon, but the rain fell in torrents and the wind was often sufficiently forceful as to break off large limbs of the fragile acacia trees which dotted the campus. There was some shanty damage, but no one was hurt during the bad part of the wet season. Our greatest difficulty came in coping with long hours of inactive confinement within the buildings. Even during brief appearances of the sun, we found the grounds soggy and muddy and useful only for passage to and from the eating areas. The wet weather bogged down even the best attempts at optimism and we became stoics as to dreams of rescue within the foreseeable future.

The Japs were still winning the war! Or so said a visitor who had been interned in the United States. This member of the Diplomatic corps had been stationed in Panama and wound up his tour of duty interned in New York City. About fifteen hundred internees had gathered, at the call of the Commandant, to listen to this gentleman tell of the mistreatment of the Japanese who had been interned in the United States. Whatever motive the Commandant had for this talk must have been a failure. When we learned that the alleged discomforts perpetrated on those poor unfortunate diplomats took place at the luxurious Greenbrier at White Sulphur Springs, West Virginia, our questions which were permitted after the speech became tongue-in-cheek and a bit of embarrassment for the Commandant.

Thanksgiving had come and gone, unnoticed save by a few who like us, were glad just to be alive. There has been nothing in the news except for fragments of the campaign in

North Africa which I learned about on one of my now monthly trips outside. This is so far away in the world that we looked upon such action with a sort of detachment as though we were hearing about a forty-second cousin, twice removed, whom we had never met.

Eleanor told me to curb my impatience. We had enough to do taking care of the children and ourselves just from day to day. The passage of time would take care of itself. And I had to admit that the frustrations most of us felt were only a waste, that the proper attitude had to have a large share of fatalism and a tinge of hope, topped off with a thin layer of faith.

We were cheered by the diminishing threat of an attack on our homeland. Whereas the Mainichi news service had boasted that such a raid was sure to materialize, the story of our victory at Midway and the lost Japanese opportunity for further naval success filtered through the lines of newsprint and made itself clear to us. There was a hobby show and display of the ingenious creations of some of our more talented internees. Wood-carving, toy making, sewing, embroidery, painting and cabinet-making demonstrated that our inventiveness was still with us. We planned a better Christmas for all of the children and the cooperation and willingness of those with the knowledge of their crafts meant that toys would be available to all for the holiday. As though God approved our efforts, an announcement was made a few days before Christmas that small "comfort kits" had arrived from Canada and South Africa and would be promptly distributed. They contained cheese, soda crackers, margarine, bacon, tea, sugar, chocolate and a bar of soap and one kit was given to each two internees as there were not enough to go around. Since it was almost a year since we had seen some of these items, it helped make Christmas a day to be thankful.

About 150 new prisoners had been brought in from Cebu and the surrounding islands. Their trip was horrible with much of the days en route spent locked up below deck in the stifling heat of the overcrowded holds. Food was scarce and the small amount of available water scummy and foul-tasting.

Nevertheless they arrived and were quickly assimilated into camp life.

Christmas Eve has reminded us through song and good fellowship that we have much to be grateful for, since the joy of the recent arrivals is a wonder to behold. Our own spirit seems, somehow, enhanced this night as we brought out hoarded goodies and gladly shared them with our neighbors. The night was clear and in the apparent relaxed atmosphere of the holiday spirit, even among our enemies, we sang Christmas carols until long beyond curfew.

XI

Internees had given their effort so that this Christmas day would provide only pleasant memories, at least to the children. The toys were distributed by a real live costumed Santa Claus who of course, needed an extra large amount of padding to be convincing. The adults enjoyed a gala sports program with soft-ball games and even an "east-west" touch football game to entertain in the American tradition. Fortunately our captors were doing a bit of celebrating on their own and left us to our own devices for the day.

My monthly trip outside took place on December 28th and I had my usual supply list and money to go with it. My guard was the same non-English-speaking fellow who had been with me on two other occasions. We reached Santa Cruz bridge at the Pasig River and to my great surprise he said in English, "You go. Come back at 3 o'clock. I see girl friend now. OK?"

I said something like *you bet*! And on I went in the calesa to Avenida Rizal and my only scheduled stop, the Farmacia TeeHanKee. Jose and his brother Luis, the co-owners, were there to greet me and load me down with things that they could supply and some merchandise they had bought for us to fill out the list I had brought on my last visit. Jose winked at me and said, "You good people have been locked up just about a year now, so I've fixed up some 'medicine' that will help you forget your troubles at least for one night, New Year's Eve."

I reminded him that there were dire penalties for anyone caught with alcoholic beverages in camp, but he explained that I had nothing to worry about because certain medicines had a highly effective alcoholic content. So he explained what he had done. He had taken a fifth of Fundador Brandy, poured it into a pharmaceutically acceptable bottle and labeled it "Elixir Paregoric," along with the prescription as if written by a physician. He immersed the cork in vanilla extract in case some curious guard might open it to smell the contents. He apologized and hoped that the vanilla extract would not lessen the delight of the fine Spanish brandy. The bottle was stashed away with other tonics and similar appearing nostrums and as the clock approached three, I left my friends with fond farewells and good wishes for our mutual coming year.

Sure enough there was my little friend waiting for me at the bridge, right on the dot of three. We moved on to the gate at Santo Tomas where I usually dropped him and went on into camp with only a cursory acknowledgment from the Sergeant.

Today, it was not the same! I stopped and my guard-friend jumped down, but the Sergeant came over and waving his bayoneted rifle said, "You get down!"

He started to poke around in the many bundles I was carrying and like a dog on the scent reached in and pulled out my precious bottle of brandy. My heart thumping, I faced him when he growled, "Hah! What this?"

I stammered, "That is medicine for babies. Cures stomach ache; helps with dysentery," I went on lamely.

To my horror, he uncorked the bottle and smelled the cork. He looked at me with what I took for anger to be followed by a rifle butt in my gut and said, "Where you live?"

I told him Shantytown, over that way and he said with the slightest hint of a grin, "Me have stomach ache. Come to your shanty for medicine later, OK?" He handed the bottle back to me and motioned me to go on and the breath which had left my body returned!

Who knows? Maybe it was the season or maybe just an errant sense of humor. So Eleanor and I agreed that it would be wise to do away with the evidence as soon as possible so we gathered together a few of our closest friends just three nights later, and celebrated New Year's Eve in an appropriate manner.

The first small "comfort kits" had turned out to be from South Africa and to our great joy, additional kits from Canada made their appearance. They contained canned goods including sardines, corned beef, precious tins of powdered milk, cigarettes and tobacco among other edibles. The perishable food was eaten first and most of the canned goods were hidden away for use in the unpredictable future.

We often wondered how the folks back home were faring. Had word gotten through as to our fate? What of our brothers, three of whom we knew to be in the army. The *Manila Tribune* printed such tripe about the hardships allegedly suffered by the American people under these wartime conditions that we either ignored or disbelieved whatever was printed. The newspaper referred to "sources of reliance" when they told of the long lines of starving people in the large cities, waiting for food and clothing all of which was supposedly under tight rationing. Many movie stars and famous sports figures had been "conscripted" into the armed forces and were fighting it out somewhere in battle.

It was not difficult to accept the demands of a wartime economy at home, but the "Nips" would have their readers believe that morale had sunk our nation to its greatest depths with the continuing reversals as reported by these same reliable sources of information. We chose eternal optimism as the only antidote to boredom and propaganda and one day our rumor factory came up with a gem! The word spread like wildfire that the French luxury liner *Normandie* had been converted to the world's largest aircraft carrier and had suddenly appeared along with a destroyer flotilla off the coast of Mariveles. If we didn't believe that, one could go and see for himself if he could sneak up on the forbidden roof area of the Main Building.

No matter how stupid this may appear in retrospect, I went up along with two other daring fools. I just had to see it with my own eyes! We climbed the last flight of stairs and found the door to the roof barred, but not locked. So we wormed our way through and, careful not to be seen from below, trained our eyes in the direction of Mariveles, some twenty-five to thirty miles across the bay. Of course we had only the naked eye which at that distance plus our eager imagination picked out what could have been the ship and its escorting vessels, but were actually no more than dots on the horizon. There was nothing else to do but admit our inability to confirm the rumor which turned out to be the wisest decision we could have made. We learned much later that the *Normandie* had been in the Navy Yard in Brooklyn to be refitted, but had unfortunately burned and remained no more than a hulk for the balance of the war.

The "rumor factory" had its good and bad points. It served to combat the propaganda which could have been devastating to our morale. On the other hand when the promised "help is on the way" failed to materialize it increased our cynicism to the real gains we made in the European theatre.

As each day passed the word "freedom" took on a new and rapturous meaning. It became the subject of our prayers, the object of our dreams and the topic of evening discussion. We had to lose it to appreciate its true value. It signified home, family, friends, security, comforts, things so far beyond our present reach. Why do we have to lose something so precious to really appreciate its meaning? We have long since realized that many of the good things we simply took for granted would not mean so much to us now as the simple everyday staples like, good piece of bread and butter! Even the perishable food from the Canadian kits was soon consumed and forgotten and then we were back to our daily ration of rice and whatever the camp could "scrounge." Now there's a good word. It is new to me but to "scrounge" has become part of our daily activities, for men, women and children, as a means to survive.

On New Year's Day Eleanor treated Roger, Donny and our selves to a feast designed around the last tin of "Spam." She had bartered for a can of corn, some pudding and some egg-nog, plenty of nourishment and a delight to the taste buds for all of us. We topped the pleasant day off with a stroll in the moonlight as a fitting way to start the New Year.

Some of Eleanor's tattered notes revealed that the family all developed bad colds for which we took aspirin and not much else. She went on to write that we felt pretty low during the day following New Years but pepped up enough to play bridge with Mark and Dorothy Mills that evening.

A few days later we remembered that January 6th would be the anniversary of my incarceration, along with many others. Dave Harvey and Don Bell, a radio personality from pre-hostility times, put together a radio parody on "The March of Times" broadcast over the loud speaker system to a crowd gathered in front of the Main Building that evening. Well done but saddening!

Today's news comes from Eleanor's diary in which she describes the monthly room cleaning as nerve-wracking, tiring and productive of a lot of bedbugs! She is still sleeping in the corner of room #31, with Roger and Donald sharing her Beautyrest mattress. Her mosquito netting is still in good shape and without it she would be a candidate for dengue and possibly malaria which has broken out in the environs of the camp.

The camp seems brighter, the morale a bit improved since we celebrated our "anniversary." Maybe it's because we suspect that we may have passed the half-way mark or maybe because we managed to survive a year of this misery. There is nothing positive to go on but the feeling is there and it is growing to a conviction that we will not be here to celebrate another anniversary.

In a camp-wide tuberculin test under the direction of Dr. C. N. Leach, a peace-time member of the Rockefeller Foundation, 18.2% of the children were found to be positive. This is deplorable, especially as there seems to be nothing we can do about it. The high percentage is blamed on the overcrowded conditions of the camp, primarily, but also to dietary deficiencies. Emphasis is being placed on fresh air and exercise for these unfortunate children.

There is now hope that the Commandant's office will lift some of the restrictions on shanty life which is now confined to the hours between 6: 30 a.m. and 6:30 p.m. Such a move would certainly ease the overcrowding and help contain the spread of disease which our present living conditions favored.

January 9, 1943 saw the Commandant raise the question of pregnancy, if such were possible under the circumstances of our questionable health and the rules and regulations prohibiting cohabitation or even touching between the sexes. The Commandant posted a notice requiring that all cases of pregnancy be reported to his office not later than January 11th. This order was further clarified by the posted statement that such a situation would be embarrassing and difficult to explain to the Military Headquarters.

The Executive Committee followed these instructions with some of their own, as follows: "In view of the confidential nature of this report, all women internees, whether married or single, who are now pregnant report to the camp medical director so that a complete report may be made."

Several days passed, days of considerable worry for the women whose names finally appeared on a list, now in the hands of the Commandant. The lid was off when it was announced that all prospective fathers (if they could be named) would be sentenced to the camp jail for violating the non-fraternization rules. Their sentences would range from thirty to sixty days and their diet would be confined to rice and water. It was amazing how the Japanese could get right to the heart of the matter! The "camp jail" was a small dark room in the front of the Main Building and its only means of ventilation was a small barred window, high above the average man's head. Its first occupant was a husband, already the father of seven children, and apparently dedicated to increasing the population despite the rigors of internment.

XII

There have been several weeks of comparative quiet. The Japs have left us alone and the incident of the expectant mothers has passed into history with no one suffering any lasting damage. The weather has been excellent, dry and sunny and not overly hot. Softball enthusiasts have been keeping the game going with considerable vigor and some talent and they have found an appreciative audience who round up a good sized crowd daily to root for their favorite team.

My talent in this field did not rest in batting or fielding prowess, although I managed to play in every game with occasional credit. It was in recruiting the very best players who could be found in camp and who might be willing to play for our team, the "Pirates." For example, I had heard that there was a truly first-rate ball player in our section of the camp, Lonnie Frey, who had manned several details with me and was friendly enough to sell on the idea of playing softball. Although reluctant at first, Lonnie finally capitulated to my pleadings and became the nucleus around which I was able to continue my recruiting. Next was Gordon Stagner, who I heard could make a softball jump like it was going up steps, when he pitched to the batter. When Gordon agreed it was with the promise that I would go after Howard Hick for first base.

I found out through my grapevine that Howard and I had been at New York University at the same time (along with 24,000 other students) and had played basketball. When I met him, I knew why! He was well over 6′ 5″ and I had to crane my neck just to meet his eyes. Howard and his lovely wife Jean had come to Manila in search of coconut for the Baker Company, and he had become their local manager. Of course a guy with this height made an ideal first baseman but it took much coaxing to come out and give it try. And so it was with the recruitment of a team which finally got together and found so much enjoyment from athletic endeavor.

None of us were that strong or that much out of condition from *la dolce vita* but sports provided a much-needed break in the daily routine to keep us from otherwise going crazy.

April 3rd was "blue Saturday" for Eleanor. Her mother would have been celebrating her fifty-seventh birthday and all she had were the letters, now almost two and one-half years old, which she read and re-read to the boys. Eleven days later we helped chubby little Donny celebrate his second birthday. He was really not all that interested though we had some of his playmates over to the shanty for lemonade and fast-disappearing cookies. He was a typical toddler, at an age where everyone thought he was cute and tried their best to spoil him. His clothes were some hand-me-downs from his older and skinnier brother, all except shoes, which he would have discarded anyhow. To go barefoot was the custom for most of the kids.

For us it was Bakias or wooden clogs, homemade with a band of rubber across the instep to hold them to the foot. After a few turned ankles we became quite accustomed to their cool comfort.

As an aftermath of Donny's little birthday celebration, he developed a temperature of 104° later on in the afternoon. It had all the appearance of a slight cold but as the evening wore on the fever reached 105.6° and had us all scared for his safety. I took him over to the hospital where Dr. Fletcher diagnosed his problem as the flu complicated by the appearance of another two-year molar. In a couple of days he was back to normal but not after giving his Mom and Dad quite a bit of worry. Poor Don, he hates the hospital mainly because he is not with his mother during the long nights.

Rumor has it that a new internment campsite is being developed. This did not surprise us since the constant admission of new prisoners has caused overcrowding in all the buildings. Some relief could have been obtained had we permission to live day and night in the shanty areas, but the

Japanese probably considered us more accountable if we were herded into the buildings for the nighttime hours. This time the rumor became fact. A new camp at Los Barios, sixty kilometers to the south, was under construction and unmarried men and other male volunteers would be transferred to the new location.

The new site was described as overlooking Laguna de Bay, a large shallow lake. The basic construction was carried out by Filipinos, but the finishing touches would be done by the new residents. It seems that the idea of the camp came from a sudden, impulsive decision on the part of the Commandant and his staff. At the same time permission was granted for the men to move out of the buildings into their shanties, if they were lucky enough to possess one. In spite of this so-called relief gesture, the women and children failed to benefit to any great degree since there immediately began an influx of elderly and sick who had been permitted to live outside in their homes until this moment. Apparently living conditions in Manilla became intolerable for the "enemy aliens" since, not only had they been deprived of food and clothing, but they were lonely, shunned by former Filipino friends and restricted to their residences.

The day came for the transfer of 800 of our men. As the required number had not been reached through volunteering, a few married men were drawn by lot, against their will and to the anguish of their families. They were promised that their wives would be permitted to join them at some future date, but the chances of that materializing were nil, as everyone knew at heart. These men were mostly young and they had been the backbone of the camp's work force. They would be sorely missed! Among Eleanor's notes was an account of her attempts to boost our morale at Easter by dressing all of us in the remnants of our pre-war clothes, hidden away and a bit moldy, but there for such special occasions, few though they might ever be. She wrote that she traded for a pair of white shoes, something equally as useless in our present state. I turned up an unused pair of shorts, purchased so long ago in Shanghai! She had knitted me a green string sweater which fit me like a shroud and for the kids, some hand-me-downs from some of our neighbors' children who had outgrown them. Somewhere Eleanor had resurrected a lovely green dress which looked well on her despite the fact that her loss of weight made it hang loose here and there.

There was an unspoken but united recognition of Easter not only in the religious ceremonies but also in the quiet parade which took place in front of the Main Building. It was sad yet a boost to our depressed spirits that we still cared enough to come out, dressed in our best to exchange the greetings of the day as well as compliments on each other's fine appearance.

We saw our second movie since internment and it was a happy occasion since we were allowed to place camp chairs in the same parade area and see the show after the normal curfew hour. This time it was Joel McCrea and Veronica Lake in *Sullivan's Travels*. There was a Japanese propaganda film showing their industrial progress in the occupied state of Manchukuo since the war began. We had been cautioned not to applaud at any time during the show. I do not think the committee was worried about our hand clapping but more likely about our natural reaction to the Jap propaganda.

Travel is broadening! Travel while you are young! This was our great plan for the early years of our marriage but our present circumstances sharply altered our philosophy. Never was our yearning for home and family anymore acute than at this time. We talked of having a little girl to round out our family. Not now of course, but when? When would this be over? Could we plan for a more permanent life-style where we could really put roots down, own our own home and be assured that our children would receive a proper education? There would be no more packing and unpacking, renting of houses for short periods, using someone else's furniture, and moving. For my part, I had had enough with almost eleven years of living abroad and my principal goal in life from now on would be the welfare and happiness of my wife and children. My career in the export business would have to take a back seat.

Here we were, talking about the future, making plans and dreaming like there was a tomorrow, and a next month and year. May be it's because the Japanese have become more surly and less communicative which rumor attributed to our successes in the Solomon Islands. This news filtered in from the outside, allegedly heard on clandestine radios out in the hills, passed by word of mouth, mile by mile into Santo Tomas where General MacArthur's friends were being held prisoner.

During early May, the Japanese Premier, Gen. Hideki Tojo paid a surprise visit to Manila. We learned about it after the fact and speculation was rife as to the purpose of his visit. The Philippines had been promised their complete independence by the United States before the Japanese invasion. Gen. Tojo, representing the current rulers of the islands, talked about independence but tying it to a more cooperative effort in the Japanese war against the Allies. The newspapers pointed out that in gratitude for all the occupying forces had done to liberate the Filipinos from their former oppressors, they should now be willing to have their sons shed their blood, alongside of the Japanese warriors, in mortal combat with the enemy. There was much resentment at this turn of affairs and it was said that much extra precaution was needed to avoid the possibility of an assassin's bullet finding its way into the Premier's heart.

Roger and I had our hair cut for the first time in weeks. The job was hardly stylish but we were cool and found to be free of any foreign animal life. Meanwhile Eleanor joined with other mothers in a general cleaning of the Annex. Bedbugs and cockroaches in abundance were given the death sentence without remorse. Mosquito nets were repaired, wooden bedsteads fumigated and mattresses turned over. Clean but worn linen was installed and the ladies celebrated their accomplishments with an impromptu party. Some husbands, if they could be found, had been pressed into service, as was I. My reward was a hug and a kiss from my Love and also a rare piece of rice cake from the other ladies.

There was a secluded area, formerly a garden kept by the seminarians, which had been cordoned off from their building and given to us for religious services, lectures and meetings. Folding chairs would usually accommodate some two hundred people and I had been flattered with an invitation to speak one evening, on the subject of beautiful Guatemala. My talk was well-received according to my severest critic, Eleanor, and as a first attempt at speaking publicly, I was pleased with myself that I did not collapse along the way. Perhaps this incident was responsible for the emergence of the "ham" in me for I joined Dave Harvey's weekly entertainment troupe as a sometime troubadour. My precious Martin ukulele had survived the hardships of the past year and a half and its music gave solace to me, at least, and perhaps to my little family who had to listen whenever the mood was upon me. Among the Harvey entertainers were several musicians and with my uke, Wally King's drums, two guitars, a piano and other fillers, we put together a Hawaiian combo that produced some fair music. My personal moments of glory came with the vocal offerings of "King Kamehameha" and "The Hawaiian War Chant," made possible because no one else in the group could or would sing!

The conductor of the Manila Male Chorus put out a call for men interested in forming a choral group. We had a stage, a talented accompanist in Melvin Toyne and the conductor, Karl Kreutz, whose call produced some fifty interested vocalists. My limited talent put me in with the second tenors and we arranged to practice once or twice a week with the goal of presenting a concert for the entertainment of the internees. Somehow, Karl managed to lay his hands on a sufficient number of arrangements of classical, spiritual and modern music to outfit the male chorus. The idea was successful because it gave those involved another outlet for their otherwise unoccupied hours, it entertained the internees and did not offend the Japs. In all of the crowded squalor of the prison camp, the power of song, as it was in concert, lifted morale and brought us back momentarily to the world of sanity and culture.

Each part of the war had its heroes. In Santo Tomas we had many, including those on the outside who risked their lives and freedom to help us. Some of the pipelines to supplies were maintained by the few people who were permitted to go into the city and purchase food, clothing and drugs. There were also buyers for sanitation, construction and general supplies, including ten or so men and one woman, a Filipina who bought vegetables and meat for the camp, when, if and when, such edibles were available . She knew her way around, as a native woman married to an American and as time went on she became known as the "Angel of Santo Tomas." Not only was she fearless in her dealings with the military but she was unbelievably successful in obtaining food in a starving city. All of the buyers traveled out into the city in the same mode. There was an armed guard in attendance and each of us was identified by an arm band. We travelled in a horse-drawn calesa and generally on the assumption that our armed guard had his eye on us all day, we were not searched upon our return.

In this manner however, much contraband passed in and out of camp. Money and notes continually moved in and out. I believe that the Japanese deliberately winked their eyes at the money since our use of it gave it a certain credibility. The outside underground was so well organized that wives heard from their soldier or sailor husbands, imprisoned in Cabanatuan a hundred or more miles to the north of Manila. Through this same torturous underground route came several recent copies of *Life* and *Reader's Digest*, probably having originated in Australia, dropped by submarine off the Luzon coast and passed hand to hand through the guerrillas to our Chinese and Filipino contact among the merchants and finally into camp along with supplies. It was a serious risk at every step but from our point of view it fanned the embers of hope that kept us alive. The "authentic" news of the progress of the war was disappointing but it did establish that we were not losing any more territory at this time.

One day in June the Commandant's office issued a warning concerning the suspected activities of the camp buyers. We had reports of being followed by Japanese in civilian clothes, and although it had not happened to me I became shaky about continuing my job. We were ordered to obtain official passes from the Commandant and would have to wear a new red armband. A new list of items to be considered as contraband was posted and it emphasized notes and money as forbidden. Hours of travel outside were shortened and a couple of the buyers were replaced on orders from the Commandant. I was not due to go out again for a few weeks so I had some time in which to consider the choice of continuing or not. There were other pharmaceutical representatives about who either had no wives or families. As it turned out, I had made my last trip.

The articles most frequently purchased by individuals through the buyers included cones of ordinary package string, which the women used for knitting sweaters, baby clothes, even brassieres. This had become a practical solution to the disappearance of clothing from the market. The cones rose in price from a pre-war forty-five cents to a current fifty dollars. Food as a purchase for individuals had become unavailable at any price and toilet articles were now becoming scarce. I received a gift of a one pound can of Dr. Lyon's Tooth powder that would certainly last for years if we didn't decide to eat it like candy.

Inside the camp, the business of barter and trade had become big and it flourished in the hands of those who were motivated by extreme selfishness. There was no room for charity or love in this market and goods were supplied only to those who were willing to pay usurious prices in cash or in promissory notes, checks, or drafts. As an example, a mother who might need a pound of powdered milk for her little one's formula would have to pay the going price of one hundred U.S. dollars cash or paper equivalent. This busy little market lasted as long as supplies could be found to stock the make-shift shelves of the stalls or shanties used for the purpose.

XIII

By June 1, 1943, certain shanty areas had been released for round the clock use by men and older children and further permission was given to lower the drops which served to cover the window space in case of bad weather. I left the Education Building with no regrets although after one and a half years of close contact with forty roommates there should have been some—over the breaking up of a perennial bridge foursome, for instance. However, the easing of the overcrowded situation in Room 212 was the topic of the day.

In early June, all male internees who had been able to take advantage of the release of certain shanty area for twenty-four hour round-the-clock habitation were living in a quasi-homelike environment. The routine was generally the same for each of us and my typical daily schedule ran as follows: at 6:30 a.m. reveille with a quick dash for the breakfast line about ten minutes later. By this time Eleanor, with the two boys in tow would have passed me in the line, on their way out to the shanty to start the charcoal fire and heat some water for our ersatz coffee. The "coffee" was made from ground peanuts, roasted, and mixed with the few remaining grains of real coffee to give it some resemblance to the real thing.

As soon as breakfast, usually a duck egg apiece or lugan, a watery mush made from rice, was finished and our "chow" dishes were cleaned and stored, we pitch in on the daily laundry. There never was very much since Donny had graduated from diapers a few weeks before. He could now make his needs known vocally although without much warning so that we had to be alert for the emergency call of nature or suffer the consequences. By nine o'clock I was ready to assume my camp detail as a high school level teacher of Spanish. The job was interesting because of my students and what great strides in learning they seemed to accomplish under these strained circumstances. I had a few exceptional learners who I knew would be successful in college once things returned to normal. There were a couple of incorrigible cutups, a boy and a girl, who had been in my class since its inception. I found a way to cope with their efforts to disrupt class since they were captives like me, with the only alternative for fifteen year-olds being a tough garden assignment. Whenever they misbehaved I would ask the class to judge them and mete out a fitting punishment. The class was tough and they enjoyed their peer position to the extent of forcing one or the other to sing a song in Spanish in front of the class! This sort of thing worked like magic and once again we would enjoy peace and quiet in the room.

By a quarter to twelve I was ready for a dash back to the shanty or to the "chow" line where I might find Roger holding a place in line with two or three buckets for whatever was available. These containers were empty vegetable or juice cans scrounged from the kitchen in the early days, fitted with a wire which served as a handle to carry them. Occasionally I was able to buy a few scarce but expensive fresh vegetables to garnish the routine mid-day ration of rice and make-believe gravy. The only condiments we had left at this time were pepper, rock salt, cinnamon and vinegar, none of which were too helpful in making our dish more palatable.

After lunch the four of us took a nap in the cool confines of our shanty. My afternoon class at the school began at 3:00 p.m. and by the time I had returned our day together had been fairly well spent. The shanties were vacated of women and small children by 6:30 and it was beddy-bye for the boys in their Annex room by 7:00. There remained two hours before the new curfew, when we could be together to enjoy the recorded music which came over the loud speakers into the plaza in front of the Main Building. Here we strolled, talked and greeted friends and enjoyed the respite from the hot sticky weather which was the Philippine summer.

Although we were accustomed to the continuing publication of new regulations either by the Commandant's office or the Executive Committee, we always welcomed them with some fear that we would be relieved of some privilege or other. It seemed as though we were to be kept off balance, not to be permitted an adjustment to any given circumstance which we could learn to live with, if we were just left in peace. Now that we were settling into the newly obtained shanty privilege the following notice was posted:

> The Executive Committee, with the approval of the Commandant has vested under its final supervision the complete control of all shanty areas...in the Shanty Area Administration (SAA). The following violations will result in the loss of shanty:
>
> 1- Possession of radios, cameras, flashlights or weapons.
> 2- Possession of alcoholic beverages.
> 3- Disorderly conduct.
> 4- Contact between sexes, appearance of intimacy, sexual intercourse, insufficient clothing of the body.
> 5- Curfew.
> 6- Construction requirement of complete view of interiors.
>
> To carry out intent of above, an internee patrol is hereby created.

Eleanor has had an opportunity to move out of the Annex which has become crowded to over flowing due to the admission of women and children arrivals from areas outside of Manila. We made the big move to Room 30 in the Main Building where she was welcomed by some old friends of pre-war days. It was cooler, much roomier, and she resumed an old time mahjong foursome from among her new roommates. In her notes she mentions some teen-age girls who took care of Donny during some daylight hours at the rate of fifty centavos a morning. There was news of an outbreak of cholera in the city and a rumor that there had also been reported a few cases of bubonic plague. Our four MDs had succeeded in getting a quantity of multi purpose vaccine from the Manila health authorities and offered to vaccinate the entire camp. The vaccine was a one shot, four disease blast and the majority took advantage of it even if we suffered some severe reactions, as long as we would have some protection against cholera, plague, dysentery and typhoid, as alleged.

Our neighbors in Shantytown, like us, lived from day to day, season to season, and we banded together in companionship to inhibit the insidiousness of boredom. We played bridge regularly with Lois and Irv Spering or Rob Strong, who shared their shanty. The Kneedler children were constant playmates with Roger and Peter Duckworth, all being not too far apart in age. The Updykes and Bill Donnelly who had engineered the "perfect" shanty were good company as were the Werffs, an older couple with two daughters in their late teens who occasionally took care of our two little ones. We all sat around in the evenings with the main subject of conversation food and how we would prepare it if we ever had our hands on it. The men became magnificent chefs in their own minds and came up with some of the most appetizing dishes imaginable. While we enjoyed these dissertations, they only served to leave us in a state of acute hunger and frustration.

Despite my continuing loss of weight, I felt good. Eleanor had trouble with one tooth which she finally decided to have taken out. It was beyond salvaging and a victim of the universal gum-line erosion that dietary deficiency helped bring about. The extraction was painless thanks to the skill of our camp dentist who still had a supply of local anesthetic. With the tooth gone, she had no more problems for the moment.

We had received our second set of cholera-plague shots and were enjoying the usual sore arms when Roger developed a serious sore throat. He had several episodes of white spots on his tonsils and this time they were quite inflamed along with the spots. Several children had gone through the same sequence and Eleanor and the other mothers got together to see if they could obtain permission to take the children to St. Luke's Hospital for tonsillectomies. At least one American doctor was still doing some surgery at St. Luke's and the mothers asked Bert Holland who acted as liaison for the internees with the commandant for the purpose of procuring passes for such matters as emergency hospitalization outside of camp.

After several days of anxious waiting, the mothers were rewarded by permission for six children to go out to St. Luke's in the company of one parent, each have their tonsils removed, stay one night at the hospital and return. Everything was just fine until the moment to leave camp arrived. To our dismay we found that the four mothers and two fathers as well as the children, would be forced to march along Manila streets to St. Luke's about one half mile distant. Not only that, they would be accompanied by several rifle-toting guards so that the small parade looked as though they might be on their way to an execution. Despite their reluctance the little band went on their way.

The tonsillectomies were a complete success and the group returned to camp the next day to tell of their pleasant overnight at the hospital as well as the ordeal of facing crowds of curious onlookers as they walked along Calle España. In the eyes of the silent people along the way they saw sympathy as well as fear, but most of all there seemed to be a lack of spirit, a resignation to the oppressive military occupation of their homeland.

A week or so later we had our third and last "shot" and fortunately with the same absence of serious reactions from anyone. Although we did not complain aloud about the sore arms, we suspected that this same vaccine would ordinarily be used on horses.

Eleanor lost another tooth in September, this time a molar taken out with aid of some local Novocaine. She did not escape so easily from after effects this time as her face swelled and she had a black eye that raised some eyebrows! The pain stayed with her for almost a week until the dentist re-dressed the cavity and packed it with aspirin. The sad part of this experience was her loss of six pounds in six days, leaving her weak and tired.

September 21st was Roger's fifth birthday and of course, there was a little party for him and his friends. Rice flour was produced from someone's precious larder and Eleanor added the rest including a brown sugar icing that the children loved. There were modest gifts and each child received a souvenir balloon and a crayon from our stores. The children played pin-the-tail-on-the-donkey and other simple games. Children's birthdays were not forgotten and the wonder was the inventiveness of the mothers who gave so much to these occasions so that no child ever felt left out.

We celebrated our seventh wedding anniversary on the 27th of September by joining the Schlessingers for "cocktails" at their shanty. I did not ask him about the alcoholic content but there was something there. They were a couple we had met before the war and he represented Johnson and Johnson, the surgical house, and as such was part of the drug fraternity.

The rainy season was well upon us and traffic about the camp was reduced to a minimum except as concerned mealtime, hospital visits and the weekly entertainment. I had done my best to make our shanty a bit more weatherproof but we could still look up and through the ceiling at the sky without having much more than an occasional drop of rain fall on us. The pitch of the roof was steep and the palm thatch, while appearing to be porous, was, because of its layered construction, almost impervious to rain. There was one serious draw-back to its use and that was the resident "bejuca" bugs. They constantly ate away the dry thatch and as a result there was a constant fall of fine dust all over the shanty and its occupants at the time. I had used several added cross bracings of bamboo poles, having seen such arrangements on my trips into the rural regions of Luzon, Panay, and Negros, the latter two being larger islands in the central part of the archipelago.

Philippine independence was "declared" October 14th, 1943. The newspaper carried the story in headlines but there was not much substance to the underlying story. We treated it as just some more Japanese propaganda and apparently the Filipinos had a similar feeling. The total effect of this momentous announcement on the camp was about nil although in an unrelated action the camp received a new head man, a Mr. Kato, a civilian in his fifties and conversant with the English language. We heard he had spent some time in the consular service in

London and when he had been interned at the outbreak of the war he had been treated "well." Mr. Kato became "Acting Commandant"—still a civilian under military direction. Mr. Kato was small and mousy-looking but far more communicative than his predecessors. By now all of the internees have been fairly well broken to the habit of bowing to the Japs who ignored us unless we failed to grant them their obeisance. Mr. Kato was another story! We bowed to him; he returned the bow. He had not yet succumbed to the doctrine of arrogance practiced by the military. At first the politeness of Mr. Kato was taken as a sign that the Japanese must be losing the war! Truly we were naive even to the extent of creating our own rumors when the news was distant and dull.

In early November, the transfer of some 200 internees, former members of the diplomatic corps, some critically ill people, and a few V. I. P.s had been effected via the use of a Japanese passenger ship, the *Teia Maru*, from Manila to a Portuguese port in the Indian Ocean and thence by the passenger liner *Gripsholm* to the United States. The returning *Teia Maru* was rumored to be en route to Manila with Red Cross supplies for Santo Tomas. If true this would be a happy development for all of us.

November 11th, Armistice Day, unnoticed by anyone, was a gloomy windy day with a portent of some worse weather to come. We had not seen a real typhoon as yet nor were anxious to do so. By Saturday, the 13th, the wind had increased in violence to the point where the old timers assured us that we were in for a typhoon of at least grade four on a scale of ten. Although there was some question as to the advisability of spending the night out in the shanty, I really had no choice if I wanted a space to sleep. Furthermore I was unwilling to trust our meager supplies to the mercy of a storm. By night fall the rain was driving across the campus, even through the cracks around the windows in the buildings, soaking the beds which could not be moved because of the crowded conditions in many of the rooms.

My refuge in the shanty became more and more precarious as I noticed the shanty swaying and creaking more than I had anticipated. Probably my neglect through the months of good weather was to blame and there seemed to be no way to get any sleep with the roar of the pouring rain and the wind. I had tied my flaps securely and it was fairly dry inside so far, even though the wind continuously lifted the thatch on the roof as each gust struck from below. The bamboo crossbeams above me groaned in the darkness and at times I could easily fancy myself being swept up into the stormy night along with parts of my blown-apart shanty! Each time the wind would momentarily die down, I could hear the voices of my neighbors calling each other to check on how we were weathering the storm. As time went on there were fewer and fewer voices as several men had decided to slog it out and return to the halls of the Main Building.

Each time the calm came, I would hope that it meant a break in the storm, but just as relentlessly, the rushing sound of the returning wind was there to greet me just about the time I stuck my head out of the front door to see if anyone was still around. Each time this happened the wind seemed to rise a few more miles per hour. It finally became so bad that the roof seemed about ready to be torn from its lashings and that would surely bring the whole shanty down around my head. I decided to retreat to safety just as a gale-force gust of wind whipped off one of the thatch-shingled drops that served us as windows. It flew off into the night with a loud "whap"! The rain then poured in and I was wet through in a matter of moments. It came in horizontally or so it seemed and so I snatched a few of our most precious possessions into a small suitcase and quickly got into an old pair of boots and an older raincoat, secured everything as best I could. I had no light and I had to feel my way down our three steps and into the darkness. It was like dropping off into a muddy, slimy pit, then sliding and slithering along the path which I could scarcely make out in the darkness, so that it was 90% by instinct and 10% by luck.

I will never forget the blackness of that wild night. It seemed as though I could hear the clouds tearing by above my head. The rain beat into my face with stinging force making me close my eyes as I tried to navigate the path which had now become a sea of mud. Well, I had often said that so many times had I walked this path, I could do it blindfolded. This night I proved that to be a fact!

When I made my way inside the Main Building I was surprised by the weird scene which greeted my eyes. Two blackout lamps faintly lighted as bedraggled a group of men as I had ever seen. They sat huddled together in a corner, shivering in their still wet clothing. The more fortunate, whose wives were living in the Main Building had been able to borrow a towel or a blanket which they now began to share with the less fortunate. I made my way to the room where Eleanor and the boys were and found her up worriedly talking to some of her roommates, speculating as to how I might be faring. It was almost 3:00 a.m. and she provided me with a warm blanket in which I might spend the rest of the night curled up in a corner outside of Room 30. I went promptly to sleep.

Next morning I awakened stiff and sore to find that the rain was still pouring down, but that the wind had abated somewhat. We held no hope that our shanty had escaped serious damage, now less than ever because floodwaters had begun to rise. The camp, as well as this section of Manila was only six feet above sea level. At this time of morning the Main Building was over crowded and filthy with mud and dampness so we decided it might be more healthy to try, at least to make our way out to the shanty.

There was nowhere near the damage we had anticipated. The structure stood fairly upright although several gaping holes were found in the roof and sides. Meanwhile a fitful rain kept coming down and Eleanor and I worked to patch up the roof with shingles of palm leaf and a few pieces of canvas which we had been saving for an emergency. By noon the mess had been cleaned up and I had a good charcoal fire burning in our native stove. The weather continued to be dismal and the temperature was down but we felt quite cheerful over the fact that we had weathered the worst part of the storm, we hoped. A few of our neighbors had lost their shacks and others found theirs under a foot or more of rising water. The Updyke's nicely constructed shanty was flat as a pancake and floating around in the floodwaters. They should have studied native construction which now proved to be the best defense against the rigors of the local weather.

The center of the typhoon, as it now turned out to be, missed Manila and was headed northwest and out to sea. The rains continued unabated and the water continued to rise. By curfew it was but eight or nine inches from our split bamboo floor. Nevertheless we decided that Eleanor should return to the relative comfort of the Main Building and her room, while I would take care of Roger and Donny in the shanty. And so I managed to put one at each end of my bed and made a sort of sleeping bag out of blankets for myself. It was sort of nice sleeping with my children after all these months.

The next day the situation had not improved and the water had risen to the three foot mark in our shanty area, just coming up to the top step of our shelter, about five inches below the floor. Other nearby shanties were under water and from passing neighbors, some of whom were actually paddling out to recover some of their possessions, we heard that other shanty areas on the opposite side of camp were completely submerged. It was pretty bad, not being able to do anything but sit and watch the water rise, hoping that by some miracle it would not dispossess us, as it had the others. Since it was impossible to return with the children to the food lines, we decided to break into our emergency rations, some canned soup, a tin of corned beef and some dry crackers. Naturally we felt guilty because mother was not there to share, but we made a promise that she should have an equal feast when we were all back together again.

I had managed to send a message to Eleanor to assure her of our safety and to ask her to stay put as we were adrift in a big lake with no way to reach her. The kids seemed to enjoy their change of scene and we had no trouble keeping entertained with each others antics. Our food would hold out for a couple of days but no more but by then surely some rescue team would have come to our aid. Our floor was just two inches away from the rising water when the flood showed signs of abating. It was November 14th, four days after the rain had started, before there was any letup. We were alone in our area most of this time and the boys were getting bored with each other. I understood that four days and evenings spent in reading and sleeping with no other kids to play with can be dull at ages five and two and a half.

After the storm and flood had abated, the camp busied itself with an enormous cleanup job. We heard that Manila had been hard hit and considerable damage done to property and crops. This certainly could not help our sorry state of affairs. The flood had been the worst suffered by Manila in many years, although the typhoon itself had scored only light damage, bypassing the city for the most part.

XIV

The military had finally taken over the direct responsibility for the administration of the camp and Mr. Kato had been replaced by an allegedly shell-shocked veteran of the Solomons' campaign, a Lt. Col. Yoshie. There was the usual tightening up of regulations and we feared that what few privileges remained to us would soon slip away. At first the Executive Committee which was the official mediator between the captors and captives, got absolutely nowhere with the new Commandant. The Commandant soon found, however, that he could not communicate directly with each of some three thousand five hundred or more multi national prisoners without help from some inside organization. He determined on a new policy.

We were summarily called to the plaza in front of the Main Building one morning to listen to this grotesque little individual, who stood no more than five feet one inch or so in his shiny leather boots, a too-long samurai sword hanging at his side. His horn-rim glasses perched dangerously at the end of his nose and he waved his arms dramatically, prior to uttering his first word. He explained in almost unintelligible English that he had learned our language only during the last two years, the hard way, from a book, and we would have to pay close attention to his words.

The gist of his talk was that as long as we caused no trouble, he likewise would give us no trouble. He summed it all up by closing with the promise that, "If you pray bawr with me, I will pray bawr with you." A real sport!

Baseball had been a major sport in Japan for many decades and the Colonel must have been quite a fan in his civilian days. He saw us attempting to organize our new softball season which would run through the dry weather, roughly January to June. Col. Yoshie witnessed our early practices in which only sixty or so able bodied players now participated. More than three times that number had formed leagues last year but that number was decimated by the transfer of so many to Los Barios and by the malnutrition of several more still in Santo Tomas, who just could not make it physically. The Colonel became a critic in his own unintelligible way, of our softball game which was only a first cousin to baseball. Obviously frustrated by our actions one day he whipped off his coat and shirt and stepping into the pitcher's box, called for the ball. We were somewhat confused by his actions but discretion prevailed and we decided to humor him. The sight of our Commandant out on the playing field brought a bit of a crowd and as we listened to some of his instructions, which had all the character of orders, we found ourselves throwing the ball overhand and generally fouling up what was to be a regular game. Finally we convinced him that we saw the error of our ways and he was content to walk off the field and return, after dressing, to his office next to the Education Building. Not wishing to be shot or suffer some lesser indignity, from that moment on, whenever Col. Yoshie approached the field, he would see us throwing the big ball with an overhand motion.

The tide of war had turned ever so slightly. The Manila Tribune carried the first story of our successful invasion of the Gilbert Islands in this fashion. Headlines stated to the effect that the American Marines had suffered great casualties in an ill-fated attempt to land at Tarawa and the news story continued inconclusively until the last couple of lines which announced that the brave defenders had evacuated several of the Gilberts in order to shorten and strengthen their lines. From this point on we knew that "strong help was on the way" as promised!

Mr. Izzawa, the consul from Panama who had passed through our camp a year ago, had said in his speech, that so long as they were winning the war, the Japanese could afford to be generous. This was a reference to the so-called "privileges" which we enjoyed then. So with the loss of the Gilberts, the tide of generosity turned to a trickle with new restrictions and more regulations.

There was still the twice daily roll-call with the ceremonial bowing toward the Emperor. Fortunately the Japs never looked behind our backs while this was going on or they might have wondered why most of us had our fingers crossed or in some other uncomplimentary position while we were bowing. Roll-call did something to me as it must have to others, watching families, as we stood there, mother, father and many small children bowing to an invisible someone who to us was the symbol of all our unhappiness. The children did not understand and would probably be grown ups some day, with no memories of this debasing act. But we did what we were told. The consequences of disobedience were not worth the effort.

We had the most peculiar experience just about this time. An old wicker basket beneath the floor of the shanty contained our charcoal and wood scrap supply. Eleanor had a souvenir button box that Ricardo had sent in on one of his visits. It was full of various buttons she had collected since our arrival in Manila and served for mending and replacing lost buttons of all of our clothing. It became a daytime plaything for the boys until one day the box fell to the floor with disastrous results. The buttons poured out and down through the spaces in our split bamboo floor to the ground below. Fortunately the ground was dry at the time and the buttons gleamed up at us through the cracks like so many blinking eyes. We sent Don and Roger off on a hunt which became a game with some small reward for the most buttons recovered. Next thing we heard was Roger calling, "Mommy, Mommy, there's an egg in the charcoal basket!"

Sure enough there was a fresh chicken egg sitting right in the middle of the charcoal just as though some friendly chicken had come and laid it. It provided a small breakfast for the two boys the next day and just out of curiosity I decided that if one egg had been laid there, why not another?

Great was my surprise when I did find another egg, in the same place as that of yesterday! That night you can imagine that Roger and I spent much of our sleep-time on watch to see if we could come face to face with our benefactor. No luck, probably because we fell asleep at the wrong time, but again the next night and the next and for thirty straight nights, some strange chicken wandered into our charcoal basket and laid one fresh egg for us. Although we never did find out where our nocturnal visitor came from, we suspected that it had to be one of the chickens kept in the next door seminary, separated from us only by a barbed wire fence. Then one day there was no egg and thus ended the saga of the mysterious chicken. For what sustenance she brought us, we all hoped that she did not end up on the table of one of our captors.

Eleanor's hand infection did not respond to the many medications tried on her by our camp doctors. She had to wear bandages much of the time and when the bandages were off the hands were purple from the application of gentian violet or some other salve. Our good friend Georgia Hamm helped with her bathing as she had to keep her hands out of water. Not only was the condition a great inconvenience but it was a constant source of embarrassment since she was sure that her roommates suspected her of being a leper or worse. We were sure that the dietary deficiency which she was experiencing was a contributing factor and once we were rescued and back in good health, this would all be over. Meanwhile there was an ever present danger that the loss of circulation plus the deep-seated infection might endanger the fingers or the hand itself.

The camp had been excited by the rumor of the arrival of Red Cross comfort kits. We still had very pleasant memories of the small kits which had come from South Africa and Canada this time last year. For once the rumor had substance and to our great joy on December 23, 1943, each internee—man, woman and child—received a twenty or so pound carton with food, toiletries and some tobacco contained therein. What a way for us to celebrate Christmas!

On this Christmas day, Santa again showed up with his bag of toys for the little ones, a little leaner perhaps, but still in costume and still with his familiar "Ho, Ho, Ho! Merry Christmas to all!" No one was ever welcomed more sincerely and noisily by the children.

New Year's Eve which followed was a time for reminiscing, taking stock of our situation and speculating on what the future might bring. The American armed forces have reached out into the mid-Pacific and retaken several important atolls, namely the Gilberts and the Marshalls, mostly U. S. Navy and Marine

Corps operations. We have been fighting with success in the Solomons and rumor has it that Gen. MacArthur is starting an island-hopping campaign on his way back to the Philippines. Ergo, 1944 came into being with renewed hope for the rescue of "MacArthur's Hostages!"

Another cholera epidemic has broken out in Manila and the camp is taking whatever precautions it can so that the disease does not strike the internees. We were again vaccinated and this time the record of sore arms and slight fever with nausea seemed to give testimony to its effectiveness. Within the camp we had our share of epidemic children's diseases, but by some miracle our two youngsters had so far escaped every one. There had been measles, mumps, whooping cough, impetigo and diphtheria but these hundreds of cases survived.

More tragic but less widespread were the epidemics of polio terminating in the death of one of our best friends, a husky six foot three athlete, Bill Waldo. At twenty-five years of age, he was one of the most popular young men in the camp and his sudden and unexpected death came as a deep shock to those who knew him.

He was married and his wife took her loss deeply. There was simply no defense against the ravages of polio which also struck a number of teenagers, leaving them partially paralyzed and with a damaged future.

Hospital facilities were extremely inadequate with too few beds to care for the hundreds who needed increasing care as less nourishment was available. Parents were prevailed upon as a last resort to isolate their children and consequently themselves, whenever infection of fever struck. Strict isolation was out of the question and consequently children's disease had a rapid spread. Out of seven hundred plus children in camp, only twelve, including our own, escaped all of the aforementioned epidemics.

As the story behind the arrival of the comfort kits began to unfold, we realized that only a portion of the original shipment made its way into the hands of the internees for whom it was intended. The Commandant had informed the Executive

Committee that relief supplies would be arriving on the *Teia Maru* which had left Goa late in October and would be arriving in Manila in early November. The shipment included among other items, comfort kits, medical supplies, athletic equipment, shoes and clothing as well as mail. Internee volunteers were employed to transfer the shipment from ship to a warehouse in the Manila port area. It wasn't until mid-December that the food kits were visible to the camp when, at that time, the Military came in to inspect them. The crowd watching the process were angered by the way the kits were manhandled. Labels were torn off cans to see if secret propaganda messages had been printed on the reverse. Old Gold cigarettes were dumped out of the kits and confiscated because of just such a message regarding our heritage of Freedom.

No bulk food supplies had been received but the kits contained such items as tinned corn beef, pork loaf, spam, powdered milk, jam, soluble coffee, chocolate, sugar, dried fruit, vitamin C tablets and soap. The packaging lent itself to storage but we were all so hungry for some of the special items we had not seen for more than two years, that they were consumed quickly with no mind given to their conservation whatsoever.

The other supplies, medicines and clothing, save for a few token cases had disappeared between the port area and Santo Tomas. We welcomed what residue finally came in for our use, and felt that any complaint to the Commandant would be useless.

XV

January 1944 signaled our second full year of captivity as well as the start of what might be a third. Men and women had thinned down to their minimum without losing at least a feeling of good health. The paunches of yester-year had melted away and those who had them were certainly better off. The children were somewhat better off because they merited and received any special dietary consideration from their parents as well as the camp authorities. But they still suffered some deprivation and it was our fear that it would manifest itself in later years.

One of the tragedies of camp life was the rash of separations which were to end up in divorce after the war. Either a husband or a wife found it impossible to cope with the stress of internment and as the ultimate solution either sought another companion or just separation. On the other hand Eleanor and I found such comfort in one another that we looked upon our confinement as a God-given opportunity to know each other's real character and to learn to accept it without reservation for the rest of our days. We found both a time and place for love even though it would have been unthinkable in ordinary circumstances. If a couple were to be seen strolling in the moonlight toward a secluded spot where the Jap guards were not permitted to patrol, and the couple carried their petate rolled under his or her arm, one could be assured that love, as it always has done, was "going to find a way!" The petate was a mat woven from palm fibers and it served so many purposes with furniture of any description almost non-existent. But it never served better than as a pad on which to lie on one's back and look up into a starry night to wonder when the sky might again be filled with our 'planes on the mission to rescue us.

This was the wettest "dry season" with intermittent rains every other day leaving us unhappy with being confined indoors at least half of the time.

Probably the unfavorable course of the war from the Japanese view caused us to become more isolated from the "outside" than before. The military had ordered the complete cutoff of the package line as of February 1st. This would mean the cessation of a small personal food supply, money and other sundries still within the financial capabilities of the internees. More importantly it cut off communication between those in camp with families and other dependents on the outside. No further entry of food would be permitted except whatever was rationed to us by the Jap military and that source was unreliable as we had already learned. There was an official announcement from the Commandant which gave us the bad news. It said, in effect, that all Filipino nurses and doctors would henceforth cease to enter camp. All cases requiring medical attention would be entirely dependent upon the resources of the camp. Certain hospitals heretofore open to internees for cases requiring more extensive therapy than that provided by Santo Tomas hospital would be permanently closed. The package line would close permanently on February 1st and shanties may now be occupied by families.

That last item brought enough joy to us so as to wipe out the sadness we felt at no longer being able to see our faithful Ricardo nor some other Swiss friends at the gate from time to time. Finally Eleanor and Donny would be joining Roger and me in the shanty and we could at least take up family life on a twenty-four hour basis. To Eleanor it meant relief from having to take care of a frisky two-and-a-half year old at night in a room crowded with some thirty other women, mostly older and without children on hand.

To add to our woes there was a large influx of older people who had either been institutionalized or permitted to remain outside because of their health. They all needed assistance as their state of health generally was poor. With able-bodied men and high school age boys manning the essential chores in the camp, there was hardly anyone to spare for the added responsibility of the new admissions. Nevertheless, with the space available from the move to the shanties, everyone was given living space and helped into the routine of the camp life. Some hallways were filled with mattresses or just blankets marking the sleeping space of those volunteers who had given up their room space to accommodate the elderly and disabled. The camp hospital was now filled to over flowing and only the desperately ill would be permitted entry.

Then came a day when the usual surliness of the Japs became even more pronounced. There was only the trickle of news into camp these days and only an occasional newspaper became available to us. Several days after the actual event we found a small item on the last page of the *Manila Tribune*, a copy of which had found its way to us. It announced that "Japanese Military forces in the Marshall Islands had withdrawn to other points in order to shorten and thus strengthen their lines." Nothing else, just that!

Our arm chair generals dug up their hidden maps of the Pacific and began to evaluate what this might mean to us. We found that the approaching Allied forces were, in truth, advancing but as far as we were concerned, too slowly to cause us any great excitement. The map showed clearly that we were employing an island to island campaign which was fine if it meant saving lives. But for each island captured then began the arduous task of consolidation, bringing in supplies and then planning for the next offensive. And there were so many Pacific islands between them and us.

Since the tightening up of contact with the outside a depression had settled over the camp. People walked around with no desire to talk with one another and even Eleanor and I gradually lost our optimism and were taking each day one by one, without hope for the next. The children had become expert in the game of scrounging. Donny who had not lost his baby fat, was an appealing youngster who brought out the motherly instincts in any woman whose path he might cross in his wanderings about camp. Result…he was never hungry!

He was usually in Roger's company which meant that they both could be found munching a cookie or even having a glass of precious powdered milk, flavored with chocolate from the comfort kits on some of our darkest days.

The boys' attitude was something of a help to our own peace of mind. They were yet too young to realize the terrible implications of war and their lives had now in large part, been spent in Santo Tomas so they had no other experience to consider save Roger's rather confused memories of his life as a baby. His few friends of pre-war Manila were here with him in camp and all of the children of that age lived for today and maybe tomorrow. So the boys settled into a routine of breakfast, then play-school or playground, lunch, nap followed by an interlude of wandering around the camp with friends until dinner. Nighttime and bedtime were simultaneous for both Roger and Donny and in the blacked-out camp we never had difficulty in getting them off to sleep.

We watched them get thinner as they grew. At five and a half years of age Roger received some instruction in his reading but Donny's learning process was strictly at his mother's knee. He was too young for the pre-kindergarten classes that volunteers would have in the morning so our parental efforts were confined to keeping him as healthy as we could.

Even though the camp was under a policy of strict isolation, the Japs found it expedient to permit a small market to be set within the camp. It was to be run by a few trusted Filipinos who had earned their privilege by the payment of "squeeze" in the proper quarters. The market supplied local fruits and vegetables at what turned out to be exorbitant prices, so high in fact that only a very few internees could afford to buy. The market was of such limited benefit that it soon folded and disappeared. One of the contributing factors to its demise was the temptation to bring in certain items which had been prohibited and before long, whiskey made an appearance. Of course there had to be a buyer for this contraband and in due course he was caught. The Commandant who may have acted with sincere concern for the internees need for additional food, was infuriated by this violation of privilege. The market would be permitted to continue its operation but the Filipino vendors were marched to the gate and sent away with threats not to return. The market was to be placed under the direction of a member of the Commandant's staff and certain select internees would man the operation. The official notice went on to say that all sales of food would be made at cost and no vendor profit would be involved.

This sounded all very humanitarian but our skepticism was great.

A price list was posted on the following Monday morning and prices were even higher than those charged by the Filipinos during their stay. We were told that there had been a sudden rise in commodity prices on the outside and this was to blame for the increase in our prices. The market served very little, if any, purpose and closed quickly.

The specter of famine haunted the city and its inhabitants and Santo Tomas suffered, even more acutely, the effects of what was happening outside of its confines. The Japanese had provided a schedule of daily food allowances which they would deliver as long as available. These included 400 grams of rice 100 grams of fish, 200 grams of green vegetables and small amounts of sugar, salt, cooking oil and tea. Powdered milk was available for children under five but considered a luxury for anyone over that age. As though to emphasize the tenuousness of this arrangement, every delivery into camp no matter how small was made under armed guard. There were always shortages in the promised amounts and the kitchens were hard pressed to stretch out what was on hand to meet the Internees' needs.

It seemed to us that the Japanese use of repressive rules was designed primarily to keep us quiet and so it did. We were asked to participate in work details such as gardening (a fruitless task in the unproductive soil of the camp), and fence building, which included the fencing off of a ten foot area along the walls and fence of the camp. This last task meant the demolishing of several shanties so that armed guards could patrol inside the camp. We just missed by a matter of a couple of feet, but it left our shanty right next to the fenced area where the guards would be walking. Since there was not enough healthy manpower to carry out these tasks to the satisfaction of the Commandant, he retaliated by a series of privilege curtailments which only added to our depression. During the month of

March we were permitted to send messages limited to twenty five words to the folks back home. After much deliberation, Eleanor and I settled on these words, addressed to her father, knowing that he would see that the news would reach all my family members. We were not told how the messages would be transmitted but it was a unique opportunity to let them know, at least, that we were still alive. The message read:

> Eleanor the boys and I are in good health. Roger is in kindergarten. Donny is walking. Be sure to tell it to the Sweeneys.

I had little faith that the message would ever get through, but if it did I was certain that my father-in-law would understand my contradiction of the last sentence which was the old slang for "baloney!"

We eventually learned that the message did get through in the most extraordinary way. The words were broadcast shortwave by a Japanese announcer in Tokyo, picked up by ham radio receivers all over the world and sent by mail to my father-in-law, even though his name and address were badly garbled by the mispronunciation of the broadcaster and the interpretation of some of the foreign receivers.

Our isolation has succeeded in starting trouble on more than one score. Nerves have become ragged through the absence of news and the prevalence of false rumors. Arguments have started between friends on the slightest provocation and morale is at an all-time low. It is hot as hades and I have little strength to do any of the routine tasks around the shanty. The boys seem oblivious of the heat although they are constantly restless and off to wander around the camp as soon as breakfast is over. Eleanor is up at the crack of dawn each day, poking at our charcoal fire to prepare coffee which she makes from grounds of roasted peanuts or God knows what. It is still hot, dark brown and stimulating.

At 6:30 a.m., the public address system, now an instrument of torture, blares out the usual announcement that roll-call will be held at eight o'clock, right after breakfast. I have to stand in two lines, both long, one for kiddies' food and one for our own.

Another disturbance to our peace of mind is the announcement that on April 1st there would be no further cooking in shanties! Allegedly there is a fire hazard but as yet there hasn't been a single such occurrence.

The new regulation would be offset by arrangements for communal cooking, which according to the Commandant, would make for a more equitable distribution of whatever foods remained in private possession among the Internees. How this was figured out, I never knew, but sharing with those who had been improvident was not a popular idea. The Commandant's concession permitted us to construct a system of community kitchens, out-of-doors, subject to the inspection of his staff. There was to be an adobe stove, large enough to permit simultaneous operation by one or more neighbors, but with no cover protection from either the broiling sun or the rains when they came. We stolidly accepted the concession and began work immediately on the constructions.

April 6th saw the transfer of 531 old men and unattached women to the camp at Los Baños. This provided some relief from the overcrowding which had been added to recently by the arrival of some 500 new prisoners from Davao. Their arrival helped us learn something of the horrible conditions under which they had been living and then forced to travel. The stories were hard to believe with the prisoners jammed below decks for days at sea, without food or water, no toilet facilities, blacked out in the unbearable heat. Yet they survived to enter our midst in physical conditions which shocked us into realizing that we were not so badly off after all!

The Easter season came on with weather which was constantly in the 100 degree area, with humidity to match. There was no relief at night and activity reached an all time low. The camp labor situation is becoming a problem with sit-down strikes stopping garden work and other maintenance chores.

For some time now there has been a persistent rumor of a second front in Europe. At first this rumor was treated as all the rest, that is, discounted when there was no confirmation after a week or so. Its importance to us was diminished when we considered that this, even if true, would be the start of a long campaign to recapture the continental territory of the Allies only after which could we hope for some effective action in the Pacific.

On May 2nd the entire camp was summoned to the plaza in front of the Main Building to hear an address by the current camp Commandant, Col. Yoshie. At 10:30 a.m. he faced us not with any electrifying announcement as we half expected, but to tell us "straight from the heart" that he understood our troubles but that military rules and regulations were of greater importance.

We left the plaza somewhat bewildered, having gained only a headache from the sun and nothing from the Commandant's undramatic speech.

Almost as though to make up for the "straight talk" of Col. Yoshie this morning, an announcement was made later that a movie would be shown out on the plaza the evening of May 5th. Curfew would be lifted for the occasion and we would be permitted to bring our camp chairs out for the occasion. It had been a long time since such entertainment had been offered and everyone became quite excited at the prospect. The film was an oldie, preceded by a Japanese propaganda short telling us about their great hydro-electric development in Manchuria. The old American film with Veronica Lake was confusing insomuch as it started with the second or third reel, followed by the last which gave the hero the girl right in the middle of the picture. The climactic fourth or fifth reel produced the very height of the action and there suddenly flashed across the screen the announcement, "THE END - A VITAPHONE SHORT." The screen went black. There just wasn't any more. Well, they tried!

Somehow a couple of copies of the *Manila Tribune* of June 6th were smuggled into camp and I was fortunate enough to see one for myself. There was a rather obscure account of the Hitler-ordered evacuation of Rome to protect the great art treasures of history from Allied vandalism, or so it claimed.

But more to the point was another story confirming the long awaited "second front" reported as a quote from an Allied news source. The text was brief and to the point. The landing was covered by 11,000 planes and a procession of battleships, cruisers, destroyers and mine-sweepers across the Straits of Dover, meeting only 25% of the expected resistance from the coastal defenses.

Although the newspaper failed to carry any news of the South Pacific, the clandestine radios had been busy and rumors began to circulate that we were having good success in the China-Burma-India theatre as well as with MacArthur's island hopping strategy which had placed our forces in New Guinea, New Britain and the Moluccas. Our maps indicated that his strategy might be to ignore Java and Singapore and try to cut the Japanese supply lines by retaking the Philippines and then heading north to Japan itself.

This was a time when our drooping spirits revived. Our morale got quite a boost from the successes which we were able to verify even if they were on a continent all the way around to the other side of the globe. The attitude of our captors became somewhat jittery and their daily stream of orders were given then countermanded and then restated until we weren't sure what we were supposed to do to comply. Meanwhile we continued to play cards with our neighbors, watch our kids develop, and try to find ways and means to cope with our sparse diet as well as the oppressive hot and humid weather.

A stern warning was issued by the Commandant's office today, June 10th, to the effect that possession or knowledge of possession of a copy of the *Manila Tribune* would be a grave offense against the military code governing Santo Tomas. This is proof that the Japanese are upset by this turn of events since the issue in question quoted speeches by cabinet members in Tokyo to the effect that any defeat suffered by the German nation would have no effect on Japan's prosecution of the war in the Pacific. It was reiterated that their original plans were for a separate campaign in each sphere with (as well as I could get the drift) 'moral' cooperation from each of the Axis partners.

Italy was now considered an enemy for the way she chose to break her ties, and the Italians had already been interned in Japanese countries and Japan proper, or so it was reported.

My thirty-second birthday was an occasion of absolutely no importance but Eleanor managed to make it a festive treat with some cake makings' that she begged, borrowed and maybe even stole! The Grimes joined us for a share of the goodies and we all sang a "happy birthday" very much empty of meaning. Larry who was a peace-time employee of Du Pont, had demonstrated his artistic talents by doing a water-color of our picturesque shanty in return for one can of corned beef *[see back cover]*. If we did not lose it somewhere along the way, the painting would be a lifetime memoir of these internee days.

Two days later we were startled by the sound of the air raid warning. With no prior announcement, we were sure it was the real thing until an announcement over the speaker system informed us that it was a drill and we were required to go to designated shelters or to our shanties as the case applied. We were under blackout rules and these prevailed for the next two nights giving us a world of speculation as to the cause. But whatever our hopes were, they had to be dashed by the following morning's "all clear."

Our eccentric midget Col. Yoshie quietly left camp and was replaced by a brutish looking Lt. Onozaki who assumed the post as "Acting Commandant" while a civilian, Mr. Hayashi, who allegedly was ill and had not yet surfaced, would be the nominal Commandant. We were now well aware that the army's representative, no matter how lowly his rank, would be the real boss.

Our entertainment committee had worked for five months to put together a real old time minstrel show. Despite the limitations of costuming and rehearsal facilities, the participants were as good as the real thing in their papier mache tuxedos and grease paint as applied by our local beauticians. The end-men were blacked out and replete with sight gags and funny stories. The "Davao Quartet" was a highlight of the program and their music sounded to us as good as the "Merry Macs" at their best. Their parodies were, to say the least, daring, and we wondered if the Japs would tumble to the double-entendre. Actually, the verses kidded us more than our captors, but we had already learned that their sense of humor was on a different wave-length from ours.

The next day we found out that the Commandant or someone on his staff had a better knowledge of English than we gave him credit for. Dave Harvey and the Davao Quartet were rebuked by Lt. Onozaki for "public criticism of the administration of the internment camp." Seems that such expressions even in song as "roll-call, Glory be! Mush! Oh gosh, oh gee!" and "lining up for no-chow" or a "hot time in Paris tonight!" were indicative of the low regard we had for our prison life. So over the threat of dire consequences for the whole show including the chorus of which I was a part, a written apology signed by Dave and the Davao Quartet was demanded, received and posted on the bulletin board. Although we laughed up our sleeves at the incident, it dampened our enthusiasm for any further super-stage productions.

Early the morning of July 15th, a huge explosion rocked the camp. Smoke was soon visible toward the port area and again speculation became the game of the day. But there were no planes nor was there any air-raid alert. Next morning our somewhat daring humorist who woke us with music daily, played a recording of "I Cover the Waterfront" without our captors getting wise to its significance. We therefore concluded that an oil barge or ammunition dump had been fired.

Our powdered milk supply originally issued to children under five had been steadily cut until the current ration scarcely clouded the water. We heard from the committee chairman of Finance and Supplies that a fifty kilo sack of the poorest grade of brown sugar now costs more than ten thousand pesos in hard currency, the latter being Filipino money or its equivalent in military pesos, about ten times that amount. The Japanese tell us that the Filipinos are starving outside and we must prepare to tighten our belts.

Loyal friends who would gladly have sacrificed anything to preserve the lives of the internee children were told, "Internees have plenty. Do not need!"

In a speech to the public in the front plaza, Earl Carroll, who was then serving as chairman of the Internee Committee, told us that we were getting a maximum of one thousand calories per day with the amount of food permitted by our captors. This is barely enough to keep a human being alive. He emphasized the seriousness of the situation and urged us to take it easy on physical exertion. We are already aware of the deteriorating conditions of our bodies and there is not one single person in the camp who has not felt the pinch. Weight loss was now serious and in particular the small amount of protein began to turn up case after case of hypoproteinemia. This condition was characterized by a gradual swelling of the ankles and the ultimate prognosis was death, literally by drowning in one's own body fluids.

The Japs keep asking us for more working hours, a larger garden production, but where is the energy to produce going to come from? At its best, the garden can produce only greens in quantity sufficient to supplement the scanty regular diet. The number of calories contained in talinum, pechay, or kang-kong is nil. In our opinion it is a lost cause, a wasted effort.

Tobacco has progressed from luxury to necessity status. No matter how rank the substitutes may be they at least diminish the craving for food. I had a lucky "flash" about a year ago when I filled an old Bakelite cigarette humidor with "dobies" as the native cigarettes are called. When I found them the cover had rusted so that it was about impossible to remove. I finally pried the lid off and found the contents to be usable but as the paper had become worm-eaten the tobacco had to be used as pipe filler. And so Eleanor became, like so many native women, a smoker of the old corn cob which I resurrected from our belongings. Although she never did adapt to pipe smoking, she did find the tobacco, moldy as it was, an appetite depressant.

Like a few other internees who did not believe that the war would be over next week or the week after, I planted a few things in our little patch of ground including one tiny banana tree, some radishes, several gabi or taro and a row of calla lilies. Since I had no choice at the time, I knew that I would need extraordinary luck and perseverance to see these plants ever grow to produce anything edible. The gabi grew well and its tubers would eventually provide some food. The radishes in full maturity measured less than a quarter of an inch. The callas bloomed with a pretty flower but their roots turned out to be inedible. The banana was our most promising venture. At nine months it was a good seven or eight feet tall, very leafy and had one small stem of bananas which would surely develop into several hands of tasty green fruit, perhaps as many as fifty or more. We watched it like hawks during the day and prayed that at night the fruit when it ripened would not be stolen.

An unusually dramatic announcement was made by the Commandant on August 1st to the effect that all moneys in the hands of the internees had to be turned in to him to be deposited in the Bank of Taiwan for the following reasons:

1. To protect internees against robbery.
2. To insure a steady supply at a rate of interest.
3. To prevent gambling.
4. To effect a balanced buying system.
5. To destroy inflation in camp.

All adults were to receive fifty pesos per month and each child twenty-five. Details would be given later, but we had four days in which to comply.

The measure has been given the faintly familiar appellation of "controlled economy." The Commandant pointed out that the arrangement could be construed to be of definite benefit to the camp, but we are no longer so naive as to believe that this measure was created for our benefit alone. On the contrary, unless similar controls were instituted outside in the city of Manila, this would be just another knot in the final strangulation of Santo Tomas. The pittance permitted us each month would not serve to purchase more than a few bananas or coconuts providing those luxuries could even be found. The camp's black market prices have soared to new heights with sugar at 150 pesos per kilo as a prime example. Buyers suddenly began dumping their money just to have some commodity to exchange in the future. Only a very few believe that they will ever see the money turned over to the Commandant's office and those who had saved rather large amounts of cash now feared being questioned as to its origin. The next four days were chaos with sums of money being offered in exchange for anything which might later be tradable.

After careful consideration we came to the conclusion that it would be wise to comply, at least in part, with the new order. I turned in 300 pesos, keeping a like amount for our future needs. These notes I concealed along with other documents and notes I had been making in a hollowed-out bamboo log, placed as though it were one of the supports of the shanty roof. According to the Jap order I would be able to draw one hundred fifty pesos a month for two months by which time, or so we all believed, we would be hearing American guns in the distance. At this time our family food reserve was down to three tins of soup, two cans of corned beef and one can of beans. This might have provided one good meal for the four of us under ordinary circumstances.

August 7, 1944, produced a strong rumor that Davao had been bombed by our forces. If it is true this will be the first attack of the campaign to retake the Philippines. Davao was some five hundred miles to the south of us, a seaport on the island of Mindanao. As though to confirm that something good was happening somewhere, the Commandant gave orders for an air raid shelter to be dug on the front lawn in front of his office, ostensibly for the personal use of him and his staff.

His laconic comment to bystanders was that air raids were an inevitable part of the hostilities.

One of our leaders called a group together and made an announcement that he had ordered three planes and three boats to take him and several close friends back to the States. Other manifestations of his irrational behavior resulted in his removal to the psychiatric hospital in Mandaluyong. Many of us felt that we, too, were close to that sort of breaking point. Probably the constant flow of rumors with only a small percentage having any basis in fact did more to raise and dash our spirits to the point where life was a matter of the daily trip to the edge of darkness.

XVI

Our new Commandant, Lt. Onozaki has placed before us an interesting document. He called in the Executive Committee and placed a "labor code" in their hands. They were dumbfounded by its terms which required vastly more labor efforts on the part of all internees at a time when our health was deteriorating day by day. It read as follows:

> A) War has become intensified and it is expected that the Manila area will be subject to bombing, in which case it will be impossible to bring foodstuffs into camp. The quantity of rice on hand will be sufficient, but no fresh vegetables or other fresh foods will be available owing to the disruption of transportation facilities caused by military activity. The internees must therefore meet this situation by placing under cultivation all available land within the camp and increasing the number of garden workers as well as the hours of labor. The garden plan, previously inaugurated, has not been successful.
> Lt. Takeda will take charge as the Commandant's representative and the internee committee must change its garden organization so that the full effort may be put into work.
> B) Labor in general. The labor situation as observed by the Commandant's office and other Japanese authorities, is considered unsatisfactory and the Executive Committee is requested to put into effect a new labor policy. Lt. Takeda will be in charge as the Commandant's representative and the Executive Committee is requested to take the following observations into consideration:
> 1. A new effort must be shown as regards gardening.
> 2. Basis of work assignment should be fundamentally:
>   3 hours daily - all women, children under 15 and men over 60
>   4 hours daily - children 15 to 17 and men 50 to 59
>   4 or more hours - men between 18 and 49 years of age.
> 3. Hours of work to be 8:30 AM to 5 PM except Sundays and Japanese holidays and Christmas.
> 4. The Japanese army will probably increase the extra money allowance for labor performed by the internees on the above basis.
>
> C) Official visitors to this camp have generally carried away the impression that the internees do not do enough work in their own interests, with the result that the authorities in direct charge of this camp have been criticized. This has also caused higher authorities to form the opinion that as long as the internees do not display a

greater effort to help themselves, the authorities need not exert themselves in assisting the camp.

Internees who have extra time should work at the spinning of hemp thread, making envelopes, sewing and other work, compensation to be paid in merchandise such as sugar, tobacco, cloth, etc.

To a neutral observer, the comments accompanying the labor code might not have seemed unreasonable. After all, life was tough just outside the walls not to mention back home in the countries which were engaged in the world conflict. But at this point in our incarceration, our physical condition such that any forced labor could mean a death sentence to some of us.

With two and one-half years' experience in dealing with the Japanese military, we were extremely cynical as to the promises offered in return for the demands on our bodies. We were sufficiently aware of the facts regarding the availability of food to know that even the Jap military could not keep their guarantees.

Furthermore the rainy season was in full swing and the entire garden area was under water ninety percent of the time. Rice would have been the only crop with a chance of survival and we were assured of an outside supply as long as our gates functioned. Just the maintenance of the camp with its population now of some four thousand souls required almost the maximum of energy we were capable of giving. Hardest hit seemed to be the families with small children since the daily stint of laundry, extra cooking and general care took all that a mother and father had to give.

When the Commandant's "labor code" was first posted everyone read it with ill-concealed indignation. We questioned the statement that there were sufficient quantities of rice on hand with our ration being limited to about 400 grams per person per day, and decreasing quietly from time to time. This was another Jap military guaranty down the drain since they had told us only a few months ago that we would be receiving one thousand grams daily per person.

As concerned the "garden plan," no matter what our efforts might be when the rains subsided, we would be faced with an unproductive soil and a limited supply of seeds and seedlings. Thus far the only crop which had shown any promise was a slimy green spinach-like leaf known as "talinum," hated by all and having only minerals as its redeeming feature.

The extra money allowances referred to repeatedly by the Commandant, in our opinion, was a figment of his imagination. Also, the type of work suggested during "extra time" might have been meant to aid the enemy and we would have starved first!

The remarks which angered us most was the reference to "higher authorities" considering untenable that we should continue to live in comparative idleness. There was no one in camp who did not have his hands full in trying to keep up with assignments, maintenance of health, laundry, and last but not least the care of the 700 camp children.

The presence of children was the strongest Japanese weapon to deter us from any aggressive action against them. The kids have been made to suffer the full consequences of this protracted war they got into innocently. Their entire lives will be affected to some degree by what they will have witnessed before it is over. Today as we look at our two youngsters we see them thin and undernourished, perhaps stunted in growth and it tears at us day in and day out, as to what this privation will do to their ultimate development into adulthood. Maybe we are becoming chronic hypochondriacs because each day seems to bring with it a new complaint of weakness or headache or skin problem. We still have a fair supply of basic vitamin-tablets smuggled in when I was fulfilling my duties as a camp buyer. Unfortunately they are a little on the heavy side with nicotinic acid, one of the B complex vitamins and each time we take one, there is a flushing of the skin along with a tingling sensation, not lasting long, thank goodness!

On August 15th we were startled from our sleep by what must have been a police siren sounding not far out of camp. Everyone thought that an air raid had to follow so our disappointment was great when nothing happened right away. However, before the night was over we had a single shocking earthquake which rocked our shanty and had me leaping out of bed to grab the boys. A bright blue flash lit up the sky in the direction of the Manila Electric Company but all this together added up to just another bit of unproductive excitement. Eleanor and I looked at the boys to find that they hadn't moved in the slightest since we had tucked them in for the night. Now, what next? We had passed through war, capture, imprisonment, typhoons, flood, cholera and earthquake.

Today, September 9th, there has been an official announcement that we are on "air-raid alert!" No one knows what is going on but the camp is wallowing in speculation. There does not seem any departure from the normal air activity of the flying "wild eagles" of Hirohito but there is no mistaking the preparations now being made in camp. There is a great to do over blackout precautions and air raid shelters. The Japanese are worried and what is more important, they are taking no pains to hide the fact. Any day might be the big one. Even the kitchen has been warned to have on hand a three day emergency feeding for the camp.

I set to work to dig out a shelter beneath our shanty but I quickly ran into water scarcely one foot into the ground. Keeping busy does my brain and our nerves more benefit than if we were to sit and wring our hands and wonder what to do in case the bombs start dropping around us once again. Donny is excited about the prospect of planes and the knowledge that their arrival would bring the end of the war that much closer. He says, "Ho boy! Soon I can go home to my Grandma's shanty and have some apples!"

It is exactly 7:50 a.m, ten minutes before that odious roll-call. We are on our way, the boys running ahead as usual.

Where do they get the energy? Suddenly the low whine of the air raid siren starts up. It changes in a moment from a growl to a screech just over our heads. We can hear the drone of motors in the distant sky as the loud speaker orders us to "take shelter immediately!"

Roll-call is forgotten or ignored as everyone rushes either to the buildings or the protection of their home-made shelters. We run to our shanty and dive underneath into the half-dug trench with the muddy bottom. We didn't fit very well but the boys enjoyed the mud while Eleanor's and my bodies made a shield for them on either side. It was hot already and the bugs had started to crawl so it was with some relief that the "all-clear" sounded just one and a quarter hours later. As we lay there really hoping for the drone of planes we realized that it was strangely silent outside of camp. The usual noisy traffic was simply not moving. When the all-clear sounded it was as if a silent movie, stopped on a single frame, suddenly started with newly discovered sound added.

Some muscovado found its way into camp and our local black marketeers were selling it for two hundred pesos a kilo! Muscovado is the lowest grade, crude sugar, used in ordinary times for horse feed. It is a black lump, half dirt and other wastes such as grass, straw and you name it. It must be boiled down, strained and boiled again. From a lump of muscovado weighing two pounds, a half pound of dark syrup might be obtained. And I bought some!

One afternoon as I was leaning against a post supporting the barbed wire enclosure where the Jap guards patrolled, one of them approached me. His smile revealed a set of gold teeth which must have been his pride and joy. Otherwise he was typical of the lowest ranking privates upon whose shoulders the responsibility of guard duty seemed to fall. His uniform, ill-fitting at best, was soiled, particularly the white collar of his shirt which had not been washed, I would guess, since his present tour of duty began. But he was smiling all the way and when he was within a few feet of me, said, "I speak English. You know San Francisco? I have many friends there!"

So as not to disappoint that square brown visage I replied that I also knew San Francisco and asked him when he had been there last. His smile grew even broader as he answered, "You know San Francisco? I have many friends there!"

I realized the limited headway we would make at this rate so I went on as though he had asked me a question to which I replied, "San Francisco is a lovely city don't you think? I wish I were there now!"

Still smiling, he answered, "You know San Francisco? I have many friends there!" And having satisfied his need to exercise his English (pronounced 'Engrish'), he waved and sauntered away.

The evening broadcast of "information" for this night, September 20th, was an unusual and cheery event from the viewpoint of the Internees. Our announcer read a statement of the actual rice situation. Our present rations were to be increased from 250 to 300 grams per day, per person. He continued, "Fifty tons of rice have been brought into camp. This will last for fifty days. This should be enough as far as this evening broadcast is concerned!"

For a moment surprised silence greeted this unusual announcement. Then a hubbub of voices broke the silence followed by overtone of subdued laughter. A bit of good news and some sly humor produced a welcome relief from the tension of the last few days.

Tomorrow is Roger's sixth birthday, his third in camp. We promised him that his next will be back home, with Grandma, Grandpa and all the folks. He prays for an air-raid.

The words of a little child...

September 21, 1944 dawned bright and early just like any other day when it didn't rain. The difference began with Roger who was up with the sun, eager to celebrate his birthday and impatient with our failure to share his enthusiasm at this early hour. "Where are my presents?" he cried as he rummaged around the few possible hiding places of our shanty.

I said, "Hey! It's not even six o'clock yet. Give your old Mom and Pop a break, willya?" But by that time he had found an old penknife that I had promised him and it didn't matter that it was a bit rusty and had one broken blade.

Eleanor had sewn together a pair of decrepit short pants to make one fairly good set and there were some shiny marbles and repainted toys which completed his "loot" and made him a happy little boy for the moment at least.

By now we were all up and around and it was time for roll-call as we had put away our meager breakfast. With this distasteful obligation out of the way, I faced up to my regular family laundry detail which took less than a half hour. My regular camp work assignment was at this time, mowing the grass in front of the isolation hospital. The mower had seen all of its good days and the lawn looked worse after I had finished cutting. I checked in at the desk at Santa Catalina hospital to see if they needed any extra help as I usually did. None was needed at this time and I started back across the campus at about 11:00 a.m. Some folks were standing around looking up at the casual performance of a few Jap "Zeros." There were always some few 'planes over this area of the city, probably patrols or just out for the exercise. However, at this moment from the northeast came a distracting drone, a hum quite out of tune with the recognizable pitch of the Japanese propeller and now very quickly identified as belonging to a large formation of distant 'planes, high in the sky, far away to the northeast. One of the bystanders remarked, "Someday they'll be ours!"

As they came nearer and more distinct, I automatically began to count them. I reached the amazing total of seventy-two when suddenly the low and electrifying wail of the air raid siren rose to a crescendo shriek! It could only mean one thing! The *real* thing!

The watching bystanders, like me, were rooted to the spot. We stood entranced and not a one of us moved until we had that final assurance that they were ours. By now sirens were moaning all over the city and we had our answer. Our hearts beat fast and our throats choked with emotion! The camp P.A. system blasted out instructions to take cover, find shelter immediately! Orders came from the Commandant's office to get out of sight or get shot at!

We all scrambled for the place where our families were — in our case, the shanty. There I found Eleanor and Roger, apparently oblivious to the fact that only a thin nipa roof separated them from falling shrapnel, spent bullets, shells and other debris from the battle which was now taking place. Roger was dancing up and down with great excitement saying, "See! I got my air-raid! That is my happy birthday present. What did I tell you?"

The planes were right overhead now and I could see them break up to drift off in different directions in flights of two, then to peel into their dives, it seemed, right overhead. They must have been heading for the airfields south of Manila and also for the Port area in the west. They had to be carrier based dive bombers.

The sky was a blanket of bursting ack-ack and small pieces of shrapnel had already started falling. I could hear the "tick" and "smack" according to the size of the pieces as they hit the ground all around us. But through all this, where was Donny? Our three year old was missing!

We had scrambled into the muddy trench beneath the shanty and in answer to my worried question, Eleanor said "He was over near the main building with a pre-kindergarten group and I'm hoping they were all taken inside to safety.

Without much conviction I said, "Oh he's sure to be safe. They just wouldn't let a tot that size run around loose."

My attempted reassurance failed to hit the mark with either of us so I decided to go and look for him. I hastily put on a red cross arm band, to which I was entitled and which was my permit to move about camp in just such a situation as this. Nevertheless I left the shanty by dropping out the rear window, out of sight of the sentry on the west wall. I immediately ran into another youngster about Donny's age, wandering around, completely unconcerned with the historic events now taking place over Santo Tomas. I recognized him, grabbed him by the hand and led him protestingly back to the frantic arms of his family. As I reached their shanty, the loud speaker came on with an announcement of a list of children who had been picked up all over the grounds and had been deposited safely within the main building. Wonder of wonders! Donny's name was first and they said exactly where he could be found!

The air battle was still in progress so I quickly made my way back to our shanty even though I knew there was a good possibility that Donny would be unhappy and maybe in tears over his plight as a temporary prisoner of some strangers. A fresh barrage of ack-ack let loose at this time and I dove into the nearest trench. As I got my bearings, I realized it was really in a mud-hole—safe for the moment but one helluva a mess! I was wet and my shirt was not only a gooey mess but I found a couple of slugs attached to my collar. I laughed and laughed when I thought of the change my spirits had undergone in these last few minutes. I scrambled back to the shanty during a lull and gave the good news to Eleanor and Roger and then decided to go and try to locate our youngest.

Still luckily dodging the falling shrapnel, I made the main building and ran up to the southeast corner of the second floor where I found Donny, not unhappy, not crying, but very unconcernedly munching on a piece of bread covered with peanut butter and jelly! Two nice ladies had been his providers.

The two elderly ladies were quick to tell me that he had been a good boy and promptly told them his name and where he lived (Shantytown) and who his Mommy and Daddy were. I'm sure our experience with a wandering child was very similar to the others whose names were announced over the loud-speaker.

Before returning to our shanty, I decided to take Donny up to the third floor to the room in which the Oblate Fathers were living. We might be able to get a good view of what was happening all around us. We found them all gathered around the windows, keeping themselves out of sight and harm's way with the protection of the overhanging ledges but still with a grandstand view of what was going on. The third raid had begun and we were able to watch the dive bombers break through the clouds and come screaming down on their targets. They had complete unconcern for the barrage of anti-aircraft fire that bracketed their dives and not one single time did I note one of our 'planes hit! Donny clapped his hands when I let him lift his head for a quick glance and I never had a greater thrill.

A good conscience and real concern made us quickly leave our vantage point and try to get back to the shanty. It was quiet for a short intermission and arrive we did to find Eleanor and Roger wondering what had become of us. The raid had been generally going on since 9:30 a.m. and it was now nearly noon. We saw clouds of smoke over the walls toward the south and west. The damage must have been terrific! Although the 'planes seemed to have departed for the time being, it was 1:30 in the afternoon before the "all-clear" sounded. Only then were we permitted free movement and a chance to get something to eat. Our release from tension was so great that we decided to splurge and open one of our few remaining and very precious emergency rations. We selected a 12 oz. tin of corned beef which we carefully divided into four equals parts, one for today, one for tomorrow, etc. We mixed it with some rice and fried it over our little charcoal stove and nothing ever tasted so good!

All during the hasty meal the boys played "air-raid and dive bomber" and Roger said over and over, "Boy! What a birthday present!" And he sure made believers out of us.

Usually the boys had an afternoon nap but we were all so high on "cloud nine" that such an idea was out of the question. Sure enough at 2:30 p.m. the air-raid warning came on loud and clear and we went to our wet and muddy "shelter" beneath the shanty. Our only protection was the mattresses we had stacked up over our heads but everyone else was in the same shape, believing as we did that our destiny now was in imminent rescue, alive and in one piece.

We thought that there was less ack-ack this time, as the 'planes went into their act. However, considerable shrapnel kept falling in our area as we could tell by the slap, whack of the jagged pieces of metal hitting the ground close by. We all had our boots on and lay huddled together, happy yet apprehensive that some errant bullet might find us. Eleanor summed it up saying, "Look, let's take no unnecessary chances now that we have come this far! Why don't we try to make the building during the next lull? It has got to be safer there."

By 3:45 all was quiet again and we peeked out to see if we could determine what damage might have been done. The Port Area was sending up billowing clouds of smoke and we counted on much damage being done there. There were continuing explosions as though delayed action bombs might have been dropped. We found the main building crowded and bursting with excitement. It was our first real cause for celebration and the Internees had made it our biggest holiday.

Taking stock, we learned that several people had been struck by shrapnel or other debris from the raid, but fortunately no one was seriously injured. We generally felt that all Japanese anti-aircraft fire had been directed over Santo Tomas, an assumption that was backed by our view of the U. S. 'planes seeming to go into their dive bombing from a point high in the sky above our camp. Of course none of these assumptions were true. The sky was an infinite place and the target areas were anything but a prison camp for the compatriots of the flyers. The lull ended at exactly 4:45 p.m. when "our boys" were back at it again! The Port Area was once again the prime target and with the continuing smoke and explosions from their previous raid, it was easy to pick out. After an hour or so of this, we realized that no thought had been given to the evening meal. Whatever happened it was going to be a late one. No matter, our appetites had flown with the air activities and as it turned out almost everyone settled for a cold snack of some sort, rather than to expect the kitchen to gear up to a regular hot evening meal. Activity in the sky ceased about 6:30 p.m. and twilight slowly softened the excitement of the day. The children fell a sleep as soon as they were put to bed and in the blackout there seemed to be no better thing to do than to join them. We were worn out physically and mentally and just as we were about to crawl in for the night, I heard, "Tom! Eleanor! Are you still up?"

The whisper was urgent and came from our near neighbors, the Duckworths. After acknowledging that we were still awake, we could not refuse a few moments' exchange of conversation which turned into an almost all-night re-cap of the meaning of the day's events, plans for the future and best of all, the time honored subject of "what we are going to do when we get out?" The Duckworths were from the English north country and their brogue was sometimes a bit difficult to follow. We had developed a warm friendship, mainly because their son Peter was Roger's best friend and playmate. They shared our excitement over Roger's "birthday present" and agreed that indeed, this was a day long to remain in our memory.

We said goodnight somewhere around four in the morning, with an exchange of "V" for victory signs and a hope that it would continue.

We slept fitfully the rest of the short night and were up, bright and early after dawn to see what the following day was to bring. I was uneasy over the effectiveness of our shelter beneath the shanty and I promised that I would get busy to improve it as soon as I had a bite to eat. This idea went the way of all other thoughts when the air-raid siren sounded its alarm right at 7:30 a.m.

Judging from the approaching sound, the 'planes were again coming from the northeast, making us certain that a task force must be operating off the Tayabas coast, the least inhabited area of the island of Luzon. By now, many rumors were floating around camp, but the most credible was that Admiral Halsey was directing a powerful striking force nearby in the China Sea.

In a very short time there were clouds of dive-bombers overhead. We watched them coming and stayed transfixed until the antiaircraft started firing. We kept our eyes on the progress of the battle, peeking around the sides of our little shanty, finding that everyone else was doing just about the same thing.

There were roving Jap guards who would threaten to shoot anyone who "exposed" themselves in this fashion. Our own jungle telegraph kept us advised when one of these fellows was approaching our area.

This raid appeared to be heavier and more sustained than yesterday's. Certainly more shrapnel landed around the camp. One piece which must have weighed five or six pounds fell with a loud whack just beyond the front of our shanty. We dug it up later and found it embedded into the ground almost two feet! These were wicked looking pieces of metal, all sizes and shapes and they began to be sought after by the children in particular, as trophies. We found a four inch shard sitting in our full water bucket which was standing behind the shanty's sink. Several shells landed in camp and exploded but most fortunately in unoccupied areas and miraculously no one was injured.

The sky above was criss-crossed by trails of smoke and now and again we could see a plane, hit either by anti-aircraft or enemy plane fire, slowly fall out of formation and start a turning, writhing descent toward earth. Before our horrified gaze, a parachute would emerge from the stricken craft only to be pursued by a Zero, showing its hated fried egg markings. The result was the tragic machine-gunning of the helpless aviator whose body could be seen, slumped over in death, his parachute now being carried by the wind to a landing who knows where.

The bombs seemed to find their targets as the ack-ack became less and less in volume. They must have located and destroyed batteries surrounding the city's military targets, but of course these could easily be replaced by other mobile units. Our hope was that strong help had to be on the way! This was the phrase that sustained us all through these months and we never for a moment doubted that such was the case.

One source of entertainment during these critical hours was the ever-changing actions of our keepers. The guards had decorated themselves with some sort of net upon which were fastened papaya leaves, twigs and any other greenery which would supposedly help them blend into the foliage of the country. They were extremely agitated over the raids and would have buried themselves in self-dug foxholes, ignoring us completely, if their superiors were not constantly on their tails with new orders. I heard a big splash not far from the shanty when the raid was at its peak and saw an embarrassed guard hauling himself out of a water-filled ditch.

The P.A. system had broadcast instructions to the Internees to take shelter during the actual raids and that moving from place to place would be severely punishable, if caught by the guards. In fact, a couple of the more adventurous among our compatriots had been brought before the Commandant for defying these orders and he told them that as long as they wished to see the combat they would have to stand out in the open campus until further orders. This meant standing in the broiling midday sun with no protection whatsoever either from its rays nor from the debris which constantly fell from the sky. They were lucky, as we later learned, surviving the day with no more than some painful sunburn.

One our close neighbors, also a "free spirit," decided that he was entitled to a front row seat and though he evaded the watchful eyes of the guard had his cure in another way. A machine gun bullet fell at his feet, just missing his shoe which was filled with a shower of dirt which he later displayed to all his neighbors, like a trophy of some sort.

All of these exciting events took place before eleven o'clock that same morning and our disappointment was great when this series of eight separate actions was followed by quiet for the rest of the day. There were huge fires in the port area and smoke drifted continually over the camp for the rest of the day. This night the moon is at the first quarter so maybe we'll have some night action. As usual the rumor mill was building and by nightfall we had the war just about over. We did have one air-raid warning but it was probably the reflex action of a nervous finger because it was not followed up.

Some of the rumors were interesting such as a detailed account of a huge landing on Corregidor with the U. S. Navy knocking on the door of Manila Bay.

The night was disappointingly quiet especially in contrast to those memorable nights of December 1941 when the Jap attackers were so successful. Eleanor and I slept lightly so we had no trouble getting up and dressed before 6:00 a.m. We sure didn't want to be caught without breakfast as had happened yesterday. One meal missed was more than any of us could afford in our present state of sub-nutrition. The boys were out hunting ack-ack souvenirs as soon as they were fed and we kept a close eye on their whereabouts in case of a new raid.

Roger had a bag full of wicked-looking shrapnel along with a few spent shells and Donny tagged along not far behind with his little bit. It wasn't until 9:15 this morning that the alarm sounded. The formations appeared high in the bright blue sky but to our chagrin failed to drop their "pennies from heaven" on this trip. They were apparently out of range of the Jap anti-aircraft fire as the enemy guns were silent. One significant change in the routine caught our attention and that was a complete absence of Japanese air interception. The all clear sounded at 11:00 a.m.

The foregoing led to the camp discussion topic of the day. "Where was the vaunted Jap air force?" Speculation had it that landings must be in progress and the enemy air power would be concentrated in a defense of the landing targets.

The Commandant's office had made an announcement that the attacking air force had always aimed for public works such as the water supply and therefore we must keep on hand a good supply of potable water. Seeming to back up the Commandant's admonition, the water pressure dropped to almost nil this morning causing a rising panic throughout the camp. Fortunately we had a supply of some twenty gallons and more of our neighbors had also provided for possible damage to the water supply.

Our supply of gas for cooking was suddenly cut off and our kitchen people worked heroically to convert their stoves to burn wood—but that material would last only as the diminishing number of trees on the Santo Tomas campus. Another concern of our Executive Committee was the cutting off of the hot water supply for the hospital, a means of providing clean linen and some sterilization. The hospital kitchen was closed and the number of meals for the camp was cut from three to two daily.

These deprivations, the increasing tension of our guards and the nearness of the shooting war made a great change in our morale. We felt we could survive any abuse short of out and out starvation. We eagerly anticipated the next attack believing that escape or release was just around the corner.

XVII

No one was up to accepting the truth of the situation. There had been no landings. Luzon was not yet a primary target. The U. S. forces were still far from a major victory in our area. Sea battles had yet to be fought and won before General MacArthur's invasion forces could safely seek a foot hold in the Philippine Islands. And here we were, our situation deteriorating to the point where people were dying of malnutrition or starvation without hope of any long-term survival under present conditions. But we faced all things good and bad with calm assurance that at long last rescue was moving our way. The only remaining question was "could we hold out?"

Our Shantytown neighbors were, for the most part, couples with small children, like ourselves, all with yet a meager stock of canned goods, set aside for the absolute emergency should it occur. We took each day as it came, sad to see our little children not progressing physically as they would have under normal living conditions, looking at each others' skinny bodies, watching for a telltale sign of swollen ankles—a forerunner of beri-beri or hypoprotenemia. Those swollen ankles meant a retention of fluid which in two weeks time could literally drown a person and certainly kill them.

Infection, uncurbed by desperately needed but unavailable medication, had taken the lives of a couple of close friends in very short order and iodine and Mercurochrome were worth their weight in gold. Skin infections were commonplace and generally no cause for alarm, although they were still unsightly and usually bothersome. Eleanor had contracted a hand infection some time back and was still hampered by a ban on using soap or soapy water. The infection had eaten so deeply into her hands that the camp doctors thought she might lose a finger or two. If it worsened now, there would certainly be no medication to allay her symptoms.

Today, Sunday, September 4th, rewarded us with an early raid. At 8:25 formations of our 'planes went over en route to the port area. We heard the cruummp of bombs and soon saw a rising pall of smoke over Manila Bay. Cavite had been hit and since this had been an important U. S. Naval Base, we assumed it had performed a similar function for the enemy Japs. We rejoiced, forgetting our immediate cares in the excitement.

The "all-clear" sounded at 1:30 p.m. and during the entire time we were prohibited any movement about the campus. This meant that no food could be prepared by the kitchen, nor, of course, could it be served. To enforce this, the Jap guards were particularly officious, emphasizing their orders with a jab of a bayoneted rifle, when someone moved too slowly to suit them. There was mutual frustration over the language difference, but as the emergencies grew, the Commandant provided us with a list of key words which would move us from place to place when necessary.

We were without indoor plumbing in Shantytown so the most widely used "key word" became the equivalent for "bathroom." "Benjo" more than served its purpose and to this day I'm not certain but that it was a slang expression used by the common soldier rather than a socially accepted word.

Occasionally one of our more daring spirits would engage a sentry in dialogue which consisted of our lad pointing to where his wrist watch would normally be and asking in English, "What time is it, you dirty sonofabitch?" This type of humor never became standard practice and was discontinued completely when Hank Hersch got an answer he was not expecting from a guard who said, "Oh HO! You, double sonofabitch-bastard!" And with this he unshouldered his rifle and swung out at Hank who had wisely taken off in the direction of the crowd in front of the main building.

Individually members of the Japanese military guard were tolerantly disposed toward us but collectively these feelings were buried under the corporal punishment system practiced by their superior officers, passed on in turn to us in the presence of the latter, for the slightest cause. We witnessed beatings of soldiers by their officers; what we considered a brutal loutishness in their treatment of us was really a passing down of the same kind of discipline. Even our children were not exempt from this type of treatment although we had always believed that the Japanese had a special love for their little ones.

The military representatives we have met during the past three years have impressed us with their conviction that the Caucasian race must be driven out of the Orient and relegated to a second class situation, if they remained in the "Greater East Asia Co-Prosperity Sphere." Our customs and culture have been ridiculed by their press and radio throughout the war without ever explaining their success achieved by copying our manufactured goods and processes, our educational systems and sports.

We look at the little brown man who is guarding our section of the wall today and find it hard to consider him as an individual. He is a proto-type, sad-sack, droopy-drawers type hardly military in bearing as one of our soldiers, his face a look-alike to all of the others we have seen. His people have been preaching a doctrine of hate since our war began in 1941 and we have absorbed some of this jingoism and now hate him, as a representative of the Rising Sun! But—he is an individual; he may even have a family back home in Japan and may not care one way or the other about the doctrines of his bosses and their political aims. At times he even looks like he would wish to talk to us, maybe about our children or even his.

We feel saddened, Eleanor and some of our friends, when we sit down of an evening, and in the darkness of the blackout, "shoot the breeze" for a while before bedtime. This artificial "hate" that dominates the lives of our captors and us, can it ever be overcome when times get back to normal? Will our wounds be too deep to even recognize the brotherhood of man and practice God's own word, "Love thy neighbor."

I lie awake that night wondering what kind of a world will we leave for our children and theirs? Will it be a constant war of survival among nations divided by language and customs which one finds unacceptable to the other? Or will the lessons of this World War II, the war that should end all wars, teach us values, in tolerance and brotherhood that will make Peace on Earth available to all mankind? I wonder.

The blackout seems to be a permanent fixture although there was no sign of a raid throughout last night or during today's daylight hours. This is rather a letdown for us after four exciting days' aerial events. Our neighbors reflect the gloom that Eleanor and I feel, caused perhaps by a sneaking suspicion that our attacking forces, wherever they might be, were perhaps repulsed. We have faith that our deliverers are on the march and that they may be attempting to set foot on Philippine soil right at this moment. But the silence only gives us an opportunity to be realistic, to know that it will take time, according to the MacArthur plan of slow, sure, island-hopping with a minimum of casualties. Will we be home for Christmas?

The silence continued through the next few days, including our eighth wedding anniversary. On that day we did have a siren go off but nothing else happened to mark our celebration. We realized that our married life had been a bit hectic with travel and living in the Dominican Republic for a year, Guatemala and El Salvador for another three or so, having our first born arrive in the latter country and our second almost en route to the Orient. Exciting and educational surely, but present circumstances seemed to be wiping out any further desire to live abroad. Of course our future plans depended entirely upon survival.

During the past two weeks an oppressive silence has hung over Manila. There is a feeling of tense waiting, a feeling which not only hangs over the outside population but also the Santo Tomas Internees and their captors. Yesterday excitement consisted of the arrival of three pigs, ostensibly to supplement our diet. Manny, Moe, and Jack wound up as pork gravy which was added to our morning mush ration the following day.

At 12:07 p.m. on October 7th came the welcome sound of the air-raid alert. But nothing happened, and the all-clear sounded, three hours later. At that time, much to our surprise Jap trucks started rolling into camp, fully loaded with a complete miscellany of war materials from parts of ships, guns, ammunition and gasoline. We were angered and frightened by the unloading of these military items at various spots on the front campus. Almost immediately an announcement of restrictions on Internee movements in or near these areas was made. We watched in stunned surprise as anti-aircraft batteries were set up only a few feet away from the buildings which housed our people. Our committee immediately put in writing a protest to the Commandant which read as follows:

> To the Commandant:
> Subject: Military Activity in the Front Grounds
> "The Internee Committee has been informed that the area in front of the Main Building, including the east and west roadways, the center path, and the entire field in front of the Education Building, will be closed temporarily to the Internees, except for those on essential camp duties. The road to the hospital is to be kept clear in order to permit the movement of trucks.
> "We were later informed that the two pavilions now used as classrooms, were to be utilized at night by Japanese soldiers for sleeping purposes. It has been reported that the soldiers, now quartered in the front grounds have taken certain camp-owned materials, such as adobe brick and iron drums from the storage area of the sanitation department, and further that the bridge leading from the west roadway to the southwest garden has been removed.
> "Also it has been noted that the soldiers have not remained in the area set aside for their use. Certain sanitary problems have arisen which have already been called to the attention of your office.
> "Generally the Internees have the impression that the front area is now being utilized for purposes of a purely military nature in no way connected with the maintenance of this camp. On behalf of the Internees we respectfully submit that:
> 1- The use of any portion of this camp and its facilities for military purposes is objectionable on the grounds that the presence of interned non-combatants is being utilized to give protection from bombardment. In any event, it is considered that such usage constitutes a potential menace to the safety of the camp.
> 2- The use or appropriation of camp-owned materials by the soldiers occupying the front grounds has not been authorized insofar as we know, and we ask your assistance in taking the necessary steps to preserve and protect camp property.
> Respectfully,

The foregoing document was signed by three members of the Internee Committee. The Commandant summoned the chairman to his office the following day and spoke with him through an interpreter. He assured the chairman that the soldiers would no longer use the pavilions for sleeping nor would they be allowed to use camp property. However, he expressed displeasure at the inference that the Imperial Japanese Army would use the Internees as a shield and considered as insulting the first paragraph of the committee's letter. Nevertheless he asked that reassurance be given the Internees that everything possible would be done to protect the Internees. At the close of the interview the Commandant requested that the chairman act quickly to relieve the anxiety on the part of the Internees and it was agreed that the substance of the Commandant's remarks should be posted on the main bulletin board.

Our concern was well documented by the inventory of what had been brought into camp at this time. It included a contingent of troop, fully armed and field equipped, a considerable number of marine engines, spare parts, shafts, cables, cranes, hoists, wire matting for airfield repair, steel plates for ships, a miscellany of guns in various states of repair and crated materials the identity of which we never could learn because of the restrictions on our movement in the area. We guessed that all of this came from the Palaus which they had lost a short time back. There were also a number of army trucks apparently from some hurried evacuation along with fuel in drums which were camouflaged and placed near our hospital where they might be less likely to suffer damage during an air-raid.

These transformed the front grounds into a genuine military encampment now reinforced by the construction of barracks to house these and additional troops. The latter were constructed on the border of our hopeful gardens and as a result most of our produce went to feed the military. We became frightened by the imminence of our being used as front-line hostages if and when the fighting might begin around Manila.

But it seemed there was little we could do about it except register our complaints with the Commandant. One thing certain, the war was approaching our area. These were the signs and from them we could and did take heart.

The publication of a series of new regulations by the Commandant must have been prompted by the military and the unfavorable course of hostilities. They amused us more from their wording than from their intent and for whatever they may be worth, they are reproduced here:

> A- Matters which are prohibited:
> - to run away or to plan to run away from camp.
> - all acts to communicate with outsiders secretly.
> - all acts to bring in or take out articles without permission.
> - communication apparatus of any kind.
> - electrical appliances, chemicals, intoxicating liquors
> - printing apparatus or materials, optical instruments-
> - implements of war, documents or pictures of anti-Axis nature.
> - maps, atlases or pictures detrimental to military operations.
> - to enter forbidden places
> - to enter the Commandant's office
> - to assemble in groups of more than four or to hold meetings.
> - to change buildings or to construct one.
> - to plan to execute any new undertaking.
>
> B- Rewards or punishments
> - are to be administered by the Commandant except that the Internee Committee is authorized to reward for good conduct, but a report is to be made.
>
> C- Entertainment only as approved by the Commandant.

There were also detailed regulations relating to education, sanitation, designation of buildings, their use and occupancy, all of which seemed to imply that punitive measures would be taken on the least pretext of overstepping our tightening bonds. We began to appreciate the peace of mind we enjoyed when we were seemingly forgotten by the military, perhaps remembered only as pawns to be kept for some future contingency.

XVIII

Friday, the thirteenth of October was neither our lucky nor unlucky day although we were treated to momentary excitement when the air-raid sirens screeched their warning. After our usual scramble for safety, nothing happened but we just knew that there had to be some war activity going on in the general vicinity. Our neighbors, Eleanor, the boys and I have settled down to a low profile of watchful waiting, entertaining each other with dreams and visions of what we would do "when we got back to the states." Men, women and children dreamed up succulent recipes which in reality might have been quite indigestible to the ordinary stomach. We talked food while we struggled with the now familiar local available talinum or gabi root or, if lucky, an occasional banana.

It rained and we played bridge, mahjong or cribbage or gin or whatever turned anyone's fancy. We expected little activity from our airmen while the weather was adverse so this became a period of boredom in which we did our stint of watchful waiting.

Sunday, October 15th, we are again under attack! It's great to be "back on bombing" as the alarm sounded early this morning. It is 8:45 a.m. and the 'planes can be seen over the Marakina Valley to the east, slowly turning in distant action while their thunder reached our ears moments later. There were heavy cloud formations which must have given some fliers help and which must have been a deterrent to others.

We were dismayed to see so many Jap 'planes in the air, but at least this type of combat cut out the ever-dangerous anti-aircraft barrages which were a menace to the civilian population. This was actually the first time that we had seen Jap 'planes in action other than as laconic patrols over the city.

We were a bit too far off to distinguish the actual battle results but among the Internees were enthusiasts who counted several Jap 'planes knocked out of the air. We saw one dog fight which results were verified by our neighbors. One Jap 'plane, diving head on toward one of our dive bombers, received a burst of cannon fire right into his nose. The Jap exploded immediately, the mess of smoking fragments marking the spot in mid air, where he had received the vital shot. I was sure of his identity as our 'plane circled, lost altitude and then zoomed low over camp in a wing-wagging sign of victory. I could see the beautiful white star on his wing.

Throughout the better part of the exciting battle, Roger and I were outside of our shelter, lying among the huge gabi leaves out of the vision of the Jap guard. Only when the smack of some falling shrapnel was heard did we scramble back into the protection of our muddy fox-hole. Each time we breathlessly described what we had seen for Eleanor and Donny's benefit. None of us seemed to pay any attention to the obvious danger which was to come along with any rescue attempt. In effect, we seemed to regard the proximity of death with some amusement, detached, as it were, from the rescue we knew was sure to come. With tongue in cheek, we told each other that there was no worry with the bullets, shrapnel and explosive shell we heard or saw. The one which might get us would be one we neither heard nor saw! So why listen? Thus far no falling object had been ticketed for any Santo Tomasite. If one did come down with your name on it, that was that.

We were out in the open again, Roger and I, watching the actions of one of our 'planes over the bay area. Several ships in the harbor were protected by barrage balloons, large gas bags attached by cable to several points of the ship's deck and meant to deter 'planes from dive-bombing. The particular 'plane we were watching had wagged his wings, dived out of formation and shot up the center-most and largest balloon. That was a maneuver of sheer exhilaration, a bit of "Watch me boys! Here I go!"

He continued his attack on the balloons until some of the ships must have been defenseless. We could see the other 'planes now start their dive bombing runs although we could not see the ships. The rising columns of smoke gave eloquent testimony later, to the success of our attack.

With tensions running high I found relief in reinforcing our fox-hole type shelter beneath the shanty. The boys and I shoveled gobs of damp earth against the sides of the hollowed-out hole, so that we had better protection against any lateral debris, but little help overhead where it really counted. It really didn't matter because our feverish activities kept us busy and our minds off our troubles. Our neighbors were doing the same. Eleanor was in charge of the shanty floor overhead which had been piled high with mattress, pillows and anything else that might slow up the fall of shrapnel. She called our activities "psychological but futile."

Time has permitted the infamous nipa worm to eat away much of the protective covering of our thatched roof. When it rains, water drips intermittently throughout our living quarters. In the dry weather fine powder drifts down on us, presumably from the activity of the worms. Our sawali-palm thatch sides are in good shape as are the drops which serve as windows. We are grateful for the durability of the bamboo poles which support our structure and the strips of the same material which serve as our floor.

Tonight was so balmy and quiet that we asked Emily and Cliff Larsen to join us for a chat. This young couple had planned to be married when the war with Japan erupted and postponed their big day. Despite their imprisonment they managed to get outside and carry out their plans. Their honeymoon in 1942 was spent apart since they were interned like the rest of us, in separate quarters. Now they were residents of shantytown, living in their own bahay a few doors removed from us. Our visit with them was cut short by a Jap guard who came along and ordered us to "go bed now!"

The following morning we were at roll-call and almost immediately the air-raid sirens started their awful wailing! We were not dismissed for a change, but forced to go through our routine of bowing toward Tokyo and the Emperor and answering to our names. Apparently the Japs were convinced that our 'planes were after strictly military targets and would not bother the camp routine. Lately our captors have strictly enforced the bowing routine which meant that every one of us, men, women and children, had to kow-tow to any Japanese soldier who came within our vision. It angered us almost to a point of revolt which of course, would have served no good purpose. I believe that if our health were back to normal, some one of us would have lost his composure and done something we all would have regretted.

Even the stimulation of the daily air-raids, such as the four hour session today, was no help to our battered mental state. Our bodies showed evidence of starvation and it kept getting worse day by day. The few men who still enjoyed the luxury of shirts were able to cover their bony torsos, but elbows, arms and legs revealed the common loss of fatty tissue. Chest-less women walked gingerly on two incredible sticks which could hardly be called "legs." Children were the most pitiful of all as they searched for something to eat, even to the cast-off garbage which was kept outside of the Japanese quarters.

To describe one's reaction to the screech of the air-raid siren, is a definition of fear laced with excitement. My insides undergo some sort of upheaval and for a moment I am paralyzed with panic. My heart races and I want to run. Even after the many raids we have lived through, as soon as a lull occurs and we are allowed to move, there is a concerted rush for the toilets. It is not the fear of being wounded but the excitement all around us which causes our action.

Wednesday, October 18th produced a short but effective raid. It began at 10 a.m. and was over less than an hour later. Several shells had landed not far from Shantytown, in the seminary garden and just outside the wall. The explosions were loud and shrapnel could be heard hitting either the building used by the seminarians or the wall. The shells had to be unexploded and of Japanese origin, probably directed to the U. S. aircraft overhead. We learned shortly after that a few of the shells, undoubtedly from machine guns, had landed in camp, perilously close to one or two shanties, spattering them with mud, fortunately smaller in caliber than those which had exploded outside our area.

At 11:45 a.m. we were permitted an hour of unrestricted movement for the purpose of securing food and "reuniting families" separated at the start of the early raid. I was but one removed from the ticket puncher at the head of the food line when, without warning there was the familiar "cruummp, boom, crruump" and they were at it again! Luckily the raid was a short one this time and the food was still warm when I was able to return to the shanty. The fact that no warning siren had sounded made us think that the Japanese were becoming disorganized with their defenses.

This sort of activity continued throughout the rest of the day, attack without warning, no alarms and no return fire, at least that we could determine. That night we sat with the Grimes and the Larsens summing up the significance of the day's events. Our morale had been given a boost by the fact that our boys had come in high over the city, undetected and out of range of the ack-ack. We attributed these facts to the superiority of our men and their equipment. We speculated that this might be IT although as far as we knew no definite attack had occurred anywhere near Manila by other than carrier borne aircraft. But with so much air activity and apparent superiority, it seemed that our day of rescue could not be far away.

As we murmured our thoughts in the darkness, we watched the flickering shadows cast by fires burning somewhere in the distance, listening hopefully for the drone of our returning aircraft which had yet to come in by night. There was a stillness in the air, of anticipation and anxiety of the destruction to come.

Sleep did not come easily for Eleanor and me. The boys slept the deep sleep of innocence, but we talked and talked mostly about the good times of former years. Then we dozed for awhile, half awake and half asleep and then wide awake as into our foggy minds came the sound of hushed movement in the distance. There was the sound of muffled voices as of a crowd of people far away. Vehicles, perhaps trucks, tanks and cars were on the move as we could tell from the sound of many gears grinding and motors running. Even the railroads seemed alive with the noise of engines huffing and whistles blowing as they moved along the rails. The total sound was one of a soft roar which had to be caused by the movement of a lot of men and materials, hopefully out of the city.

We couldn't help but wonder if tomorrow, or some day soon perhaps, we would awaken to a camp abandoned by our captors along with a city populated once more only by civilians. As we tried to continue our sleep, the noise wandered away in the distance and finally all was quiet again. I'm sure that Eleanor was as disappointed as I was since the brevity of the incident could not have meant a total evacuation of the occupation forces from Manila.

Next morning we arose, not at all refreshed by last night's sporadic rest but eager for the new day and what events would follow. Eleanor asked, "What time do you think they'll be over?"

Jokingly, I answered, "Oh any minute now!"

I glanced at my watch just to see how long it would take to make my words come true. It was 7:23 a.m. and as I looked up we heard them! Talk about calling the shots, they really made me look good as a forecaster for the moment. This was a big one. We counted more than a hundred 'planes in the first wave and when they dropped their cargo the earth rumbled and rocked with detonation of hundreds of bombs. The noise was deafening and the damage must have been devastating. Clouds of smoke mushroomed into the skies from oil and fuel dumps, the port area, Cavite and some of the air fields outside of the city limits. The day was bright and clear, ideal I suppose for air action.

This raid lasted only a half hour but it was followed by four more, all of equal intensity and brevity. From our vantage point they came in with the traditional sun at their backs, almost invisible to us and probably impossible targets for any effective defense.

We could not only see the evidence of destruction, we could smell it! Burning oil, the sharp acrid smell of explosives and fire were proof of the success of today's action. All of us, our neighbors and friends were a bit more daring now and we witnessed much of the air activity outside of our shelters. The guards paid us less and less attention, realizing, I suppose, that their days of victory were rapidly vanishing. The actions were far enough away from Santo Tomas so that there was a minimum of debris either from the skies or from the ground fire to endanger us.

We will long remember that day although we did not learn why, until the next when word of a landing attempt by our forces had been made near Dulag, on the coast of Leyte, a large island just south of Luzon! The detailed account, appropriately slanted in favor of the Japanese defending forces, had appeared in yesterday's *Manila Tribune* and somehow the account had filtered into camp.

This was the news we had been waiting for! This was the first step in the re-taking of the Philippines, the first landing! It seemed that the newspaper had minimized all of the facts pertaining to our role in the landing, keeping that part of it to a bare acknowledgment that we did indeed have a foothold. Our losses were emphasized and magnified in the fashion of propaganda. Yesterday's super air activity was undoubtedly meant to be a distraction to Japanese military headquarters in Manila.

The news washed over camp like a flood and I'm sure that our captors were concerned with its effect on the Internees. But we contained our enthusiasm mostly with the rationalization that Dulag was a long way from Manila and that the daily deliverance that we were hoping for was still a long way off. Nevertheless, we celebrated in small groups even to the extent of finding a few drams of spirits which had been squirreled away for such a momentous occasion.

There was some air activity of the port area this same day but its importance to us was shrouded by the momentous news of yesterday. As the day came to a close, we heard the usual recorded music over the loud speaker system and at the close of the program our announcer said, "Good night! Better Leyte than never!"

There were no more air-raids for the next few days. We assumed our boys were busy consolidating their landing success at Dulag.

XIX

The siren was busy today, October 25th, although we were unable to find a single American 'plane over the city at any time. A few Jap "Wild Eagles" now called "Mild Eagles" by the Santo Tomasites were seen nervously patrolling the area. We could not easily identify the Jap 'planes, not knowing the difference between a "Zero" and a "Betsy," but we were sure experts in identifying our own. We knew about P- 38s, P-51s, J3-25s, etcetera, but we had not yet seen a four-engined bomber which would mean land-based 'planes were finally in action.

The rumor factory is in full swing and we have heard about landings large scale and small scale, on about every size-able island in the Philippines. Luzon has not escaped our fancies and the Legaspi Peninsula is a favorite topic of speculation. The fact that every rumor differs in the details makes obvious their lack of credibility. Among other items Eleanor heard that Luzon was under a special alert, one rumor which was probably based in fact. We have had a constant struggle not to accept many of the choicest rumors as truth, so we try to keep our eagerness under control and sort things out with logic rather than emotion.

Bob Russell came by and stopped for a minute to chat. He asked, "Have you heard the latest?" Bob was a great athlete and had been a superstar at our camp softball league games. He had won a decathlon sometime back before the war and was a hero to all the young fry in Shantytown.

I answered, "If it's more then an hour old, I haven't."

"Last night's *Vanguardia* announced an attack which was repulsed, somewhere near Antimonan on the east coast off Luzon and this morning a radio broadcast said that a large convoy was seen of the Tayabas coast."

"Bob, I've got mixed feelings about these news reports. I believe them because I want to, but at the same time I think they cause most of us to drop our guard. I know I want to dive in and eat up our reserve and in reality, how far away can rescue really be?"

"Yeah. You're right, but we are still starving for good news as well as food, and logic just isn't popular in a situation like this!"

He went on, stopping at the Werffs to spread the word. I went up into the shanty, told Eleanor what Bob had said and then went to the back "window" to see if Jerry Updyke and Bill Donnelly were camping out tonight. They weren't so I said to Eleanor, "It's getting late, why don't we hit the hay?"

Sleep did not come easy and sometime beyond the middle of the night I awoke to a discreet but significant cough from beyond the front of the shanty. I figured that it must be one of the Jap guards, outside but beyond the barbed wire. Curiosity prompted me to see what he was up to, so I crept out of bed and went to the front door which was partly open for better ventilation. As soon as my head appeared, he made frantic motions for me to come out. I came down the steps with my heart in my mouth, barefoot and very, very wary.

"Ugh! You...sato...watchee?"

I guessed that "sato" was that awful brown solid sugar since he held a decrepit bag containing a brown sticky mess which could not have been anything else. He apparently wanted to know if I would trade or buy it, since he said, "You have watchee?"

I thought for a moment how much we would appreciate something to sweeten our morning mush so I said, "No have watchee. You want pesos?"

He thought for a moment and then said, "six hundred ok!"

This staggered me but I thought how little the few hundred "Mickey Mouse" pesos meant to us. I had about four hundred pesos at that time and so I offered it to him. He hemmed and hawed mostly in his own unintelligible tongue but finally gave in and told me that the bag contained two kilos, which was far from the truth, but I was glad enough to get it.

I had to go inside for the money and found Eleanor was awake and very concerned about what might have been going on. I put her fears to rest and went back to my very nervous trader who probably anticipated an unexpected appearance by his corporal or sergeant at any moment. He grabbed the notes, counted them in the darkness, quickly turned and trudged off, happy that he had made a good bargain.

I lost no time in returning to bed, after safely stowing away our new found treasure. That miserable little bag made us happier than a full-course Thanksgiving dinner at home might have done.

Next day our usual alert sounded at 7:50 a.m. and it again failed to stop roll-call. Evidently our captors wanted to impress upon us that not even the serious business of an air-raid would permit us relaxation from the daily homage to the Emperor and Tokyo! And how we hated it! Even with fingers crossed behind our backs and other hidden obscenities our frustration smoldered and bubbled beneath the surface.

More reports of epidemics in the city and more precautionary injections were ordered. Today the four of us lined up for another combination shot of cholera, dysentery and typhoid. This one hurt and the boys found it hard not to let a teardrop or two fall. Today was the first in a series of three shots and with the sore arms, some fever and nausea which followed, there weren't many of us who intended to complete the series if we could avoid doing so.

Even though the effect of our injections lasted through Sunday morning we found sudden recovery in a very heavy air-raid which started early that day. As usual, a great many pieces of shrapnel fell in and around camp and afterwards the children had a field day in recovering souvenirs, among them some pretty wicked-looking pieces of jagged metal fragments.

That same night the moon was almost full and shone bright and silvery in a clear night sky. We talked about the beautiful colors of autumn back home, the harvests which neither of the boys had ever seen in their short lives. We talked of the countryside where some day they would see for themselves the hay piled high and the leaves turning red and coppery, falling from the trees with each gust of an October wind. Hallowe'en was only a day away and that was one holiday neither Roger nor Donny knew anything about. Snow, frost, icy mornings and turkeys gobbling somewhere waiting to be the star of a Thanksgiving celebration were existing far away under the same moon that made our evening a time for dreaming. As much as we promised one another not to do so, we returned to our favorite topic, food! Cooking and recipes are no longer the exclusive province of the women. Men and children have displayed fertile imaginations in concocting dream meals to prepare and eat once we are out of Santo Tomas.

Next day was dreary and drizzly without letup in the smothering heat of the tropical rainy season, an environment which seemed to make us feel more imprisoned than ever. Our mush tasted much better with the addition of some melted brown sugar although it retained an ever-penetrating moldy over-taste. I had a day's wash to do and I searched for some excuse to skip it but without success. I finally got it finished and watched it hang, flapping wetly on a line which I had strung under the overhang because of the constant rain. There was a light breeze but in this humidity I felt that my labors were wasted. Just about the moment I concluded my work, the loud speaker blared out with the announcement that a typhoon was on the way. The barometer had dropped sharply in the past two hours and the Commandant had ordered the warning. This had to be serious! We had survived other typhoons, mostly of diminished intensity, since their centers had not passed over Manila. Apparently this would be different. Our standing instructions were to evacuate the shanty areas during the most intense period of the storm of this magnitude. "Typhoon Alley" was a path across Luzon from southeast to northwest with the storm eventually dying out in either the North or South China seas. Most of the storms by-passed Manila with the greatest damage occurring along the coastal areas both southeast and north of the capital city.

Our camp weather experts estimated that the eye of the storm would hit Manila late this night but so far into the evening we were experiencing only the continuing soggy drizzle with perhaps a few additional gusts of wind now and then. Eleanor and the boys were tucked in ready to be moved if and when the change in weather demanded. By 7 p.m. it was pitch black and the wind was rising unmistakably, to judge from the shanty, which rustled like dry corn stalks in late autumn. The temperature was dropping and I got out of bed to fix one of the drops which had broken loose and was flapping against the side of the shanty. I could feel a cold breeze blowing up through the split bamboo floor but I was reassured as to the steadiness of my cross-braced bamboo, since the shanty seemed firm as a rock despite the gusty wind outside.

Until now the rain had been only a drizzle but suddenly some huge raindrops splattered the roof with a sound like hail on corrugated metal. By 10 p.m. the wind was almost a gale and there was no doubt but that the shanty would suffer some loss of its thatched roof and sides. It was colder than before and I decided to get everyone up and dressed, ready for flight to the Annex some hundred yards away. The shanty continued to holds its own and we sat huddled awaiting our fate. We were continually amazed by the roaring gusts of wind which whipped out of the night toward the shanty and we would brace ourselves for the shock we knew had to come only to find that the roar suddenly swept up and off into the night with little or no movement of the shanty. The threatened deluge did not materialize but a steady rain beat down around for the rest of the night. The wind continued to roar and moan alternately but not once did its full force strike the shanty. We could hear the ripping away of some of the limbs of nearby acacia trees and then their crashing to the ground, maybe taking along a shanty roof here and there. We were not in the danger zone at any rate and it seemed also that an invisible wall of some sort of protection kept us from harm.

Toward morning the wind suddenly died down and just as suddenly began pouring down torrents of rain. Our roof leaked and the sides of the shanty were soon water-soaked but we guessed happily that the typhoon had unexpectedly veered away from Manila before its anticipated arrival. Eleanor and the boys had actually fallen asleep during the early hours of the morning, waking up to find me busily patching leaks in the roof. It is wet and muddy outside and there has been some flooding of the lower areas of the camp. Otherwise the camp returned to its normal routine.

It is wet and cold this morning and we are weary with our long night's vigil. Bill Donnelly called over to see how we had fared and imparted the news that yesterday's paper had carried an item to the effect that a relief ship, laden with 1500 tons of war relief supplies for prisoners in Japan, Manchukuo, Formosa, and the Philippines has left Vladivostok. As a matter of fact the materials had already landed in Manila sometime in June of this year and had been awaiting "arrangements" ever since!

We had an announcement from the Commandant this morning in the form of a warning that violations of the regulation concerning the bowing of all prisoners to Japanese officers has now been extended to any representative of His Imperial Highness, military or civilian. Neither children nor the aged are exempt from this regulation.

Further to the foregoing a "generous concession has been made regarding the required attendance of the sick and aged at roll-call. They may now be seated except whenever any representative of the Commandant's office may be present." Not much help, really, considering the fact that there is present, practically always, a member of the Commandant's staff.

XX

A new month has arrived November reminds us again of home. It is cold and overcast and could be a typical autumn day in the northeast. But in Manila, this day was just about as cold as it would get for the entire year. We could also expect rain nearly every day, either stormy downpours or cold continuing drizzle until every bit of furniture and clothing was covered with a glaze of mildew. Humidity and mud ran hand in hand and as a result we spent most of our daytimes indoors, in the shanty or wandering around the Main Building.

The camp medical board, our four doctors, warned us against hoarding food reserve stocks except possibly those which were in sealed containers. Even our captors admitted that we were being short-changed in the deliveries of camp rice rations and then told us that these shortages would have to be made up from our camp reserve stocks. Two months before, the doctors had recognized that severe malnutrition was fast approaching the camp population and that camp reserve stocks of M & V (meat and vegetable) rations originally supplied by the Red Cross would have to be tapped. This translated into six ounces per person per week of M & V or corned beef of which there was also a small supply.

This went on as long as they would last, which turned out to be about two months. So, today, November 1, saw the last of this nourishment used in the general mess. We lingered over our "stew" gravely aware that at this point the going would henceforth be rough as to the preservation of our health. Individuals were indeed lucky if they still had a can or two of the Red Cross rations on hand. Naturally the topic of general discussion is food or rather, the lack of it! Housewives gather between air-raids and discuss all means of making the morning mush more palatable, garnishing it, perhaps with talinum (yuk!) or camote tops if any become available. Gravies are whipped up with casava flour (if one is lucky to have some), and all of the ideas inhibited by the disappointment of a camp garden which falls far short of production needs. Every conversation overheard seems to start with the phrase, "You take the morning mush…"

I heard one woman say to another in the chow line, "We've run out of the cooking oil which we had taken from our coconut oil lamp and filtered and I've tried some face creams which were hidden away all this time, but they are perfumed. Eleanor Lewis has some Albolene which does not have any scent in it and I think I'll make some kind of a trade with her."

Of course I was proud of Eleanor's resourcefulness and I realized that her "delicious" fried rice dish owed its succulence to good old Albolene!

When I told her of the overheard conversation she said that it was unlikely they would have anything edible to trade and if they were thinking about face cream, forget it. She had stopped using it almost three years ago!

Fuel has become a scarce commodity and there is no one who has not already started chopping up their meager furnishing, including their shanties. All of the campus trees have been trimmed to their main trunks and high branches and some of them are about to come down for all time. We understand that conditions outside the walls are as bad or worse than ours. The islands were never self-sufficient in agricultural production and with no outside shipping other than warships getting through these days, we began to hear rumors of famine in the nearby islands of Samar and Mindoro.

We are fairly certain that MacArthur and Sergio Osmena, the provisional Filipino President, are in Leyte. Supposedly the news came from outside sources and has been substantiated by clandestine radios even though the Japanese daily has carried not a single word of such landing. A substantial landing had occurred on Friday, October 20, both on Leyte and the adjoining island of Samar, so we were convinced when our camp announcer, during a routine broadcast over the loud speaker system, said, "Better Leyte than never!"

The Japanese reaction next day was noted to be depressed and nervous. Even the lowliest private on guard duty was uncommunicative and obviously not interested in looking our way. The commandant complained about our deportment at roll-call and also about the noise he claimed we were making near his office. On the other hand the camp was brighter and cheerier and people who had been sitting around, inactive and withdrawn, now came out to see what they could do to lighten each other's load.

My own optimism was dampened by the news that in the last twelve hours there had been four deaths in the camp hospital, all directly due to malnutrition. Everyone seems apprehensive that they might find swollen ankles on getting up in the morning, the same being a sign of early beri-beri or hypoprotenemia, which was more likely. Once the swelling was noted there was not much hope for survival since proteins in any form were simply not available. General opinion had it that death could occur within two to three weeks once the fluid started accumulating in the lower extremities.

Air-raids are almost daily now and they last for hours on end. We have been reasonably safe so far but the uncertainty and the noise and destruction around us has made us all nervous wrecks. We have seen only one- and two-engine 'planes, a few P-38s but no big bombers which we knew had to come to our rescue.

Each night we go to bed with our clothing and boots neatly stowed by our mattresses. We have given up running to the comparative safety of the Main Building and have elected the unprotected comfort of our shanty simply because of the energy required to run.

Something has been added to our diet of less than two pounds of rice per person per week. It is a soup made from dilus, a tiny bony minnow-like fish with scarcely a milligram of meat on its frame. The soup is given only to the children at midday and despite its thinness it is much appreciated by the little ones. There is not a child in camp who does not show the effects of privation. Their growth has undoubtedly been retarded to some degree and their bones just seem to stick out all over and pitifully. The vaunted Japanese reverence for children is certainly not apparent from our point of view!

We were awakened with a rude shock at 4:20 a.m the morning of November 6th by the siren screaming its ugly warning of another air-raid! At almost the same moment we heard the steady drone of 'planes. Of course there was absolutely nothing to see in the pitch black pre-dawn hours and this caused our normal fear to grow into terror. Somewhere nearby a series of explosions rocked the ground. We couldn't use our shelter since it was still ankle deep in mud and it took a lot courage or foolhardiness to stay where we were. The loud speaker warned us that we were forbidden to move anywhere in camp during the raid thus removing all doubt as to where we would spend our immediate future.

There was no further sleep for us as the raid continued for about an hour. Dawn followed with no all clear although the bombing had now become silent. Shortly after daylight the raid began with even greater fury than before, with more 'planes and more forceful bombing than ever before. The camp seemed to be in the very center of anti-aircraft fire and shrapnel was coming down with the sounds of a heavy hailstorm. We were no doubt in a very vulnerable spot, unprotected by any standard, and so we finally scrambled into our shelter mud and all!

Despite our discomfort and having to eat our food in the dark smelly dampness, we found a contradictory lift in our spirits as the boys fought imaginary air battles and maintained their unconcern over the real dangers about them. Eleanor's composure under these stresses was marvelous and it gave me strength to be both fatalistic and philosophical about the eventual rescue which would be ours.

There was no "all clear" all of this day and we stayed put, crawling out of our dank prison from time to time for a stretch and no one complained!

By evening things had returned to a tentative calm. Although no "all clear" ever did sound, we were permitted to move around, obtain our evening meal, and finally go to bed in the blackout.

Next day I was able to return to my grass-cutting detail only to find that the growth, due to the heavy rainfall, was too great to allow me to use the ancient lawn-mower. I had to resort to the sickle, a job far too taxing for me to continue for more than a short while. The vicarious enjoyment which I obtained from keeping a respectable lawn in front of the hospital was gone. It was replaced by a feeling of need to be with my family at all times during what had to be our last days of this interminable confinement. All over camp there was a notable laxity in the performance of duties which had become so routine in the maintenance of our camp life. Of course, the ever noticeable diminishing of physical capacities impaired the services and their performance which we had come to take for granted in the daily life of Santo Tomas.

November 9th found the barometer falling again and we know well what that means! Our burning question is whether the old shanty can take another onslaught of a typhoon. Our weather forecasters have given their opinions that a quick-moving typhoon, starting somewhere in the vicinity of the Palaus, is rapidly moving in our direction.

I busied myself checking our moorings, making things a bit tighter here and there in an effort to give a feeling of more confidence in our flimsy home. By 10 p.m. there was a good deal of thunder and lightning and suddenly the rains and wind came. Torrents poured down and the wind reached gale proportions while we huddled together in uncertain safety. The nipa flaps slapped up and down and our roof gave signs of flying away as we huddled together in our bed. The boys unbelievably had fallen asleep and were undisturbed by the howling of the wind and roar of the rain about us. The braces which I had checked groaned and rattled and finally the bookcase with its load of well-used books tumbled away from the wall with a crash. I had to get out from under the mosquito netting and re-fasten it with a handy rope. The night outside was wild and I wondered whether we would make it through until dawn. The huge leaves of our gabi plants were whacking against the walls and Eleanor kept calming my fears with the comment that it sounded much worse than it really was.

We had occasional periods of quiet during which we thanked God for the durability of the old shanty. I was thankful that we followed the design of the many Filipino babays that I had seen in my travels through the islands before the war. They knew how to survive the tempestuous weather of October and November.

Toward dawn the weather abated in its fury although the rain and wind were still with us. We were wet inside and out. In the daylight I could see patches of roof which had disintegrated but because of its slope and the thickness of the nipa palm, worm-eaten though it was, we could still find dry areas in the shanty. I couldn't help but remember that this abode had been our home for a longer period of time than anywhere else during our years of marriage and travel.

Our water came from a spigot some twenty-five yards from our front steps. The water works and network of mains had survived both the Japanese and our bombs and time and again we thanked the wonderful U. S. Engineers who had built the system many years ago, thanked them in our minds and hearts, that is. Among our life's necessities were the water buckets we used to haul that sweet precious life-maintaining fluid. Our own bamboo plumbing had not yet failed us and still provided bathing and sanitation facilities without interruption. The narrow muddy path which led from the corner of Shantytown, past our shanty and along the barbed wire fence was our "main street" and in the wet season its gooey surface made even bakias dangerous to wear. So we slithered barefoot along the way, each of us on his own particular errand of survival.

November 11, 1944, Armistice Day at one time or other, found us in something of a depressed mood. I offered Eleanor a penny for her thoughts. She said, "I wonder if there is any Armistice Day, anywhere in the world, anymore."

Roger asked, "Daddy, what's an Armistice Day?"

I tried without success to explain that at one time the peoples at war agreed to stop fighting each other. I found myself floundering as to how I could make my sons understand that it was not likely to happen now, with both sides in our war claiming victories and neither one thinking that it was time to give up the fight.

We took out our frustration by dipping into our meager cash reserve and buying a quarter pound of laundry starch for 38 pesos (Mickey Mouse money). Eleanor had the idea that she could convert it into some kind of pudding and her efforts were rewarded with a lumpy, mass of slightly sweetened brownish goo. It had some value as a source of carbohydrate and of course it reduced the hunger pangs for a while. Since today was rice distribution day our boys followed their playmates to the counters and went down underneath in search of the few grains that were bound to be spilt here and there. Even those few grains were welcomed if only to stretch the morning mush a tiny bit, the next day.

Two days later our spirits were again lifted by activity in the air. Today's raids left fire all over the city but our special thrill came from a formation of six dive bombers who dove and raced almost at eye level, along the length of España Boulevard, directly in front of Santo Tomas. Their primary job was not necessarily to give us a thrill, but to strafe the Far Eastern University buildings, a few blocks away. Those buildings housed the Japanese military command and had heretofore escaped any attack.

During all of the day's air attack there wasn't a sign of the defending aircraft. At sunset, just after the departure of our 'planes, the Japs took to the air, not in pursuit surely, but probably to assess the day's damage. We are still under strict blackout regulations including orders to stay put and not move around the camp. All during the night there was continued air activity by the Japs and we wondered if they were evacuating some of their 'planes and equipment. With the guards more in evidence than ever before and the tenseness of the Internees over the nearby day's activities, we wondered what might be in the minds of our captors. Anything was possible, even to the annihilation of all of their civilian prisoners—and this idea did not escape us.

We rushed to finish our early morning chores the next day, anticipating a repetition of yesterday's action. We were not disappointed. Almost on the dot of 7:30 a.m. our lads were at it again! This raid was heavy and lasted throughout the morning. We all witnessed a dogfight between three Jap zeros and one of our Corsairs in which battle the outmaneuvered Japs were each one finally disposed of. Even to us who cheered on the eventual winner, the sight of a 'plane suddenly exploding into fragments high in the sky, then falling as twisting, burning debris with no sign of a crew who might have escaped by parachute, produced a sick feeling in the pit of our stomachs. We knew that several brave men, believing in their own cause, had died in that moment of conflict. But then, war is mostly death and destruction!

Two uneventful days followed and then, on the seventeenth, the word was passed along to us that the Japs had just started an unannounced search of shanties. No one knew the reason but we all possessed items of some suspicion such as currency, diaries, even a few clandestine radios and cameras, forbidden weapons such as the ancient Derringer which I had long since hidden deep in the recess of one of our hollow bamboo supports. I had thought of this contingency and had long ago stuffed away my notes as they were written, under the shanty in a false bamboo support for our floor. Of course, if the Japs were really suspicious of anyone, they would more than likely tear a shanty down to the ground to have their search be rewarding. What little currency we had left, was a "no-no," so I quickly stuffed the notes up among the nipa shingles of our roof.

There was no doubt as to the seriousness of their search. This time they cordoned off various sections of the camp, placing guards at the perimeters so that no traffic in and out of the area would be possible. Some of our neighbors had real concern over their possessions such as flashlights, photographs of camp life along with their camera equipment and even some U.S. dollars. At times like this strange bargains are made and because my shanty offered more secure hiding places, we wound up with some of our neighbors compromising keepsakes in exchange for a "consideration" such as a cup of cassava flour and a couple of ounces of precious sugar, brown and dirty as it was.

I made a few random notes on this week's air-raids and they wound up as crumpled bits of scrap paper, stuffed into the pockets of my skimpy shorts. When the Japs show up at the shanty, I'll just stuff them under a handy shrub or something. The search goes on section by section and it appears as though Shantytown will be the last to be hit. If the Japs hope to uncover anything seditious, they have certainly chosen a ridiculous system of covering the camp. Most everyone is taking advantage of the fact that once an area has been covered and searched, those who are still to be visited by the inquisitors have been passing on to their friends in the searched area those items of value which may or may not be found compromising. While there is always the possibility that the searchers may cross everyone up and make a second pass at the area, so far it has not happened. The whole procedure makes me wonder whether they are just carrying out this maneuver to please the Kempi Tai or maybe to keep busy in the face of mounting military losses all around the area.

Tuesday, November 21st, we were routed out of bed by a 4:30 a.m. air-raid siren. We awaited the usual sounds of bombs falling and anti-aircraft fire sending its staccato shots out into the night skies, but other than a distant drone of high flying 'planes, no action took place. Our captors have apparently doubled the guard. The soldiers are marching their perimeters two abreast. They apparently fear that our debilitated Internees might hatch some kind of a plot to break out and capture the camp, at least!

XXI

The next day, Wednesday, the ax fell. We were treated to a visit by the feared inspection team! We saw the group of three Japs, led by the hated Lt. Abiko, nominal military head of Santo Tomas. There was Lt. Shiraji, and an interpreter who I could not identify. Abiko had made himself quite unpopular with the prisoners by instituting some new regulations which we felt unnecessary and productive only of hardship. Some of these included the maintaining of a bowing position not only during roll-call but anytime a Japanese soldier of any rank happened to pass by. We were told that he treated infractions of the rules quite harshly, not only our rules but also rules broken by the soldiers who might get slapped or knocked around, at the discretion of their superiors. Abiko soon became known as "S.O.B.-ko" and his approaching presence caused our little family to quake in our shoes.

The call was certainly not a social one as they insisted on examining everything we had including the inside of the ancient hibachi that served as our stove. The boys sat silently in a corner, on the floor with their hands folded meekly in their laps while Eleanor and I moved beds, suitcases and our other sparse furnishings in order to make them sense our desire to cooperate. Neither Eleanor nor I could muster a smile and I'm sure our silent lips and serious faces had to be regarded as unfriendly. Our hearts beat more rapidly whenever it appeared as though they might consider us as anything more than just a couple of the ordinary prisoners, stuck in the Godforsaken hole for the war's duration. We were constantly mindful of the caches of our incriminating possessions and we studiously kept our eyes off the spots where these items were hidden.

As the search progressed Shiraji and the interpreter became increasingly bored, seemingly anxious for their visit to be over. Abiko persisted, making us more nervous by the minute, for it seemed that he was looking for some specific thing, probably a radio or some weapons. Our neighboring shanties were absolutely quiet anticipating the visits which had to be theirs after we had been cleared. Or perhaps, they were meditating on the kind of gracious hospitality to extend to the foreign dignitaries who were about to grace their humble abodes.

Like all good things, their visit came to an end with their filing silently out, down our steps to move on to the next shanty. We were exhausted! The strain of that inspection will live with us for a long time to come. Our knees were weak and watery and even the children seemed very subdued, probably just from looking at the expressions on our faces. We sighed with great relief!

To describe Lt. Abiko is to explain some of the dislike we held for him. He was a well-built dark-skinned Japanese, taller than most and with a face that was never seen with a smile. He was quite military in his bearing and inclined to bully his inferior soldiers according to witnesses who had seen him slap several for reasons that were not apparent to the watchers. He had heavy brows which were slightly hidden by thick horn-rimmed glasses. He was an active leader around camp and never missed a roll-call that I can remember. Lt. Shiraji, on the other hand, was obviously from civilian background and behaved with courtesy to the prisoners. He was of slender build, lighter in complexion, and a bit shorter than Abiko. We had some difficulty following the many changes in the camp's command. At times we have had a civilian Commandant who always seemed subservient to the military presence no matter how low the rank of the officer-in-charge. The interpreter who accompanied Abiko and Shiraji on their visit to our shanty was never again seen by me which leads me to believe that he may have been a local Japanese civilian pressed into service on a temporary assignment.

As far as anyone had been able to find out, eventually, nothing whatsoever of any military significance had been turned up throughout the camp. We hoped that their experience with the prisoners would convince them, once and for all, of our spirit of cooperation and innocence. There was no indication of any kind from the Commandant's office, nor would there be any, of whether they accepted their search as final and not feel that they would have to intrude on our "privacy" again.

The rumor mill has been busy again and with it we have become aware of the progress of our armed forces in Europe, the collapse of Italy, Russia's success in pushing back the invading German forces, and at the same time the fact that no good news is reaching us as to the progress of the war in our area. We feel strongly that a campaign to re-take Luzon must be just around the corner but our forces have been able to keep a tight lid on what may be planned and what is actually happening on a day to day basis.

Meanwhile our strength is slowly but surely disappearing. It is an effort now to attend roll-call and then to have to hike in and pick up our meals. Some garlic was offered for sale today and since it has food value, I bought a clove for ten pesos. Eleanor can use it to flavor our rice.

A very nice shelter has been constructed beneath what used to be our camp dining shed. It is to be used for the storage of the commanding general's car and will deprive prisoners of the most generally used shelter during the seasonal rains. In fact it was the only outdoor shelter area where people could gather during the day, be it rainy or blisteringly hot as in the dry season! We have been warned, naturally, that to approach the vicinity of the "garage" will be considered a serious offense against the Emperor and be subject to grave "consequences." Odd isn't it? We have just noted that the General's car is the former property of one of our fellow Internees.

I have been working like a beaver to develop a garden that might produce something edible, ever since September. But it is like pounding my head against a stone wall! Through the kindness of the Philippine Department of Agriculture and the unexpected cooperation of the Commandant, the camp was given seed of various vegetables indigenous to the island of Luzon. As it turned out, the land inside the old University of Santo Tomas was excluded from this fecundity. After carefully planting, nurturing, cultivating and keeping from drowning these seeds of tomato, corn, cabbage, radish, talinum and pigweed, only the latter three even emerged from the ground. Even their maturation provided only a few meals of "side dish vegetables" and these in the form of a mucilaginous, disagreeably green mass which required force to get our two boys to eat.

No one had been able to produce a garden that was worth the effort, and that included the ambitious "camp garden" with the slight advantage of fertilizer provided by our captors. I believe that most of the willingness on the part of the garden workers came from their acceptance of the assignment as a relief from boredom. The entire production of the camp garden went into the central kitchen to become part of the "stew" which came our way now and then. I consoled myself with the thought that the Japanese soldiers, not to mention the entire Philippine population, could not have been faring much better than we were.

We heard that there was large-scale famine in parts of the islands where our forces had successfully blockaded against the arrival of supplies from the larger and more productive islands. Mindoro, a large island visible across the narrow strait from Batangas, itself some sixty miles due south of Manila, was one of those islands. In peace time it was not a crop producer, being considered a sort of hunting preserve for the more affluent citizens of Luzon. It was here that the smaller cousin of the carabao was hunted in its wild state. One of the genus of the fierce wild water buffalo, this animal was the Tamarao. Sharply-horned, it stood only six or seven feet in height, but was the uncontested king of his Mindoro jungle and as such provided an exciting target for the hunter.

This morning Roger woke me up to tell me that he had been chased in his dreams by a large turkey! Why not? We had talked about today, Thursday, November 23, 1944, Thanksgiving day somewhere else in the world. We had so many good memories of this day in years past, with Eleanor exerting her finest culinary art to fill the house with spicy scents, the delicious odor of a big bird in the oven, stuffing, cranberry sauce, pumpkin pie and all the trimmin's. Now we loved to talk about it until our insides were growling at the thought of all those goodies and nothing to soften the pain except the usual morning "mush."

"Next year, I promise you, on this day we will have the biggest and best Thanksgiving feast you ever experienced." This I told the boys even though Donny had never tasted the delight of a turkey. After all, he was only just three and a half years old now and 80% of his life had been spent in Santo Tomas! We and our neighbors were a bit depressed by the non-celebration of Thanksgiving as well as a complete lack of air activity for the day. We conceded that even the busy American fliers deserved a day off to celebrate in the fashion we could only talk about.

Two days later the cycle began again. Daily air-raids, diving for shelter, sneaking witness to what was going on in the skies around us, keeping out of the way of the obviously glum and disturbed Japanese guards, was our routine which no longer gave us belly cramps and cold sweats.

XXII

For the world at peace, December was a month of happy anticipation of the holidays to come. For us, we might happily anticipate the beginning of the end if there were any real change in the daily routine. But the Japs were on the prowl again, searching through areas at random, perhaps hoping to surprise someone with contraband or something else illegal. I think it was merely a subterfuge to keep busy, like our garden workers. But it became a war of nerves, and we were showing it.

Lt. Abiko has paid us another visit, and again went away empty and disappointed. He and his coterie have been at it for two weeks now and I was told by a "reliable source" that all he had unearthed was a pre-war Texaco map of Arkansas.

One day all of us had an opportunity to weigh ourselves at the hospital. We knew we had lost, particularly Eleanor and me. She just barely cleared 100 pounds, losing 25 from her normal weight. I was down to 129, having dropped some 64 pounds from my pre-war figure. But what is more significant, we showed a weight loss in the six weeks since November 1 of 15 pounds for Eleanor and 21 for me. We were much more concerned for what was happening to Roger and Donny. At a time when they should have been gaining along with a normal rate of growth, both had *lost* a couple of pounds in the same interval of time. At ages six and three, their ribs were showing, the color of their skin as well as its texture showed the effects of malnutrition and there was no sign of growth!

The very next day, the Japs who had been busy searching buildings and other shanty areas, returned for the second time in a week. This trip Lt. Abiko was accompanied by an interpreter and two private soldiers. But apparently they had been busy at their task for some time and were a mite tired when they reached our place. They pointed to one of our dilapidated suitcases had me pull it out and open it. The clothing it contained was as old and dilapidated as the suitcase and they quickly turned around without a word and marched out and down the steps, away, we hope for the last time.

Again my "reliable source" reported that Abiko and his gang had uncovered a sizeable amount of military "Mickey Mouse" pesos in the hands of one of the camp's shadier characters. Our small supply of Jap money, Philippine pesos, and a few U.S. dollars was still stashed among the nipa shingles of our shanty roof.

After this excitement it wasn't too difficult to adjust to our daily mutual commiseration. Eleanor found some amusement in describing her experiences in the ladies' shower, pointedly reminding me of so and so who had been such an attractive "sexpot" before the war, or so I had said, now was quite skinny indeed, with nothing to show where had formerly reposed two delightful and ample mammary appendages. All skin and bones and a sorry looking lot they made, those social dowagers, matrons and young women who had contributed so much to Manila's very gay night life in the days before the war! The men were even more notable in the loss of tons and tons of fat so carefully and expensively acquired during those pre-war days of "la dolce vita."

We all clung to our social habits, dressing up each evening in our finest clean shorts and a shirt if we were lucky and the women tried hard indeed to maintain morale by carefully tending their hair, using what makeup they had left among their meager supplies. Socially, we played bridge until curfew or listened to lectures which had no real practical theme save to fill up the space of time. There were no more pregnancies let alone births, but there were many separations which would later become final divorces, a sad commentary on couples' inability to cope with each other under the pressure of our circumstances.

We continued to teach our children in the makeshift school and at home in our shanties, never faltering for a moment in the belief that rescue would come and soon! Kindergarten was still an important function for the teachers and parents and one useful purpose served was the education each of these youngsters received as to the rights of one another. Behavior had not been any problem with the young people in Santo Tomas and particularly at this point when their energies had reached a lifetime low. Both Roger and Donny were already accomplished readers of children's books and our own small library was well used by us and our friends to the point where books were always in danger of falling apart. We kept them in good repair however and some precious tomes like Lin Yutang's *Moment in Peking* would be with us as long as I could carry it.

The Commandant's office formally advised us that our cereal supply is running dangerously low and no word has yet been received from higher military sources that anything can or will be done about it. Our Executive Committee has been applying every possible pressure on the seemingly not-too-concerned Commandant, and without any satisfactory response. This leaves the Internees with a new depth of hopelessness. It is mid-December and our friends and neighbors are all showing the unmistakable signs of malnutrition which will lead surely and rapidly to death.

A rather unusual raid occurred today December 15th at 8:00 a.m. when two groups of eight 'planes each, ours, were seen streaking across the sky, motors silent until at a given signal, they peeled off in dives, with all power on, motors roaring, and bombed and strafed an area which seemed right close by. Their action apparently caught the Jap defenders unawares, as there was a substantial pause before the antiaircraft batteries got into action.

This marked the end of a long lull in our air attack and gave us momentary hope that it might signal a final thrust of our forces toward Manila. We had to take cover as that response to the nearby target area brought a shower of shrapnel and flak into the camp grounds once again. The usual restrictions on our movements were enforced more firmly than ever and as a failure to take cover during the raid, three Internees were forced to stand bareheaded in the sun, for a total of eight hours without relief. We protested the inhuman treatment pointing out the exposure to falling debris, but the Commandant's representative was adamant, reminding the Executive Committee members that we were as much involved in this state of war as they were, civilian status notwithstanding.

After the initial bombardment by our 'planes, and for the rest of the day, three or four 'planes seemed to remain in the vicinity, possibly for the purpose of tying up traffic in and around Manila. They flew out of reach of the anti-aircraft batteries and seemed to spend their time with a few strafing runs on desultory targets. We were under constant "air-raid alert" and our movement about camp was limited to meal times and other emergencies. Needless to say we carried out such movement with extreme caution.

Our fliers continued their patrols throughout the night for the first time and in so doing they apparently paralyzed Japanese air activities in the area. Nevertheless one lone Jap flier sneaked into the area just before dawn, landing in Grace field just north of Santo Tomas. He came in very low and fast, eluding our 'planes which were probably ten thousand feet above him. Apparently he came in to refuel, for after a short interval of silence, his motors roared to life again and he started his takeoff just as dawn broke. I was up with the first sounds of the 'plane's motors and I saw him, a "Zero," as he flew directly over the camp heading for his rendezvous, wherever it might be. Ten seconds later my hair stood on end as the scream of diving 'planes filled my ears. Eleanor and the children were out of bed in a flash, and to the windows of the shanty to witness an electrifying sight. Three U.S. "Hellcats" had come from nowhere, diving on the tail of the Jap, blasting him from the rear, while as we watched, the "Zero" faltered, suddenly belched smoke and plummeted earthward in a nose-dive that left no doubt as to his fate! This was an unforgettable sight, long to be remembered by our children and ourselves, witnesses to the horrible death that comes to the fighting man in war.

The sequel appeared in Monday's *Tribune* which chronicled the heroic death of flying ace, Major Kodama, recently assigned to Manila's air defenses for the purpose of improving their situation. We were all witnesses to his arrival and untimely departure from this world!

Day after grueling day in and out of our rude air-raid shelters as our fliers kept up the attacks, we became like automatons in our reactions. The children followed us like tiny robots, but never complained. We continued our games with the neighbors of "What are you going to do when you get back to the States?" We have high hopes followed by severe depression, almost in tune with the weather or the time of the day. Early morning was always a time of high spirits, boundless hope and conviction that it had to be but a matter of days. Then as the day and reality as to our actual chances moved on, spirits dragged and the morale sagged. No rescue could be expected that soon and when it came it had to bring casualties along with the action.

Just a week away from Christmas Eve, Sunday, December 17, we were still under the rules of "air-raid" alert and so we busied ourselves with cook books, planning theoretical Christmas Day dinners, women copying each other's favorite recipes, all of which was described to us by one of the camp physicians as a sure sign of approaching insanity! However, Eleanor and I had it all figured out. "When we get to New York...breakfast, and what a breakfast, in bed at some fine hotel. There'll be hot cereal with thick cream for the boys, oranges and grapefruit and a real country combination of ham and eggs and hot cakes for all of us, real coffee and a big cheese danish to top it off." We went on, and planned a whole day, most of which was spent in our favorite restaurants along Fifth Avenue and Broadway—and that was just the *first* day!

Our stomachs well taken care of, we then turned our thoughts to entertainment. We would visit the museums which should thrill Roger and Donny, and then plan to see a movie or two in one of New York's palatial theaters like the Roxy or Radio City Music Hall. Of course we will have to dress warmly because it will still be winter, or will it?

Despite our daydreams, the days went on, each one dragging after the other with interminable slowness. We live each long day for what it brings us, with no thought of tomorrow or plan for same until we awakened to find that nothing has changed. The same walls surround us, the same barbed wire fence decorates our front yard and the same little brown men are in evidence, slowly patrolling their beat, sullenly carrying the weight of their world on their shoulders. The old popular greeting of "What's new?" has fallen into complete disuse and our neighbors and friends now pass each other with scarcely a nod of the head. Maybe our depression has deepened because of the proximity of Christmas, our third in Santo Tomas. Add to that the Christmas we tried to celebrate during the Jap bombings of Manila and we come up with four of a kind!

There has been no action in the pre-holiday week as far as air-raids or even alerts are concerned. Our morale sinks deeper than ever as the Commandant's office announces that our total cereal allowance per day has been reduced from 1000 kilos to 700 due to the shortages existing in the city! To add to our depression, one camp doctor told a group of us that deaths from malnutrition have averaged two per day for the last ten days. The Japanese are insisting that the certified cause of death be stated as "heart disease." Looking at our own bodies I wonder how long we will be able to hold out. Donny, our chubby baby is now a scrawny three and a half year old, showing his knobby joints though a thin layer of dry skin. His ribs, like Roger's, are countable and his energies have diminished to an unhealthy apathy. Neither boy has any desire to attend their kindergarten and first grade classes and we have just learned that the school is about to close for lack of attendance.

Eleanor and I have scoured our possessions to try to come up with something for the children, but with very little success. I haven't even told Eleanor, but I have a can of Spam hidden away. This will last for four days of Christmas week. The portions will be small by any former standard but they will be a treat for our taste buds since we have had nothing outside of our camp mush since Thanksgiving. Just before Christmas, our cereal (rice) ration had dwindled to its lowest ebb, 180 grams, per person, per day. This was not enough to live on and would soon result in an epidemic of death by starvation throughout the camp.

By Friday, December 22, our lot appeared hopeless when we were boosted to the skies with announcement from the Commandant that the International Y.M.C.A. had been permitted to send some foodstuffs into the camp. Our bonanza included 650 kilos of assorted beans, 100 pounds of sugar, small quantities of peanuts and cocoa, topped off by a sufficient quantity of cigars to provide one each to the male population! The military held the cigars "in custody" but the rest of the food was sent to the kitchen immediately. As it turned out, the camp received but a small part of what was offered by the "Y," the rest being turned down by our captors with a curt "The Internees have plenty. They do not need anymore."

Just to bring us back to earth again, the same night the Commandant's office announced that in view of the serious shortage of fuel, only two meals would henceforth be served. The total daily allowance would, however, remain the same.

If it is the aim of the Japanese military to keep its prisoners in a state of abject misery, they are certainly succeeding.

There is now a consensus of opinion that all but the most vital camp work will be discontinued by the New Year or we will simply be hastening our death through malnutrition. In order to carry out this idea without antagonizing our captors, we will continue to show up for our assignments but by tacit understanding, our labor would be token only, and with frequent rest periods interspersed. Our garden efforts had hardly been fruitful so no one really felt betrayed by our plans.

Despite the bleak outlook for this Christmas, the children maintained their enthusiasm and high hopes. We have assured them that Santa will not forget them, but that due to the dangers of war he will leave their toys and presents with Grandma so that they may have them when they get back home. Although they are quite disappointed they chose to look on the bright side, pointing out to us that Mommy and Daddy shouldn't be sad, because we would be seeing Grandma in only a few weeks!

During the afternoon of Saturday, December 23, some plainclothes Japs, probably the military police, came into our area, stopped at Cliff Larsen's shanty, just three away from ours, went in, pushed Emily aside, sat Cliff in a corner and proceeded to tear their shanty apart! We watched in fear and wonderment as to why Cliff, a quiet unassuming prisoner, who, like ourselves minded our business, did what we were told and in no way violated the rules of the camp. As we watched from the cover of our shanty, we were horrified to see the Japs practically drag him off toward the main building while Emily stood helplessly by. Her next door neighbors and we did what we could to comfort her and try to come up with some surmises as to what had and was going to happen and why?

I had a few uneasy moments of my own trying to hide notes- I had been collecting and writing since the early days. Since they had many references to the recent air-raids, I felt that they might be regarded in an unfriendly light by the Japanese and so I dug a hole beneath our banana tree and buried them temporarily. Emily and Cliff were our close friends and we knew that they were absolutely innocent of any intrigue which might have made them dangerous in the eyes of our captors. It had to be a case of mistaken identity! Meanwhile Emily and her shanty were under guard so our contact with her was temporarily discontinued.

Later on that evening, we learned that Cliff, along with Carroll Grinnell, the Chairman of the Executive Committee and A. F. Duggleby, a member of the Finance and Supplies Committee had all been confined in the camp jail. We had plenty to think about since all three men were kept incommunicado and the Commandant's office would give out no information whatsoever. A fourth man had been picked up by the same group and had been taken out of camp to the headquarters of the military police, or so we supposed. That was the dreaded

Fort Santigo in the Walled City. From all accounts, of those who were taken to Fort Santiago, very few ever made it back out!

Emily was heroic in the face of her uncertain destiny. She had been barely able to say goodbye to Cliff. Her guards, who were from the regular camp garrison were polite but not at all accommodating. She chose to believe that he was just being held for questioning and would be back with her for Christmas Day.

Christmas Eve was a dull dreary day, overcast like our spirits. There was no news of the four men taken prisoner and no indication from the Commandant's office that anything could or would be done to effect their release in time for Christmas. This situation was the chief topic of conversation throughout the day and there was much speculation that Cliff and the others had been the unfortunate victims of a period of "cracking down" by the authorities because of the war's turn of events. Needless to say, there were no usual Christmas carols nor other sign of the holiday spirit anywhere in Santo Tomas. We were still under blackout conditions and we wound up the day turning into our beds at eight-thirty.

XXIII

Christmas Day, 1944 saw a resurgence of the old never-say-die spirit! We awakened to a new day, greeting friends with a smile and a Merry Christmas! It was almost catching. It seemed as though everyone we met must have received some sort of good news during the night and somewhere along the way, we added to our greeting, "It won't be long now!"

An amazing resurrection of old toys, reconditioned and even repainted had come to light and all of the children shared in the surprise prepared by several dedicated ex-carpenters, woodworkers, painters and other craftsmen who had banded together for the sole purpose of giving our children a real Christmas! Among some small items our boys received a bag of marbles, a couple of pre-primer books with a drawing pencil and crayon.

The Commandant in an unexpected burst of generosity, permitted us to purchase for five pesos, a bar of coconut candy measuring three inches by one-half inch square! Lord only knew where it came from, but it was edible and available to the few parents, including myself who had a five peso Mickey Mouse note.

We found out today that among the items received from the Y.M.C.A. were many tins of jam and they were now carefully divided up so that each Internee received one-twelfth of a can. For us this meant a total of about ten ounces and was it welcome!

Roger, with much help from Mommy, fashioned a paper tree which we hung from the rafters, having decorated it with bits of cotton and bells, cut out of paper and colored by Donny. Our family achievement was admired by our friends and neighbors who visited during the day. Everyone around us in Shantytown had done something marvelous in decorating their homes, ingeniously putting to work every resource available from acacia pods, to palm leaves. The whole day sent our spirits soaring!

Even the food ration became an occasion. The kitchen had, perhaps improvidently, but who cared, put into our morning mush every bit of the seventy-six pounds of sugar received from the Y.M.C.A. and it tasted wonderful! To top off the day for the evening meal we each received a double scoop of rice!

The best present for all of us came with the appearance, for the first time, of four-engine bombers, Liberators, B-24s! Nothing had ever seemed so beautiful as the flight of high-flying majestic birds which told us that at last, there were land-based 'planes operating in the skies on our behalf. We heard later in the day that leaflets had been dropped during the night, on which was inscribed a Christmas message to the Filipinos, wishing them fulfillment of their dreams for a happy and peaceful New Year.

There was no bombing activity and the peaceful evening descended upon us with special permission to sit outside of our shanties until 9:00 p.m, a two hour extension of the regular curfew hour. We sang softly to the children until they were deep in sleep. With nothing else to do but enjoy each other's company, dressed in our best unpatched finery, we sat and held hands until our drooping eyelids forced us to go to bed.

The days following Christmas were anticlimactic. Our bubble of holiday joy collapsed as the uneventful week drew to a close. Sunday was New Year's Eve and despite advice from friends to stay away from the scales, we decided to weigh ourselves to record for history's sake, the way we were on the last day of 1944. Well, it only deepened our concern since I was barely able to make 120 and Eleanor just 100 pounds!

There was just no way to stop this continuing loss of weight and what was even more serious, the boys were both losing a little at the same time. Here-to-fore they had managed a steady but small weight gain as part of their growth process, but now their tiny ribs became more discernible with the passing of every day. There was no visible answer to the problem and all we could do was pray that our deliverance would not be too far away.

Beri beri and hypoprotenemia are spreading and the death rate mounts as we see our friends and neighbors still walking around, doing their household chores despite swollen ankles and legs. There are some who have progressed to the state where their faces are swollen, bloated as in a florid balloon-like mask. They are almost unrecognizable with their legs and arms puffed up with fluid and wherever the skin is touched, a dent remains. These are the superficial symptoms while the heart is invariably involved and will function with diminished capacity until it gives out. It is a sad and bizarre sight with so many affected, each one aware of their consequences but facing death with acceptance and calm. It is a tragic situation indeed.

We watch our bodies for the first sign of deterioration, staving off, we believe, that dreaded final collapse with our meager supply of vitamins, the one can of Spam and anything we can scrounge which may contain protein.

Further shock and disappointment was caused by the removal from the camp jail of Cliff, Grinnell, and Duggleby to, we supposed, Fort Santiago. There was absolutely no word as to their fate and we comforted Emily as best we could. At least the guards had been removed from her shanty and she was left in an uncertain peace.

New Year's Day 1945 began the year which would be either the most memorable in our lives…or the last! This Monday morning the kitchen again exercised their ingenuity by serving coffee, even though it was ersatz, made from ground roasted peanuts. We didn't care! It not only tasted good but served to remind us of good times past. An even greater treat was served to us by the appearance of two formations of about twenty Liberators each, bearing eastward, probably after troop formations or fortifications in that direction.

Their flight was away from the harbor suggesting that they might be using an air field in nearby Mindoro and they were accompanied by escorts of P-38s and their joint appearance gave us hope that the final push was underway!

As each day goes by the number of our planes in the air increases. Even the Japs have become less strict about taking cover since the action now is almost constant. The bombing and strafing is distant though audible to all.

By the end of the week our diet suddenly improved by the addition of camotes (sweet potatoes) to the menu. The Japs brought a few truckloads into camp, they said, in place of rice which has become scarcer then ever. The quantity in weight per person has not changed but the camote is far more filling and nourishing than rice. Eleanor with great imagination took about a half cup of rice which we had been hoarding, soft cooked it, added a bit of cocoa which had also been tucked away in a corner and all but forgotten, and made a rice pudding! Even without sugar it was a happy change for all of us. To top off this delightful Sunday meal, I lit up one of my ten cigars which had finally been issued to us on Christmas Day, puffed away in relative contentment and even let Eleanor take a puff or two as part of the special occasion.

We were still on the 180 gram per person per day food allowance and the kitchen had resolved the distribution problem of the camotes by boiling them together with their skins and eventually ladling out a representative mass to each person, man, woman and child. This little development gave camp morale a real boost!

The Day of the Three Kings, "El Dia de los Tres Reyes" in Latin America is the celebration of gift giving and this January 6th exemplified this custom by the appearance of a sky full of our planes, bombs dropping on the enemy from 7:30 a.m. until sunset, without respite except for a brief time off for recess in the afternoon. It was the most sustained raid to date and our magi from the East brought us these gifts of hope and rescue! This was their message of love and concern for our fate, telling us by their actions, to bear up with fortitude, to survive!

The long raid went on and in the brief moments of suspended activity, I weeded my sad little garden. A Japanese soldier, passing by stopped a moment, looking at the garden and me. He said something I failed to understand but as he was obviously referring to the budding cabbages, I risked a response. I said, "No good! No grow!" They were sorry looking indeed; worm eaten and a bare two inches above the ground, although planted two months before.

The soldier looked at me and proceeded to make what I took to be suggestions about how the ground should have been better prepared, fertilized and tended. The only real impression I got from him was the amount of gold in his front teeth. They shone so beautifully in the sunlight. He sported a Tojo type mustache and wore the usual horn-rim glasses and was about five foot two. Finally the soldier asked if I had "bebbies." I nodded and held up two fingers for Donny and Roger and also indicated their size by placing the palm of my hand at my hip and my thigh.

He gave me a dazzling smile and held out two sticks of bukayo, a kind of coconut candy. His apparent generosity floored me and not wishing to offend him, I held out my hand through the barbed wire and took them quickly. Being somewhat cautious, I told him I had no money. There was no response so I thanked with a hearty "aregato!"

The boys were ecstatic when they saw their goodies and only a bit of special persuasion on my part caused them to agree to ration the candy so that it would last for about a week, cut up into small pieces.

Every day some small miracle takes place, keeping us going. We were almost to the point of believing these good things were going to continue to happen to us every day and it was with some difficulty that we agreed not to count on them.

The very next day, as I was returning from the breakfast "chow-line," I ran into a group of excited Internees discussing the latest camp development. Lt. Shiraji of the Commandant's staff had made an announcement to the monitors after roll-call. He stated bluntly that a certain department of the Japanese camp administration had received orders to leave camp immediately. Certain supplies belonging to them had already been removed from the warehouse. Everything in the office was "piggly-wiggly" and it would be closed for the rest of the day. The status of the Internees would remain the same and strict discipline would be expected!

It can easily be imagined what an effect this had on the camp. There was a blaze of conjecture, but absolutely nothing authentic as to what all this meant. The guards were in animated conversation all around the walls and as usual our planes were buzzing around overhead to add to the confusion. We were ordered to take cover and I made my way back to the shanty only to find my benefactor of yesterday standing by the barbed wire fence, waiting for me, gold teeth and all. He was very much in a hurry, it seemed and without preamble he said, "You have money?"

I was dismayed and pretended that I did not understand. My apparent innocence cut no ice for he then said, "I give bukayo, you give six hundred pesos!" No matter how limited his English was, this I had to understand!

It sure looked bad for awhile as he was obviously angry, had a rifle with a fixed bayonet and certainly meant business. Weakly, I tried to explain that I thought the candy was a gift for my poor starving "bebbies" and that he must surely understand the difficulty of our situation and that besides, I had no money, certainly not the large sum he was demanding. His answer was simple and straightforward, he said, "You give me six hundred pesos!"

We were getting nowhere.

So I told him the worst. I had no money. Then he got mad. He poked his bayoneted rifle through the fence in my direction as I stepped back out of reach as gracefully and as well as I dared. He said, "You get money. I come back tonight."

Eleanor and I had christened this little fellow, "Toothie" and my rather unpleasant interview with him was cut short by the arrival of two sentries who were apparently reporting to him for their next assignment. It seemed that he was the corporal-of-the-guard.

This was no little item to add to our already overloaded bag of troubles but I was determined that he would not get money from me if I had to duck out of his sight every time he came by.

Later in the morning, while on an errand to the "Ed" building whose floors were divided between the Commandant's staff offices and single male prisoners, the former being on the first and our people on the second and third floors, the sky became alive suddenly with Liberators. There were forty-eight B-24s criss-crossing overhead, apparently bound for the airfield just northeast of camp, Grace Park. Traffic within the camp was paralyzed and I was marooned in the "Ed" building.

This was the show of shows! The big bombers were in action for the first time right before our eyes. There were a dozen or so men with me in the large room which constituted the upper floor of the building and we were able to move from the front to the rear windows to see the devastating attack. We watched the flight of our planes right out to the vicinity of the airfield. As they reached the area of their target we could see the actual descent of the silvery missiles and quickly the sudden wake of white flashes followed by mountainous towers of smoke rising geyser-like from each hit. For a short pause all was silent and then it was as if a series of severe earthquakes had hit us. The building shook like a frail tree in a typhoon. Everything which had been hanging on the walls came down with a crash along with the tinkling of glass from broken windows. Again there was silence.

Someone said, "My God!"

That was all. The stunning shock of the noise and the explosions left everyone of us in a frightened daze. It took a few moments to connect the sight and the sound. What could remain standing after such a dreadful blow?

I felt concern for my little family but as there had been no indication of any damage to Santo Tomas beyond those things which had been jarred loose from their hangings on walls, I expected that they were safe. Nevertheless they must have been at least as frightened as I had been and I had to get back to them just as soon as movement was permitted.

My impatience sped that decision and I decided to sneak out the back way, hoping to follow the hedges and any other shelter all the way to the shanty without being discovered. I did so, luckily, and when I got there I found Eleanor and the boys in high spirits, all anxious to tell me what they had seen from their restricted vantage point. When they finally quieted down I was able to add my experience. When they learned of my front row view of the entire performance they were breathless with excitement. Our neighbors could not help but overhear the enthusiastic reaction to my account and within a few minutes we had a small crowd of visitors anxious for further details! I was a bit concerned over the possible reaction of the Jap guards but our friends told us the happy news that all of the guards had momentarily disappeared.

In the middle of my recital, our boys came back for a repeat performance and this time we all went outside of our shelter to witness first hand what was happening. Our view was cut off by the wall and the seminary building but the sounds of battle brought joy to our hearts. There was absolutely no return anti-aircraft fire, possibly due to the ineffectual range of the Jap guns.

This was the first time in our memory that there were no Jap guards anywhere to be seen. The sentry boxes were empty and so we stayed out of our shelters, watching the glorious giants of the sky passing back and forth over the camp.

With the Japs gone, I got the idea of calling across the wall to the seminary, in the faint hope that either my old friend the Filipino gardener or perhaps a seminarian might hear me. Someone answered and I said the first thing that came into my head, "We're hungry! Have you anything to eat? Anything…?"

Eleanor, the boys and I waited tensely for some answer, but none came. Our friends had gone back to their shanties and we were alone for the moment quietly wondering if we had been heard. Not knowing who had answered my call, I did not dare to call again despite the apparent golden opportunity. But while

I was debating what to do I heard a smack in my garden and lo! Manna from heaven! There was a hand of beautiful, ripe, yellow bananas! There wasn't a sound of footsteps nor any sign of life on the other side of the wall. I called softly, "Thank you and God bless you."

I knew the risk taken by our benefactor was great as contact with the seminary was, of course, absolutely forbidden. Our gift was to us, at this time more precious than gold and we made every morsel count a hundred times. There were twelve nutritious golden bananas which were divided up so that the boys each had something extra for the next six days!

The constant "alarm" was in effect for two full days and the camp was virtually paralyzed as a result. Our planes came back the next day at about 10 a.m. with a group of twenty Liberators soaring majestically overhead. The anti-aircraft was again silent and with no guards visible we stood out in the open drinking in the exciting sight. We learned through our usual grapevine that the guards had not left camp, but were merely going through some sort of a training exercise in the cordoned off area of the camp.

As the planes came directly overhead there was a sudden furious burst of anti-aircraft fire from nearby. For the first time their shots were effective. The shells seemed to burst right in the path of the high-flying planes and we were suddenly appalled to see the first direct hit just below the right wing of the outside right hand plane in the first formation.

At first there seemed to be no real damage save a slight wavering in the flight of the plane but then it slowly began to trail a thickening column of black smoke. To our horror we saw the smoke turn into a sheet of flame covering the plane from wing to tail. Apparently still under control it broke formation, flying upwards and to the right, to avoid contact with the others.

It must have been an excruciating moment for the other members of the squadron to witness their comrade's misfortune and to be able to do nothing except sail on and away from the path of the doomed plane. All of us on the ground lived those last awful moments with the crew of the ill-fated B-24 watching it start its death dive with a series of slow spirals down, down to the earth! We held our breath, hoping that somehow the crew might escape and after an interminable vigil, we saw three white dots separate themselves from the flaming wreckage. One of the three was lost as a tiny bright spurt of flame indicated that his chute must have caught fire leaving a tumbling black object falling earthward to his certain death. There may have been others still aboard the plane which was now breaking up into pieces of wreckage, still burning, still smoking as it plunged on downward. Part of the wings, with some of the forward fuselage was about all we could identify as it passed from our vision, out of sight to the west of the city. The pilot had apparently done all that was in his power not only to avoid damage to the rest of the squadron, but also to the residential area of the city.

We lost sight of the two tiny remaining parachutes but we did learn later that the Japs announced the capture of two airmen from today's action.

This was the first time we had actually witnessed the destruction of one of our planes and particularly the death of one of our airmen. If it had been possible, the camp would have immediately set aside a day of mourning for the gallant fliers who had met their death today. We took this loss to heart since we looked upon these men and this action as part of our rescue attempt! Each of us took today's losses personally and prayed for the souls of those who had been lost.

During this dramatic episode no one had thought of shelter or personal safety but suddenly we realized that shrapnel had been falling and was continuing to be heard slapping the ground here and there in Shantytown. Nevertheless the hand of Providence seemed to stay the danger and we found that no one had been hit. Roger and Donny were crying despite Eleanor's comforting ministrations and I realized that my face was wet also with tears of anger and frustration over the sights we had just witnessed.

As the day drew to a close the quiet mood we found ourselves experiencing was mute testimony to the realization that the rescue of the Internees could not possibly be carried out without costly sacrifice. We were calling upon sons, brothers, and friends to come and take us back home, at the risk of their lives and possibly even ours, but come and quickly! Our sense of values had been severely warped by time and deprivation. Weren't there others, also prisoners, perhaps worse off than we were? Why should we expect to be a top priority in the scheme of things? I began to have doubts of the imminence of our rescue.

In a military sense why wouldn't it be less costly to by-pass the Philippines and strike right at the heart of Japan? The military strategy carried out by civilized countries demanded that the winning of a war should be sought with a minimum loss of life. Where did 4000 or so hostages fit into such a plan? This was a dangerous speculation and if my family were to share my thoughts they would certainly become super-depressed!

The air-raid "alarm" has continued for a couple of days without any "all clear" relief being sounded. Our people were in good spirits as we felt this to be one sign of impending rescue. During the night of January 9th, we heard a series of distant explosions and the occasional hum of a plane. We scanned the skies looking for some tell-tale sign of what might be going on, but with no success. At least we did not see the customary red and green navigational lights which would have identified Jap planes, so it had to be our boys in the air. We speculated that the distant explosions might have been demolition, the thought of which gave us a thrill. Some three years ago, the same sound had signaled the evacuation of our own armed forces from Greater Manila.

In the early daylight hours there were a few American medium bombers active over the Jap-held airfields. All was quiet in our immediate vicinity until 10 a.m. when two fleets of Liberators appeared in the sky. They approached from different angles to the approximate spot where the B-24 was shot down yesterday. Perhaps by design they criss-crossed each other so that a cross was formed in the sky, meant, we supposed, as a tribute to their fallen comrade. The planes were almost a transparent silver in the sunlight, so far above the usual anti-aircraft fire that the Japs did not even shoot.

Their tribute completed, the two squadrons went about their assignments each with a different objective. The bay area was the target of a furious bombing and troop concentration northeast of Manila was the other recipient of our fury. As the morning became afternoon the air attacks ceased but the obvious demolition explosions went on at an ever increasing intensity. They were not far distant and before long the sky was filled with a smoky overcast. There was a taste and smell of oil and gasoline in the air and we said to each other, "That's all to the good!" As we visited each other's shanties, the conversation was geared only to how much longer it would be before our rescue would take place.

"Three weeks!" That was the consensus. But even that relatively short time seemed interminable. We had to stick it out although there were those among us who were obviously not going to make it! We were determined to try and help those in the latter category by bartering, even with our captors, for any kind of nourishment that would stave off death by malnutrition. Even in our despair came another straw to grasp. On January 10th, the kitchen announced that it was going to be able serve rice, fried in pork fat, for this evening's meal. They added, "Unfortunately, the portions will be small!" And they were, amounting to about 60 grams (2 ounces) per person.

Donny and Roger were so excited at the prospect of something to eat besides the customary mush, that it was hard to face their disappointment when they saw the two small mounds of food their measured portions came to when they sat down to eat. So Eleanor and I shared half an ounce with them and took some left over mush and mixed our remainder with it. The result wasn't too bad as we both imagined a faint remaining taste of pork as we ate our unusual meal.

There is still no word regarding the four men who were taken out of camp and Emily has not given up hope for one minute that Cliff is still alive. We are all more than ever resigned to what may have happened to those men even though there is not the slightest idea around as to why they were taken. Each of our friends and neighbors live with the thought that it might have been or may still be their fate, to be taken, suddenly, without warning.

A notice from the Commandant is passed on to us by the remaining members of the Executive Committee. "In order to avoid bloodshed in camp, the Commandant has decided to remain. His main concern is for the Internee welfare, especially with regard to food. Although food is practically impossible to obtain in Manila, every effort will be made to secure whatever is available for the Internees. It is expected that the same rigid discipline as heretofore maintained, will be carried on."

Whatever did this mean? We have had no prior hint of the Commandant's possible departure and why the insistent assurance that he will be doing his best for our welfare? Could he be worried? Is his conscience, or perhaps fear of reprisal after his inevitable capture by our advancing army getting to him? And what did he mean by avoiding bloodshed?

At first we were puzzled and disturbed by this announcement but considering the usual inexplicable actions of our captors we settled down and took it all in stride. As far as we knew, despite announcements and rumors to the contrary, the only Japs to have left camp, were one contingent of the guard, including our friend and benefactor, "Toothie," thank God!

Despite the Commandant's protestations of difficulty in procuring food, we witnessed truckloads of supplies including whole dressed pigs and a complete assortment of other meats as they passed us by en route to the Commandant's quarters. The Japanese fed themselves well and there seemed to be a series of parties going on in their offices, almost constantly. Despite these obvious goings-on, Lt. Shiraji told our representatives, in a voice packed with emotion, that "Even the military garrison is on a starvation diet because of the naval blockade in the China Sea!" It is a sad sight indeed to see some of our people, pride completely tucked away, scavenging at the garbage pile behind the Commandant's offices. Pitiful are the old men, bodies wasted by starvation, swollen with beri-beri, half buried in the depths of a fifty-five gallon drum, dragging out the remains of a well-eaten roast pig or perhaps some camote peelings or other unidentifiable garbage. They are even draining the beer bottles stacked in cases along with the rest of the garbage, all of which is to be taken away in the weekly visit of the "honey-wagon." How we miss the coconut milk and occasional sugar which flavored our mush!

Our only compensation is that our stomachs have shrunken to the point where our hunger and our appetite is reduced accordingly. We have quit worrying over loss of weight and after I reached a low of 118 pounds, I have sworn off looking at any scale for the duration.

The big event of the day turned out to be the moving of our people from the second floor of the "Ed" building to make room for a contingent of Japanese men in and out of uniform. Great speculation arose from the move which was carried out without a word from the Commandant. Perhaps the camp at Los Baños had already been liberated and this could have been the garrison on duty there. Despite all of the conversation on the subjects we never did find out where these people came from, who they were, or why they were here. However, they did inherit a front row view of the cluster bombing of Grace Field which went on day after day until it seemed that nothing above ground could have survived the tons of explosives.

January 11, 1945 started out like any other day but it quickly turned into one of the most memorable in our lives! Someone had overheard a broadcast this morning, over the wall. A friendly Filipino had turned his radio volume up, loud enough to be heard over the wall. The news report told of an attempted landing by "enemy" forces north of Manila at Lingayen. The Jap radio station KZRH gave the usual bull--- about terrific enemy losses incurred in throwing back the invading forces but after three years of reading and hearing Jap propaganda we drew our own much more favorable conclusions.

Needless to say the word spread throughout camp like wildfire in a parched prairie. Even the most conservative among our friends and neighbors turned into believers of this news. The newspaper would undoubtedly carry the story in its next edition and we wondered how they could possibly play it down to the laconic tone of the radio broadcast of this morning.

We had landed! It was true! We can guess the whole story, a repetition on a hundred-fold larger scale, of the Gilberts, the Marshall, Biak, Halmahera, and Leyte. It would have been done with a complete assurance of success by the planners, for this was the big one! General MacArthur said he would return and he was talking about Manila, from whence he so hastily departed in 1941, leaving us as his guaranty to the Philippine nation. Our hostage days were numbered. *They* were on their way!

XXIV

The Beginning of the End

What a difference a day makes! Today's happy faces lit up the camp in contrast to the darkness of yesterday's mood. We visited with one another, shook hands, slapped each other's backs, cried a bit and laughed a lot.

Don Kneedler told me that someone had seen eleven guards with full packs leave camp last night. He added that the night guard in our area had left his post at 8 a.m. and no one had yet appeared in relief. I got real brave and decided to take a chance, crawl through the barbed wire fence separating the patrol path from the prisoners, and take a peek over the top of the sawale wall which cut off our view of the seminary garden. Don Kneedler was almost as nervous as me, but he helped hold the wire so that I would not be hung up in its barbs. Over the wall I saw Conrado, our old friend the gardener, working as usual, this time pruning their banana trees. I called over to him, probably scaring him out of his wits, "Hey Conrado! We have no guards. Can you spare us a few bananas?"

He looked at me for a moment, not sure who I might be, took a long look around and then, satisfied that no one was watching, sought out a pair of ripe hands of bananas, tossed them over the fence into my eager and waiting hands, I thanked him profusely, scrambled back through the wire, gave one hand of the fruit to Don and joyfully brought the balance to my family. This would provide a little more nourishment for a few more days.

A while later as I was returning from an errand to the Annex, I met one of our neighbors who was openly conversing with a Jap guard, attempting to trade a gold watch for some rice. He called me over to help him as he did not know the Japanese equivalent of "rice." In the midst of what was now a three way conversation, I heard the sudden roar of some low flying planes and looked up sharply to catch the beautiful sight of two U. S. planes, not over two hundred feet up, hellbent for the Bay area.

This was my first sight of the new insignia, the star bisected with a dash, visible as they wagged their wings in greeting. In spite of all previous warnings, the camp rang with loud cheers. The soldier standing in front of us didn't know quite what to do. He held his rifle by his side, followed the flight of the planes with his eyes and with his mouth wide open in disbelief. When the planes had passed, he looked at us, frowned, then grinned sheepishly and walked slowly away. The conversation was ended and its purpose forgotten.

There is a tremendous difference in camp morale since the events of the last couple of days. Hope has blossomed like a beautiful rose. Each day now brings deliverance that much closer. The bombing runs now seem concentrated on troop movements to the north of us, starting early each morning and continuing throughout the day, now that the weather has moved into the dry season. The Jap supply lines are taking a pounding and demolition goes on at an accelerated pace around the fringes of Manila. We hear the movement of heavy equipment toward the north, probably to counter the U. S. offensive which must be mounting around Lingayen.

Our captors seem to get stricter and nastier as the days wear on. Contrary to our way of thinking, they seem to give no consideration to the possibility that they may be in our shoes before too long. Several persons have been slapped without provocation or warning and roll call has become an opportunity for Jap officers to vent their spleen on us. Often we are forced to stand at strict attention for long periods of time apparently only at the whim of some lesser official. We are constantly warned that our deportment must be within the strictest bounds of propriety according to the Japanese code of ethics and courtesy. More than ever the war of nerves continues and accelerates.

Despite the great boost to our spirits, our health continues its downward plunge. Our weight loss has speeded up alarmingly and more and more of our friends and neighbors are being confined either to hospital beds or their own.

Like many of the men, my weight has now dropped to what it was at age twelve, 105 pounds. The children have not gained an ounce in a month and Eleanor is finally below one hundred pounds! She deprives herself of what little sustenance is available to give to the boys and her mental state is fast becoming apathetic. We keep watching our ankles for that telltale swelling, each morning as we awaken, knowing that we have perhaps only a few days until the first signs must appear. I have no energy and even a short stroll tires me to the point where I must sit and rest. And so it is with all of our neighbors who are in similar straits, perhaps even a little worse off than we are. We still have a small store of the vitamins which my Chinese friends had gotten to us and to those we probably owe our freedom from the dread symptoms of beri-beri. Those who have fallen victim to its ravages have faces bloated almost beyond recognition. These cases are hopeless, their death warrants sealed. We are reluctant to look at them, knowing that only a few days of life remained. Sadder is the knowledge that only a simple diet would save them.

Eleanor used the last of her Albolene face cream to fry our small remaining portion of rice. There is a brisk business of trading with the soldiers now, as discipline from their superiors in this regard seems to have been relaxed. Watches, rings and other long-hidden personal treasures are finding their way into the hands of the enemy in exchange for a half kilo of rice or precious sugar. The Commandant publicly denounces any such trafficking, but we think he privately profits by the trading.

There have been mysterious goings and comings from the guarded warehouse in which our food stores are kept. Eye-witnesses claim that sacks are being removed during the night by both Jap officers and men and that the loot is being taken out the "back gate," apparently to avoid direct accusation by the prisoners. This may explain the daily weight shortages reported by our commissary people who are charged with receiving into the kitchen the designated number of fifty pound sacks of rice or cereal, each day. These sacks rarely weighing more than forty or forty-two pounds now. Since the honor of the Japanese military is above reproach, any accusation on our part would be a direct insult to His Imperial Highness, the Emperor and treated with according harshness. Probably as a result of all this chicanery, our ration has now been cut to 160 grams, daily, of rice or corn meal, whichever is available.

Each day our theater of war draws closer. We can feel it and can certainly hear it. What is happening on the outside? How we would like a first-hand look at the city and its preparations for the final defense. Larry Grimes and I sat out on our shanty steps each night and speculated as to exactly what would happen when our rescue attempt cranked up. We were certainly not expert in the field of military tactics and our conversations became quite heated as we differed in our opinions. I listened to Larry who ordinarily was a quiet, even taciturn man, given only to short pointed comments without the waste of unnecessary words.

"The Nips are not going to leave Manila alive! We are going to have to kill every damn one of them and probably destroy the city in the process. What matters to me is what happens to my wife and kid during all this. I wouldn't be surprised if the military chief, Abiko already has orders to kill us all if they have to fall back before our guys."

"You may be right Larry, but what would they gain by killing us?"

"They sure don't stop to think about gain or loss when a Kamikaze hits his target, so why would things be any different with us? We are the enemy and so far their attitude is destroy and kill."

"Wow! That shakes me to the core! They could easily do it. There are two hundred armed men in the garrison, against three thousand weak and sick unarmed men, women and children. We wouldn't stand a chance."

Our conversation gave me a sick feeling in the pit of my stomach. It was better that we did not share these opinions with our wives as it would certainly upset them and serve no real purpose.

God! What could we do? Our leadership was pretty well shattered and able to come up with only the advice to keep calm, do nothing that would put us all in jeopardy, and pray!

Pray that our armed forces would recognize the danger in which we found ourselves and somehow effect a rescue without a loss of Internee life, perhaps by negotiation. The Jap attitude made this last idea untenable as their newspaper and radio broadcasts hammered the point across that they would die to the last man before surrendering Manila.

There were so many rumors around that no one knew what to believe, but among the generally accepted items was the presence of some 25,000 Jap Marines to whom would be entrusted the final defense of the city. We knew also that there was heavy fighting some 90-100 miles to the north and that the territory in between would be the scene of some long and bloody battles. Our time continued to run out and each day that we remained alive was a super achievement. People were still dying of starvation, now at the rate of ten per day! A new graveyard had been created between the hospital and the former east gate. It was filling up fast.

Three years and the better part of a month of imprisonment had passed as we reached the end of January 1945. Our lives during this period had but few moments of happiness and these through an escape from reality with the help of morale-building groups such as the Entertainment Committee and the Athletic and Recreation Committee. Their efforts at diversion were very productive even without the most important ingredient of professional talent except for Dave Harvey. Through their efforts we had a series of entertaining shows, concerts by groups of male and female singers, softball teams and simulated radio broadcasts with the help of a homemade loud speaker system. The Japs permitted the latter only because it was useful in getting their messages across to their prisoners.

Today these things are all of the past. Malnutrition has taken its toll and the grounds available for some of the programs have been preempted by the Japs for their own use. Our only pleasure now is the fantasy world of hopes and dreams of what used to be and might be again.

Early February's weather is beautiful! Each day has dawned bright and clear with the sky cloudless and infinitely blue.

The rainy season has given way and if weather were the only consideration in our lives, we'd really have something to cheer about. In the past this would have been the season for outdoor sports with softball league activity in full swing and with it surcease from the reality of our imprisoned plight. Now it is difficult even to move about the camp. Restrictions tie us down to our shanties, constantly under "air-raid" alert. Our energies had been sapped to the point where it is imperative to spend every possible moment resting.

I am uneasy as I note a faint swelling of my ankles each evening and the fear of beri-beri or hypoprotenemia was checked only by my almost constant apathy. I thanked God that neither Eleanor nor the boys showed any of the familiar signs, although their bones daily became more prominent and their skin drier.

Our medical staff, overworked to exhaustion and just as malnourished as the rest of us, did what they could to prevent chaos, but even their ministrations were limited to advice. "Stay off your feet! Rest as much as possible!"

One of our doctors, sorely needed as he was, ended up in the camp jail, committed because he refused to sign a death certificate stating that a starvation death was due to "heart disease" according to the Commandant. His original certifications of various deaths due to "starvation" or "malnutrition" were looked upon as an insult to the Imperial Japanese Army.

We continue to answer roll-call each morning and evening, standing at attention while some bandy-legged runty Nip lieutenant strides arrogantly before us, complete disdain in his expression while we must bow low, facing the distant Emperor Hirohito!

Air activity and demolition continues although at some distance away. The rumble of artillery to the north gives us hope that the battle lines are approaching but the camp is quiet as is the surrounding neighborhood. We pay little attention to the rumors now, because we feel so close to the real thing! It can only be a matter of days and the burning question with all of us is, "Will we survive?"

Surprisingly, our greatest craving is for sugar. The few grains that occasionally come our way more effectively assuage the pangs of hunger, better even than corn meal or rice mush except in some quantity. One of my neighbors had established a contact with a Jap guard and between them, they carried on some extraordinary trading. I gave him a gold Bulova watch which I had given Eleanor for the Christmas just prior to our imprisonment and he obtained two pounds of "sugar", almost black, solid and with straw and other debris mixed in liberally. Nevertheless it was cleaned, strained and filtered before it was doled out at the rate of one-half teaspoonful on each one's morning mush, making that meal the most popular of the day!

XXV

FEBRUARY 3rd, 1945!

The early morning sun shone bright and orange in an azure sky as we trudged grumpily to roll-call. There were a few soft fleecy clouds high above us and the day promised to be perfect, weather-wise. Outside of camp there was a stillness in the city, the usual noises of people movement muffled by the diminution of available transportation other than walking. Although we were constantly reminded of the problems of the civilian population, this morning's quiet seemed to me to have an added ingredient, that of anticipation. It was as though the city was awaiting something special to happen.

After roll-call and breakfast, like most everyone else, I played truant from my garden assignment. My ankles were swollen this morning, noticeably, and so I decided to conserve my energy by remaining with my family at the shanty. Our labors at the garden produced less than enough talinum for one good camp meal. Nothing else would grow to useful proportions and we were left with a crop of the green, sticky unpalatable mess which was talinum.

Back in the shanty, I threw myself across the bed. The boys had tired themselves out just with their brief period of play after morning mush and were now sound asleep although it was barely 10 a.m. Eleanor was reading her favorite cook-book and groaning aloud at some of the colorful pictorial displays of food. We all dozed or slept until noon when I woke up to the noise of some outside movement.

As I stuck my head out of the front of the shanty, Irv Spering, who was slowly walking toward his shanty, greeted me and said, "Tom, do you hear what I hear? That's not bombing! It's got to be artillery!" Irv was a banker in peace time and like me, not an expert at military sounds, but like all of us, anxious to diagnose and speculate on just such situations as this might be.

"Boy! If you're right that means the army is moving nearer Manila." I listened as he did for more of the rumbles to see if we could better pinpoint its identity.

"I heard this morning that our guys have reached San Fernando. That's only eighty-five miles north of here!" Irv was always the optimist and who could blame him. Just to survive we had to have faith, believing each day that strong help was on the way.

"I hope you're right but it still will take a good while before they get to Manila." I didn't add that by then it might be too late.

Irv went on his way and I turned to Eleanor and the boys and said how about a little stroll to the Main Building to see if we could pick up any more news.

There was a continuing distant muttering of guns easily distinguishable from the crump of bombs. As we passed friends' and neighbors' shanties, we saw them standing in their doorways silent and expectant, some looking toward the north as though an answer could be found in the still clear blue sky. I noticed one of the Jap sentries standing still, also looking to the north waiting, watching and wondering what was going on out there on the battlefield. His face was a mask of worry and I suppose he was thinking how much better off he was, in the relative safety of a prison camp rather than out on the battlefield with his brothers, engaged maybe, in hand-to-hand combat with the enemy.

The Main Building was agog with speculation but there was no real confirmation that the battle lines were drawing nearer Manila. No one had seen a newspaper for a couple of days and contact with our meager outside sources had been completely cut off. The Commandant and his staff were surly and unresponsive as ever. There was a minor bright note in the advice given by our camp doctors. The word had been passed that in the process of rescue we would have plenty of food available to us, but since our stomachs had shrunk and our metabolism was very low, we were cautioned to eat sparingly at the start.

We talked to friends we had not seen for days and even weeks. The change in their appearance, like in ours, was shocking. Just in this short period of time there had been a substantial weight loss on everyone's part. Some of the men were, by now, walking skeletons and I suppose Eleanor and I shocked a few of our friends by our appearance. Children fared only slightly better and again our concern for the seven hundred or so kids and their future remained top priority in the order of camp action.

Back to the shanty and our afternoon naps. Roger said to me, "Daddy, is there a typhoon coming?" His question came from the generally tense atmosphere of the camp. The unusual quiet broken only by the distant mutter of gunfire, created an uneasiness that filtered down to the children. It has a calm-before-the-storm feeling, anticipation mingled with fear.

Later in the day as we stood on the evening "chow line" the usual cheery banter was noticeably missing and in its place a few soft conversational tones could be heard. People were tired and so fed up with the monotony of camp life, what was there to say? The sky was a dull red, unusual for this time of year and sunset was around 6:30 p.m. I gave the ticket-puncher my usual line, "Tonight's the night!" But he ignored my remark, as though he had not even heard me.

Supper finished, roll-call over, we washed the boys and dressed them for bed. As usual we sat on the front steps for a while, tonight chatting with Larry Grimes and his wife, swapping ideas about food and going home, irresistibly drawn to the subject of favorite recipes— *and then I heard a siren*. Not an air-raid warning, but more like that of an old-fashioned bicycle siren, over toward Rizal Avenue, a strange sound which came closer and closer. It was neither a police nor an ambulance siren, but just the steady undulating high scream of a small, perhaps toy, device. Suddenly, not far from camp, and from the north burst upon our ears the unmistakable roar and clank of tanks! Jap tanks had never sounded like these. They had to be ours!

The wild cheering from inside and outside of camp confirmed our guesses. For a brief moment we could not untangle the webs of confusion in our brains, but then Eleanor looked at me and said, "Tom! It's the Americans ! It is our own blessed army! They've come at last!"

"You're right, Dearest! Oh God! Thanks and thanks and thanks! They're coming this way. Do you hear the cheering? It has got to be them! Oh God, let it be them!"

By this time there was shooting and in the gathering darkness it produced an enormous display of fire-works so that we started to think of our safety. The children were speechless with wonderment and sensing the meaning of our excitement started dancing around the shanty, hugging us and laughing. While all of this was taking place we stood in front of the shanty looking at the tracers and listening to the sounds of battle over the north hall. The Grimes had left for their own shanty and as we stood, I spied one of the Jap guards coming toward me. I told Eleanor to take the kids and disappear into the shanty while I found out what he was after. He motioned for me to come to the barbed-wire fence. Although he had his rifle at the ready with bayonet pointed generally in my direction, he did not otherwise appear threatening. I went over as slowly as I could in order to give Eleanor and the children a chance to get out of sight and when I reached the fence he silently dug in his pocket and pulled out a handful of soybeans.

He said, "Take. For bebbies!"

I thanked him with understandable relief. I had a handful of salted soy beans, toasted, which only yesterday had been sold about camp for about one hundred dollars a pound. My courage rose so fast that I found myself asking the sentry what the excitement outside was. The only answer I got was a worried shrug of his shoulders and a negative shake of his head. He wasted no time in getting back to his sentry box from where he could see over the wall, but not much more in the early darkness.

It was only a matter of minutes before the sound of battle had risen to a crescendo of guns, tanks, sirens and cheering. It was like a gigantic stage show but in complete darkness from this camp audience. Every prisoner who could make it was standing out in front of his shanty, some crying, some laughing but all in the throes of great exultation at this sudden turn of events. We were still under strict Jap orders not to move about camp at night under threat of being shot unless authorization had been given. There was also the very uncertain factor of the activity of the Jap garrison. We knew that they had been set up in various posts of defense around the camp with appropriate machine-gun emplacement, fox holes, and breastworks.

The rumbling, clanking tanks had passed along Rizal Avenue, beyond camp, toward the heart of Manila. Suddenly there was a brilliant display of fireworks and machine-gun fire from the direction of Far Eastern University toward the west.

Our boys must have run into serious combat here at the headquarters of the military command. And then there was silence…ominous silence!

It was now 7:30 p.m. and every Internee was listening to the progress of battle, standing outside shanties, in small groups, shielded from the view of the patrol path and sentry box by the intervening shanties. Suddenly there was the sound of running feet. One of our more daring friends had sneaked out to see what was going on. He reported that four other guards had come running by with their rifles in firing position, picked up our guard and had disappeared in the direction of the Main Building and the Commandant's office. Perhaps they were going to man their fox-holes, maybe in an attempt to hold off our rescuers by digging in and using us for a shield. Well! That was okay by us. We knew that our forces would win in the end!

The complete darkness of the blackout now hemmed us in and we were all aware that the silence might indicate that the attack may well have only been a skirmish which could have ended in disaster. There was no question in our minds however, concerning the Japanese vow to defend Manila to the last man! Now there was a glow to the west in the vicinity of the Far Eastern University and many bright flashes followed immediately by the sound of some heavy artillery.

Suddenly a brilliant greenish flare lit up the sky beyond the Main Building and hundreds of voices from that direction rose in cheers and screaming. There was flurry of shooting, small arms and some machine-guns but despite the obvious danger we, our families, friends and neighbors started a race for the Main Building and an unforgettable and welcome sight!

As we breathlessly reached the front of the Main Building area we were completely overwhelmed by the sight before us. Two huge fiery, roaring, tanks, thirty-ton Shermans we were told, stood there with searchlights prying out the remnants of the Jap garrison. In this moment of great emotion no one was coherent. The moment the tanks stopped moving, men, women and children alike clambered up the sides of the muddy, grimy monster which had given us our deliverance. And then the men appeared! The hatches opened and out crawled human beings who looked like men from another planet!

The tank crews were engulfed by hysterical men and women and children, pushing, shouting, hugging, kissing and raising the protesting men to skinny shoulders while others were kissing the muddy tanks, crying, praying thanks to God on their knees. Women were crying, men were bawling aloud and only children in their wonder showed any composure. The soldiers in their turn, wept with deep emotion at their first sight of Americans, their fellow-countrymen, so thin, so starved, so weak and so emaciated. Eleanor and I were crying and laughing while Roger and Donny were in the arms of a great big Texan who was trying to tell them how much they reminded him of his own kids, way back home. Now Eleanor was kissing a soldier who kept trying to fend her off with the comment, "But lady, I'm awfully dirty!"

By now everyone was shouting a confused babel of directions as to where the remaining Japs might be hidden. From the tangled mass of prisoners and soldiers, there wasn't a possibility of trying to restore order. We were still in danger, perfect targets for the remnants of the Jap garrison who had not left Santo Tomas.

In this melee we lost track of the children who were bent on informing themselves without our help. We soon spied Roger calling from the top of a tank while Donny was ambitiously trying to join his brother. Needless to say they were both covered with grime and hardly recognizable. We called to them to get down as it was obviously time to seek shelter. Eleanor's soldier, who was a six-foot-five Texan, had joined us to help all of us to a safer haven.

Most of the soldiers seemed to be from Texas, which was not strange in view of the fact that the tanks were part of the famed First Cavalry and known as the Texas Rangers. On all sides the weeping and laughing continued, both the soldiers and the Internees sharing the shock of each others unexpected appearance and condition. The women were special since most of them had not seen a white female since leaving home as long a three years ago. I heard one G. I. say, "'cept WACS of course, but in a uniform they just ain't got no glamour!"

All four of us plus the soldier hurried to the safety of the Main Building, finding a place of shelter in the corner of one patio. Food and coffee was beginning to appear as if by magic. Meanwhile the search for the Jap stragglers continued. The crowd trying to be helpful, actually impeded the efforts of the tank crews to find anyone. Suddenly someone shouted "There's Ohashi and Hiroshi dug in a foxhole over there! A tank on the move, had come up to the front corner of the Main Building with its searchlights playing around in the direction indicated by the Internees.

Someone shouted, "Come out with your hands in the air! We have you covered! Come out! Surrender or else..."

Suddenly four figures arose from a well-camouflaged foxhole opposite where I now stood in a crowd at the entrance to the Main Building. We recognized the lead figure as that of Mr. Hiroshi, a civilian aid to the Commandant. The brilliant searchlights all but blinded him and the other three figures as they came toward the tank with their arms high in the air. The second figure turned out to be Mr. Ohashi, the other civilian who, along with Hiroshi, had tried at times to aid Internees who had families on the outside, Filipina wives and children living in Manila by getting messages to and from them.

The fourth figure suddenly dodged away from the shaft of light and came running toward the tank, holding in his outstretched hand, an object which proved to be a .45 automatic revolver. Whatever were his intentions will never be known. He was stopped in his tracks by a staccato burst of automatic gunfire from the tank.

I heard a soldier say, "I guess that got him!"

The Jap who was wearing a lieutenant's uniform turned out to be none other than our number one arch enemy, Lt. Abiko, acting military Commandant of the camp. He had been shot several times in the abdomen, but he was not yet dead. His unconscious form lay twisted on the pavement and a curious crowd quickly gathered around him, The other three Japs were meanwhile lined up against the wall of the building, stony-faced and paying no attention to the plight of their companion.

It was some time before the barely breathing body of "S. O. Biko" as Lt. Abiko was generally called behind his back, was carried into the Main Building's makeshift first-aid station where some of our injured soldiers were now being cared for. Ironically, a heroic attempt to save Abiko's life was made by the same doctor who had been imprisoned only a few weeks ago for refusing to falsify the death certificates of prisoners who had died from malnutrition and starvation. Abiko was mortally wounded though, and nothing could be done to save him. He was moved to the old camp jail to await his end.

All of the rooms in the front of the Main Building were being converted to a makeshift hospital as we pieced together the story of our rescue. Bedding including towels, sheets and other linens were turned over to the army after the latter two items were converted to bandages by our willing ladies. A large number of more seriously wounded American soldiers were arriving from what was an ambush at the Far Eastern

University. We had suffered many casualties there and at the first contact with the Japanese forces holding the northern perimeter of the city. As our mobile units had roared down Rizal Avenue, damaging fire had rained down on them from the buildings lining the street. Grenades and mortar fire had taken a heavy toll on the troop carriers and jeeps which had followed the tanks. Our men reported that Filipino guerrillas came up as rapidly as possible and had cleaned out the Japs from behind, as quickly as we pushed them back.

As bits of information were pieced together, we found ourselves facing a rather uncertain future. It appeared that our rescue was effected by a flying column composed of about 700 men who had broken through the Jap lines about ninety miles to the north of Manila, supported by the 37th Infantry Division. Traveling day and night with their small motorized force, they proceeded far in advance of our regular lines, on schedule to reach Santo Tomas by February 4th, a date that was to have much significance for us.

No contact had yet been made with the 37th since the arrival of the flying column and it was anybody's guess as to how far away they were at the moment. Until such contact was made, the whole north side of Manila was being held by fewer than 700 Americans, at the mercy of an estimated 25,000 Jap marines who had retreated to the banks of the Pasig River in the center of the city, believing that the invasion was backed by division strength.

The flying column had forded streams with their bridges blown, fought their way through road blocks, tank traps, pill boxes and every possible defense the Japs could throw up when they learned of the Lingayen landing. From their present position in and around Santo Tomas, the Rangers of the First Cavalry had only the advantage of surprise and the disruption of Jap communications which would have revealed their unprotected plight. It later became apparent that the Japs now busied themselves with occupying the south bank of the Pasig and fortifying the surrounding buildings for their last desperate defense of the city.

Another exciting and disturbing development came with the news that some sixty-odd members of the camp garrison had holed themselves up in the Education Building, taking with them as hostages the old men and a group of boys who had been living in the top floor of the building. The Commandant's staff had recently taken over the first two floors of the concrete building, leaving the top floor for the oldest and youngest of the former prisoners who had called this building home for the last few years. The building itself stood about one hundred yards to the right of the front of the Main Building, but its entrances were so located that there was no way in which to effect a covert entry without the danger of being fired upon. With the hostage situation our boys were forced to admit a stalemate and it looked bad for the old men and boys held there.

Meanwhile we were told of the action at the front gate where our tanks had smashed their way through, shooting up and destroying the Jap detail on guard at the time. One of our braver Internees had materialized in the darkness and had directed the invaders forward toward the plaza in front of the Main Building. Our first signal of rescue had come from a Very light which had been rocketed into the air over the camp and which signaled our hasty departure from our shanty. Since securing their objective, our soldiers had set up protected gun emplacements on the front plaza, covering not only a possible outside attack, but also the situation in the Education Building, from which some sporadic firing had been coming from the Japs. This fire was not returned for fear of hitting one of the hostages who, it was apparent, had been forced to take their places among the Jap defenders on the top floor.

The parents of the youngsters who ranged in age from eight to fifteen, were frantic with concern over their children. They were in a huddle with the temporary command post and it was obvious that some kind of a parley had to be arranged. Meanwhile a number of us had wandered out onto the plaza and with sporadic bursts of machine gun and small arms fire from the Education Building, it was apparent that we were only in the way. Everyone was finally ordered off the plaza and back into the comparative safety of the Main Building.

Outside of the walls, the darkened city of Manila was ominously quiet. Where was the infantry? How long would the bluff of the flying column work in holding off the defending Japs? Even though we were full of the joy of the moment, some fear began to enter our thoughts. We heard artillery to the east of the city and hoped that it might signal the arrival of some back up forces.

Despite the predicament of our fellows in the Education Building, despite the sobering effect of the goodly number of wounded Americans being brought in continually, and despite the fact that our present situation was in the hands of only a few American soldiers, the night proceeded into an incredible orgy of happiness and thanksgiving. There was no thought of sleep for any except the youngest children. Even our two little ones stood around wide-eyed at the G. I. s, and showing not the slightest inclination for sleep. As the shanty areas were considered unsafe for the time being, we looked to borrow some space to permit the boys to go to sleep. As many of our friends had no intention of going to bed, we easily found two beds next to each other in the safer southwest corner of the building. Both Roger and Donny had been fed and fed and fed. Their little tummies filled with all sorts of goodies, stuck out like small bay windows. They were quite sleepy now and in dreamland in a jiffy when tucked into their unfamiliar beds.

We stayed awake, humming with excitement. We swapped stories with eager G.I.s welcoming as brothers and soldiers ones who came from the east. One G.I. from New York state hunted us out and showered us with food, candy, and cigarettes which we gobbled up as though it were our last meal on earth. The camp kitchen was opened and coffee materialized by the gallon. Our New York G.I. told us that our meeting gave him the happiest moment since he had left home three years ago. They all tried to tell us how glad they were to see us at the same time we were giving them the same message.

One pre-War acquaintance who now returned as a war correspondent with the Associated Press saw me, was appropriately shocked at my changed appearance, and proceeded to tell us of his hairy escape from Corregidor in December 1941. He had managed somehow to get to Australia and subsequently returned with MacArthur's forces to Luzon. We took him around, introducing him to some of our fellow Internees, proud of the fact that someone we actually knew personally had been part of our rescue.

Everyone was eating! All medical advice forgotten or ignored in the frenzy of filling one's stomach with unaccustomed "real" food. We had a banquet of D-ration chocolate bars, eaten whole, despite the printed instructions to consume sparingly over a four hour period. Canned meats were ripped open and gobbled up with fingers serving as utensils. Those delicious army biscuits! One after another consumed as though they were cookies and not hard, dry, tasteless hardtack! They were as welcome as the premier production of Oscar of the Waldorf! These, the boys gave us to eat gladly, without a thought for themselves, though they had started out their drive forty-eight hours ago, carrying rations for only four days. There were very few of them who expected their supply line to catch up with them on schedule and they would probably have to go hungry unless circumstances changed for the better. Yet they swore it did them more good to see us eat. By morning they would surely have nothing left and we could produce no more than a rash of enjoyable stomach-aches!

The wounded continued to arrive in a steady stream. There was an abundance of volunteer help, most of which was born of gratitude for our heroic rescue. The first aid station, now a veritable field hospital, was over flowing with wounded men, some of them dying, between whose beds scurried doctors, nurses, Internees and war correspondents. The din was terrific, but happiness was everywhere, engraved on the faces of pain-wracked soldiers, wounded on the way to their goal, Santo

Tomas. Order was yet beyond the comprehension of the still-delirious celebrants. Momentarily, someone would come to the fore with a command to "make way!" Other commands, mostly ignored, were to clear the dispensary or to quiet down! But in a moment or two even the person whose voice had given the command was noisily celebrating with the rest of us.

Unfortunately there had been no hospital unit with the flying column and doctors found it almost beyond them to keep up with the emergency surgery that confronted their efforts. The front hall was now taken up by a line of stretchers until even this space was exhausted.

The men who composed the Rangers were half-dead from lack of sleep, but the furious emotions of the past hours continued to carry them along, almost zombie-like, with no time nor desire to sleep nor rest, now that both were available. As the morning drew nearer, the men around us began dropping, almost in their tracks, to lie in an instant death-like sleep of complete exhaustion. They sought no special comforts, choosing only the nearest clear spot large enough to permit them to stretch out at full length. Our beds, offered happily to any soldier who would do us the honor, were mostly taken up by this time and the stone floor of the Main Building began to receive more than its share of fully-uniformed bodies, side by side with their precious boots and carbines.

A notable exception was the group of war correspondents, anxious to piece out the dramatic rescue of some 3000 and American, British, and other Allied subjects. They had the responsibility of letting the folks back home know that their loved ones had finally been released from their prison of more than three years. As they talked with us, we began too, to think of the anguish of our own family at home and how they must have been tormented with the lack of any news of our survival, if we did survive. We began to think of the many changes in lifestyle which must have developed during our imprisonment and how we would have to cope with them.

Our own families back home would be changed by years of aging, births, marriages, and deaths. Of these we would learn only when our first mail came through.

Eric and Lynette Sanders, Eleanor and I sat in a secluded stairwell just before dawn, sleepily reviewing the events of the past few hours. We had played an occasional game of bridge with the Sanders and found them to be a very compatible couple, and their daughter Pam, a lovely fourteen year old, had baby-sat for us on those few occasions. We drowsed more than we talked and almost before we realized it the first light of dawn showed faintly through the front entrance of the building.

"Another day, alive and free, but we are not out of the woods yet!" I communicated my thoughts to our little group, hoping to arouse them to the new day with all its exciting prospects.

In the corridors beyond our secure perch, the babel of voices rose from a soft murmur to a noisy clamor as more folks realized that the new day had arrived. The same fired-up energy which carried our rescuers for the last three days was now transmitted to the Internees who seemed ready and rarin' to go. The morning food line had started serving at 7 a.m. and even though such luxuries as milk and sugar were not yet available to the entire Internee body, the quantities of thick rice mush were unlimited.

I decided to risk going out to the shanty to see if it would be safe for Eleanor and the boys to join me and get away from the noise and confusion of the Main Building. I got as far as the water spigot, some fifty feet from the shanty, when a couple of rifle shots sang by over my head. We had been warned of enemy snipers occupying the buildings outside of the camp but feeling somewhat immortal, now that I had survived the last three years, I raced for cover and dodged in among the neighboring shanties until I reached ours. I gathered a few things that would add to our comfort, while we stayed indoors and practically crawled all the way back to the shelter of that old stone castle which we had so lovingly designated as "The Main Building" since day one! Almost immediately the loud speaker system which apparently had not been damaged, announced that all shanty areas were "off limits" and considered unsafe for the time being.

In comparing notes with the children, who were not feeling too well, Eleanor and I found that they had eaten three or four G. I. biscuits each, a couple of boiled eggs, candy and more candy and reconstituted milk and now were not in the slightest interested in breakfast. From the look of their protruding tummies, I thought that a dose of castor oil might be in order. I became their arch enemy when I succeeded in dosing them with a small teaspoonful obtained from the Annex dispensary, but they felt much better after the desired result had been attained. Eleanor and I compared notes as to what we had "put away" last night. Our little banquet had included one dozen fresh eggs, scrambled, served up by our New York G.I. friend along with some Spam or Treet or something. The dry, hard G. I. biscuits coated with real butter accompanied the eggs down our starving gullets, all washed down with quarts of coffee. Cigarettes and D-ration chocolate topped off this repast and gave the big Ha - Ha to the well-intentioned cautions of our good camp physicians, only a few days ago!

We just had to weigh ourselves, if only for history and at the Annex dispensary. Eleanor tipped the scales barely at a flat-breasted, hip-less, bony unbelievable 81 pounds! My own skeleton-like frame moved the needle only a bit beyond to 104 pounds! This last week must have been the worst and we devoutly thanked God that rescue came when it did. The several Oblate Fathers were saying Mass continually in the open or any spot where all of us had an opportunity to thank our Maker for the timely deliverance. More than anything else, we realized that our faith, the faith of all the Internees, had carried us through. There may have been moments of doubt, but the light of faith in God and our country prevailed. I hope we never forget!

The tense situation in the Education Building had not changed. There was talk of attempting a parley under a flag of truce, utilizing the services of one of the Jap interpreters now relaxing in the camp jail. Lt. Abiko had died during the night and his body had been removed.

Along with crowds of other Internees, the four of us wandered around the corridors, the children alongside, wide-eyed and full of questions. We stopped at frequent intervals to exchange conversation with some of the G. I.s. Their greatest wonderment was over the survival of the children and before long both of the boys were thoroughly enjoying rides atop the shoulders of two soldiers, undoubtedly weary, but their fatigue forgotten in their enjoyment of the boys' wonderment.

Even as we walked along, other G. I.s gave the two kids candy and chewing gum and also some American cigarettes for their parents. We had now learned that there was no shame in saying "Thank you!" instead of "No thank you!" at least under present circumstances. The boys sat astride their human pack-horses, soon laden down with candy, chewing gum, concentrated fruit bars, D-ration chocolate, enough for now, later, and possibly forever!

Now that our little portion of the war had changed hands, the fences quickly came down. The sawale walls and barbed wire which protected the Jap bodega or supply depot were torn away and looted by us in a somewhat orderly manner, by transferring all edible supplies to the kitchen storage. The fences between the seminary and our Shantytown were removed and sacks of beans were transported from somewhere deep in the seminary to the kitchen. This food supply had been carefully hidden from the eyes of the Japs by the daring of the Father Provincial. Prevented from helping the Internees during their confinement, he had sent food through secret channels many times, beans which had nourished our midday soup ration and grain which had provided similar sustenance to the dreary morning mush!

The Commandant's private stores gave up beans, sugar and rice which were given to the kitchen in order to provide the next few meals until army rations would catch up with us. At least, now we could offer our most welcome guests a meal of sorts, "plain but wholesome" as the Jap Red Cross often described our food to the rest of the world.

Sounds of battle had increased as the morning wore on. The entire area in the front of the camp, formerly the main campus was declared "unsafe" and we were confined to the Main Building and the area just behind it. It was expected that the Jap forces, after setting up their defenses south and west of the university grounds, would surely start lobbing mortar shells into the temporary U. S. Army headquarters now dug in around the front campus. A few desultory shells had already zoomed in and caused a few casualties among the soldiers who were busy setting up their own defenses with sand bags and slit trenches.

At eleven o'clock some trucks rolled into camp and momentarily we thought they might belong to the hoped-for reinforcements. But they only carried other contingents of the Rangers who had pursued the Japs further on down to the banks of the Pasig River. We learned that a terrific battle was now taking place in the vicinity of the Quezon Bridge, which we were trying to capture in one piece. It seemed that the Japs had again set a trap and at least one of our Sherman tanks had been destroyed. The bridge itself was undoubtedly heavily mined and would be blown as soon as the Jap troops had safely reached the other bank of the river.

There wasn't a thing we could do except mourn for the men who were out there sacrificing their lives on our behalf. The casualties were heavy and we had to be witness to the steady stream of wounded being brought into the building.

Suddenly there was a terrific blast which rattled every window in the university, and literally drove the breath from our lungs. We were in the main lobby at the moment and we could see outside, to the west, a huge mushroom of black, dense smoke arise from the vicinity of the bridge. The Japs had done it! They had blown the bridge!

This meant that at least one of the four bridges which connected north and south Manila had been lost. Everyone in the building surged toward the main entrance hopeful of hearing what had actually happened in detail.

We knew that if things had gone badly for our boys, it was quite possible that the Japs might attempt a recapture of the camp, now the only vulnerable military target in the northern part of Manila.

Still no word from the 37th! Although we could not be sure, we thought that the sound of artillery to the east of Manila might indicate that their advance might be approaching from that area. Until they arrived, the courageous Rangers had neither artillery nor air support. Eric came back after the evening meal to report to Lynette and our family something of the day's events. By noon, we had lost three bridges, Quezon, the Santa Cruz and the Jones Bridge. The Quezon Bridge, largest and newest of the four structures, having been completed in 1941, crossed the river in a direct-line from Santo Tomas University. Our boys had raced up and arrived on the scene in time to catch a withering fire from a road block set up just two blocks before the bridge. This signaled its destruction, which we heard, felt and saw, earlier in the day.

One contingent of our forces had pursued a retreating column of Japs down Rizal Avenue toward the Pasig, fighting a hail of bullets from buildings lining the street until their losses became a disadvantage. Apparently all of the bridges had been mined in order to protect the Jap escape route and as soon as the major numbers had gotten across the river, the bridges were blown. The one bridge still standing was the Ayala, deep in Jap held territory.

We were so worn out by the excitement of the past twenty-four hours that the floor beneath the blankets I had retrieved from the shanty, seemed as welcome as a downy mattress. All of us were in dreamland by eight o'clock. The blackout was still in effect as Jap planes could still be in the area. During the night our sleep was broken by the blast of nearby explosions but we were immediately reassured by a patrolling G. I. that it was only the Japs, setting off demolition mines in the business area remotely from their defense posts across the river. I hoped he was right!

We awoke early Monday morning to the blast of "75s" set up as field pieces in our front campus area. They were plastering Jap positions in the Escolta area, the downtown business section which was systematically being razed by demolition teams. Jap mortars were beginning to answer as shells screamed overhead and fell beyond the rear of the campus.

At 7 a.m. we witnessed the result of yesterday's parley between the Japs holed up in the Education Building and our truce team. Lt. Col. Hayashi, the senior officer present (who had been in charge of supplies for the camp) led a column of sixty-nine Japs, armed and in full uniform, out of the building. In exchange for their delivery, under armed escort, to the vicinity of their own front lines, our men and boys were released safe and sound to their family and friends, as we watched.

Although the sixty-nine Japs retained their weapons, they were not provided with ammunition and when the agreed-upon point of deliverance was reached they broke ranks in terror, seeking cover from the hoards of menacing Filipinos who had gathered behind the unusual procession as it marched down the length of a Manila side street. The final report eventually reaching us said that some Filipino guerrillas had gotten wind of the transfer and were awaiting them further along the way. Only twenty soldiers escaped and were later re-captured by our forces.

Even more splendid news came our way with the announcement that the 37th had, during the night, made contact with the Rangers, having come in from the east as we suspected, and were presently joining in the bombardment of the Jap positions downtown. Our fire drew Jap fire and we were all warned about the danger outside of the Main Building. Already some of our Internees had been hit and an American woman had been killed when a mortar shell landed squarely on top of her flimsy air-raid shelter, in the open shanty area. She had just been trying to get a few things together to bring back to the Main Building.

The firing increased and the steady stream of mortar shells, many landing somewhere in camp, was a nerve-racking experience. We instinctively ducked with the sound of every screaming shell, but we found comfort in the durability of those old thick stone walls.

Despite the very active war going on in our front yard, the supply trucks kept rolling in, bringing in all the things we had so long been without. Hundreds of trucks kept moving in and out of camp, completely ignoring the shells bursting nearby. We saw the American Red Cross setting up shop for the purpose of delivering mail, cigarettes, chocolate, and matches.

Along with some other Internees, I busied myself locating bridge tables and chairs so that the Red Cross officials could carry out their task in an orderly fashion. Nevertheless when a small group of civilians, unfamiliar with life in a prison camp, attempted to distribute seven thousand packs of cigarettes, a like number of matches and chocolate bars, they should have listened to some practical advice. Watching the Red Cross people set themselves up, I decided to question the feasibility of such a distribution without the usual and accustomed method of rationing by means of tickets, such as we used for our meals.

He looked at me with a paternal air and said, "We want to make the Internees realize that by making these cigarettes, matches and chocolate bars freely available at this desk, there will be plenty more where they came from, and there will be absolutely no need for any rush to obtain each one's individual share" He continued profoundly, "We wish to do more than just rehabilitate these people! Their mental attitude must be helped back to normal."

I shrugged my shoulders and said, "If I were you, I would follow our old and customary methods of distribution, if only just for this first time."

He laughed and replied in dismissal, "Don't you worry! It'll work out."

Before any official announcement was made of the distribution, there was a line twice around the walls of the inside of the Main Building of people anxiously awaiting the signal. Every cigarette, match, and chocolate bar was gone in less time than it takes to tell and many went without!

On the following day, the loud speaker announced that the distribution of cigarettes, matches and chocolate bars would be made at meal times on the regular "chowline" and upon presentation of meal tickets only.

The Army had taken over the management of the camp with the aid of the Internee Executive Committee who would be replaced as soon as the detailed plans for our survival could be worked out. Lines for this and lines for that were still the order of the day. Our habits were not going to be done away with easily and since they were developed under stressful conditions, there was no better way than to continue for the time being the routines we had so long carried out. And thus began the orderly transition from prison life to freedom!

The next day was the third of our rescue. We wondered at the fate of the 2000 men and women imprisoned at Los Baños. Officially we learned that an airborne landing had been made on the south coast, several miles from Los Baños. However as far an we knew, the camp was deep in enemy territory and it would be a problem to effect a rescue of those unfortunate prisoners.

Many Internees, long hospitalized in the Philippine General, had yet to be heard from. Their potential fate was less promising than that of Los Baños because the hospital was located in the heart of present Jap defenses on the south side of Manila. It was quite possible that the Japs would destroy the hospital and its occupants as being in the way and expendable. At this moment that section of town was reported as being under heavy artillery fire by our forces while the Japs were demolishing every building in sight except those which they might fortify and possibly hold. If our boys advanced they would face nothing but rubble, which was their present experience on this side of the river.

Both the Rangers and the 37th were fighting desperate battles, striving to pierce the Pasig defenses with some small contingents having already crossed the river at weaker defense points. Their hold on the other side was tenuous at best. Their goal was the Philippine General Hospital, to reach it before it was too late. Our original rescuers were in the thick of the fighting, having had the luxury of a one-day rest, and they were finding the Japs a formidable foe, unwilling to surrender and willing to die in a lost cause.

The Air Force had finally made its appearance and support was coming in the form of P-38s which streaked across the sky to pour their brand of death into the enemy ranks. Here and there we saw Piper Cubs, artillery spotters, effectively pinpointing enemy positions so that the heavy U.S. guns could have a vulnerable target. These pilots were heroes in their own right since their planes carried no armor and their low-level missions brought them within range of Jap small arms.

Emergency first-aid and hospital stations were set up in every available, reasonably safe spot in camp.

The Japs continued to pour a comparatively heavy concentration of mortar fire in the area of the front campus grounds which was still serving as our temporary military headquarters. The shells frequently hit the facade of the Main Building and much damage was done to the windows and walls facing the southeast and south. The building shook with the impact of the shells and our shelter was, at best, precarious. Our own artillery seemed to have much difficulty in finding the Jap mortar positions as the latter's plan seemed to be based on mobility. They would fire a few rounds and then move their mobile guns to another position. This strategy reflected the pre-rescue activity of the Japs who set up well-camouflaged gun posts throughout the many side streets in our sector of the city.

Our losses were serious during this day, as the Internees were still in a state of confusion, not quite understanding the danger that faced them from enemy fire. I suppose we all felt a bit immortal now that we had survived more than one thousand days of imprisonment.

Many of our troops, temporarily billeted in the front grounds, had no better cover than the fox-holes which they had dug for themselves. They were pinned down by the desultory fire from the Jap mortars and until the aid of the Filipino guerrillas could become effective, that type of warfare was going to be most effective. Some of the shots seemed to come from very nearby and it was probably that some of the gun positions had been set up in the neighborhood houses bordering the camp grounds. These positions were manned by "suicide squads" as there could be no escape now that the main body of defenders had left them and crossed the river.

Toward evening, the fire seemed to diminish and we speculated that at last the Filipino guerrillas had begun to smoke out their positions. The front campus was dotted with "75s" and a few "105s," now continually in use. The din was terrific!

As soon as darkness fell, I made another dash out to the shanty, which, being in the rear campus grounds, was not likely to be hit by mortar fire. Of course, there was the ever-present danger of snipers, but the boys needed warmer clothing and I gathered up everything I could carry. From some where behind camp, our artillery was now answering the Japs. As I ran, I could hear the "pop...pop...pop" of our own mortars and then the ominous "swish" of the shells as they flew over head. I had the feeling that I could look up and see them as they zoomed through the air, but of course, they were traveling at too great a speed. Artillerymen will tell you that a mortar shell can be followed plainly, if watched from behind the gun. These swishes seemed so close that I could not but help look up every time one was fired, in the pitch darkness of the night. A short pause followed the swish and then came a bright flash followed immediately by a roaring *hrummpf!*

Occasionally a Jap shell would come from the other direction, but I never heard the warning "pop!" There would simply be another "swish" and then a flash and a roar where the shell had struck, mostly behind the camp, well outside of our walls. They were trying to still the U.S. gun positions to the north of the campus.

Traveling quickly, on foot, with an armful of household goods and clothes, cannot be done gracefully. I slipped, tripped, and finally fell on the narrow dirt path which led back to the Main Building. Trying to outrun the shells made little sense so I slowed my efforts to a deliberate walk, comforting myself with the old soldier adage, that one need never fear the shell he hears.

We all breathed a sigh of relief when I finally made it back to the corner of the building where I had left my family. We needed rest so badly that not even the unending noisy passage of shells overhead disturbed our slumbers.

By next morning, the fourth of our rescue, the mortar and sniper fire seemed to come from points further away than yesterday. The reported house-to-house search by the Filipinos had done us a lot of good, or so it seemed. We were cheered by the evident increase in the presence of our air power as we knew that it held the key to eliminating the possibility of Jap reinforcements being brought into our local action.

Already the excitement-packed weekend of our rescue was past history and seemed to be something which happened ages ago. So greatly has the meaning of our lives been changed by these events, that the memories of our long and bitter imprisonment are beginning to fade into half-forgotten dreams. The thought of returning to the United States, home, was uppermost in our minds and in our conversations. No one knew how or when we might be able to get away. There were major land and sea battles going on in and around Luzon. We were kept fairly well posted as to the progress of our armed forces by a daily bulletin, in the form of a mimeographed sheet, published by the First Cavalry, nicknamed the "Rangers." The Japs continued to put up fierce resistance in Manila and to the south of us and the territory surrounding Manila Bay was still very much in their hands.

The news bulletin told of the valiant actions of our troops in rooting out pockets of Jap resistance, almost on a one-to-one basis, since they were determined to die rather than surrender. We knew that the countless acts of heroism could never be recorded in full since there was an accompanying heavy loss of life in our own forces. The Rangers, with their amazing tanks, were up in the front lines, now engaged in pushing the Japs out of their positions on the many military airstrips to the south of the city. This was an important battle factor since their capture would provide bases for our fighters and transport planes.

In camp, the regeneration of the Internees had begun. A mechanism was being set up for our registration and we were beginning to feel like U.S. citizens again. Most of the Internee traffic was still confined to the area in and behind the Main Building and we liked to think of the rear exit as our version of Broadway and Forty-second Street.

Scattered Jap mortar fire continued to dampen our spirits, but each day brought us one step nearer home.

The somber, drizzly dawn which hailed our fifth day of freedom seemed to bring with it a hint of menace. We certainly were not yet out of the woods. Even though we knew that we were fighting a winning war, the Jap shells continued to land in and about the campus. I had moved family and belongings to a room midway along the corridor in the rear of the Main Building. This was Room 27, now filled with families like our own, crowded into temporary corners, but without complaint from any of its regular occupants. We were all inclined to share with others any of our meager possessions, now that we were no longer at the mercy of our captors. Mosquito netting covered the room in a filmy maze, from floor halfway to the ceiling. That netting was, for the moment, our only privacy and at night a sort of subdued confusion existed until everyone was safely tucked away in their beds.

During the past night the crashing of shells against the front of the building seemed to increase, as though the Japs were taking out their fury against us, their former prisoners. As we had gone to bed just after 7 p.m. in the total blackout, we did not hear of the sad news of the tragic deaths of several Internees, late last night, until we lined up for breakfast this morning.

Just before midnight, the mortar barrage ceased entirely for more than an hour. Some of our friends, believing that it would be safe to go to their rooms in the front of the building in order to retrieve some of their belongings from the wreckage already there, made several short dashes without harm when suddenly the terrorizing scream of shells warned of the reopening of the barrage. A half dozen shells struck the front of the building simultaneously, one of which came through the broken window of the corner room on the main floor, Room 4, exploding against the wall, killing one man and two women instantly, and severely injuring several others. Mrs. Walter Foley, wife of the Reverend Walter, good friends of ours, lost her arm as she saw her husband lose his life. She was in critical condition and little hope was held for her survival, but she eventually and miraculously recovered.

In another room on the same floor, a lovely young girl was killed when a shell exploded in her face and in a third room, a prominent Manila attorney lost his life when shrapnel from a nearby shell shredded his body. Another shell entered a room on the third floor hideously maiming a young girl who was not expected to live. Even out in the shanty areas, death had been dealt to a wealthy Manila realtor while his wife suffered severe injury when a shell struck their shanty. They had chosen to escape the crowded babel of the Main Building for the fairly safe area in which their shanty was located. A shell must have ricocheted from the roof of the seminary and landed on their shanty.

A child who had wandered out onto the front plaza early this morning was rescued by a G. I. who, while attempting to carry the child to safety, was struck by shrapnel from a shell which had exploded not far behind him. He died as he pushed the child across the threshold of the front entrance to safety. One final tragic report was of another Internee who had received a direct hit while lying in his air-raid shelter.

If we had heeded all warnings, this needless loss of life would not have occurred. The grave lesson we had learned left us with feelings of guilt, but also with a new spirit of togetherness and patience with the conditions under which we must exist for now.

The front of the Main Building now became a "no man's land." The shanty areas were cleared once and for all. Fortunately the Education Building had not been a target of the shelling and the hospital went on with its life saving chores without interruption.

As the morning wore on the shelling seemed to cease altogether. We could only hope that this was to be a permanent development, but there was no relaxing of our precautions until the afternoon when an exciting event took place. The loud speakers suddenly came to life to announce that truckloads of bread, real bread, were now entering the front gates! With this announcement the Internees rushed out the front door of the Main Building, lining up on either side of the road to welcome the trucks carrying these beautiful golden brown loaves of the "staff of life," a commodity we had sorely missed for the past three years. The bread had been baked at army headquarters at Tarlac to the north and rushed to us as soon as the road into Manila had been secured and re-conditioned. The convoy had only suffered some sniper attacks but as it was heavily guarded there had been no casualties, and no delay.

The bread was distributed at the evening meal, one slice per person. Every time I lined up for meals now, I carried seven empty tins of various sizes, each one fashioned with a wire handle, much the same as granddad's old bear bucket. They held from one to five pounds of food and when I reached the end of the line, everyone was filled to overflowing and I needed help from Roger and Donny to carry them back to our room.

While we cheered this practice, there was a good deal of waste as the well-intentioned G.I.s who handled the serving lines gave no half-portions, anxious that we were getting enough to eat. We actually had to argue with them to ease up with their serving ladles, and then they were still unconvinced!

Our strength was slowly returning and we were anxious to put our new-found energies to work in any way which would speed the process of getting us back to normal civilian life. It was hard to accept the fact that the war was still raging all around us and there was just no way to release us yet. We all needed much more patience than we were able to give this waiting period.

The meals we were getting consisted of delicious stews, plenty of fresh beef, vegetables, dehydrated potatoes, fruit, fruit juices, bread, butter, milk and sugar, plenty of cigarettes, candy and chewing gum so that our dietary and social needs were fast being re-established.

For the first time our soldier friends told us of the hardships the folks back home had to face during the war period. Many of the staples we were now receiving in such bountiful supply, were rationed for the most part. Also gasoline, so necessary for all forms of transportation back home, was doled out against coupons. We were only slightly impressed in view of our own history of hardship, but it did make us realize that war did place burdens on those who had to stay behind and keep the machines running. No mail had reached us yet so we were still anxious about Eleanor's and my family and how they survived and what changes might have occurred.

The shanty area behind the seminary has now been cleared for use during the day. No shells have fallen into camp since last night and early morning and we are glad to get out of the mob scene and back to the relative quiet of Shantytown. Two soldiers, invited by Roger, dropped in at the shanty, told us they were from Ohio and also that the guns which had done so much damage last night were located in a house only five blocks from camp. They were operated by Japanese soldiers dressed in women's clothing until a group of Filipino partisans had discovered them. Apparently the guns had been set up sometime back as they were trained in a fixed position on the campus. No wonder that their fire was so accurate! As we sat and talked we hear a new barrage of fire and again the swish... swish of shells going overhead in both directions.

Each of the soldiers grabbed a boy and we all dashed for the shelter of the good old Main Building. Although a few Jap shells had hit in the front of the camp, the majority of the firing seemed to be toward our artillery positions to the east of the campus. As we scrambled along the path, we passed some rubble among which was an unexploded "75" shell not a yard away from us. Toy fingers of fear sped us along even faster so that we arrived at the rear of the building out of breath and with pounding hearts. The kids thoroughly enjoyed their "piggy-back" rides and they asked me if I would go back and retrieve the shell for them as a souvenir! That request and the fact that we were still bent over as though to protect us from shellfire caused a good deal of hysterical laughter from Eleanor and me. We thanked the soldiers and they went on to other duties.

Along toward sunset, there having been no further firing, our confidence returned so we decided that it might be more enjoyable to move out to the shanty for the night as well as the day. Almost at the same time as the first serving of supper was announced, a fresh barrage of shellfire was heard and that just about eliminated any further thought of returning to the shanty for the night.

The weather now is ideal. The days are clear and bright, not hot for Manila and under other circumstances time for golf and other outdoor recreation. Things are moving apace with Filipino labor being brought into camp on Friday, the 9th of February, to take over the arduous tasks of cleaning up. For the first time in years, the bathrooms and showers were cleaned up by someone other than the Internees. They were spotless. Accumulated waste, garbage, and debris was quickly removed by the paid laborers. Grass was trimmed and paths improved and for a day or so the camp was a beehive of rehabilitation.

The Filipinos were supervised by the army non-coms who tended to give them free reign. The laborers were being paid U.S. $1.25 per day and their meals but as soon as they learned the "ropes" they would have their time cards punched and then disappear until meal time. They followed that procedure again in the afternoon much to the chagrin of their supervisors. Prior to the war, the average wage for common labor was about U.S. $12.50 per month.

Centers were being established in the sectors of the city under our control, where Filipinos could purchase sacks of rice, sugar, and corn for a very nominal sum. Cigarettes, candy, and chewing gum and other luxuries were given away freely by the incoming G.I.s even though they were never sure of their next source of supply. Their generosity was amazing to the Filipinos who responded with the now familiar, "Hello Joe! You got a cigarette?"

On one unforgettable occasion, our Jap Commandant had obtained a Jap newsreel and shown it on our makeshift screen. The scene was Manila and the occasion was the welcoming of some high official from Tokyo. There was much flag-waving by the assembled Filipino crowd, but by picturing them as supporters of the military regime, it left a particularly bad taste in our mouths at the time. Undoubtedly, the large majority of the Filipinos had loyal leanings toward the United States but underneath it all, the arrival of the Japs was just another occupation by foreigners.

Today's news bulletin gives the text of a speech by the Commonwealth President Sergio Osmena who had succeeded Pres. Manuel Quezon upon his death. Pointing out the problems his people will be facing, he is asking for prompt relief from the United States. He estimates that there will be a need for a half billion U.S. dollars to finance reconstruction and rehabilitation. The Philippines have also been promised their independence just as soon as practical after the cessation of hostilities.

One week ago tonight we were sitting down to our customary ration of mush and soy bean stew with thoughts of the indefinite future and what might be in store for us and then...

The distant sounds of gunfire toward the north, then twilight becoming the pitch dark of a blackout, the strange noise of an approaching caravan around seven p.m. and then the most memorable five hours of our lives—that was Saturday night, one week ago!

The heroic bluff of 700 men in the face of overwhelming odds and their capture of Santo Tomas was a feat which must go down in the history books among the great military achievements of all time. Twenty-five or more thousands of Japanese troops were thrown into a panic of confusion, convinced that the might of an entire division was being thrown against them. They retreated to take up previously prepared defense positions and, in the melee, lost Santo Tomas to its rescuers!

We are still somewhat bewildered by the turn of our fortunes and our confusion was heightened by the renewed shelling of the front of the campus. An occasional shell now damaged the entrance to the Education Building and the hospital, and a large Red Cross flag draped across the front of that building was actually torn by shellfire.

I was standing near the entrance to the Education Building when I heard the screech of a shell. I ran toward the back of the building, meaning to put it between myself and danger. Behind me one of the "old-timers" from the gym shuffled along as fast as he could, with me prodding him along with, "C'mon, you can make it!"

He needed help and as I stopped to wait for him, just a few yards from safety, a Jap shell hit the side of the building above us, sending me flying headlong with its concussion while the old man behind me grunted and fell across my outstretched legs. His warm and sticky blood splashed on the side of my face and I was horrified to see that a large piece of shrapnel had almost beheaded him!

As I slowly regained my wits, but still in a state of shock, I pulled him as gently as I could, to safety behind the building. He was dying and obviously beyond the help of anyone so I got up and ran to the nearest window shouting for help, for a doctor and for a priest, as I knew there were some Catholic fathers living in one of the rooms on the top floor. It was a priest who came through the window first and as the old man died in his arms he did administer last rites.

It took me some time and a glass of raw whiskey (which had been hidden by the doctor) before I felt anything like myself again. I was deeply moved by the death of the old man even though I did not know him. Death had been that close to me! I realized how lucky I had been to have escaped the hail of shrapnel. My legs were shaky and when I finally set off for the Main Building where Eleanor and the boys had earlier sought safety, I decided to keep my story to myself until some later and more favorable time. Two other Catholic priests had been severely wounded in that shelling, I now found out. They had been busy helping people to shelter when the barrage came. One lost parts of both feet and the other lost a leg!

We heard for the first time that another landing had been successfully carried out in southern Luzon and was fighting its way northward to effect a junction with the airborne group holding onto Los Baños and with the 37th Division fighting in Manila. If they succeed, the Japs will be hopelessly cut in two. But their fighting is one of great desperation. They will not surrender. Their determination to fight to the death is causing our forces more than their customary share of casualties. In Manila they are making their last stands from buildings which they have fortified with every possible implement of war. Anti-aircraft guns are seeing service as cannons. Concrete pill-boxes with machine gun emplacements guard every possible street corner. They have hidden machine guns in the sewers and storm drains and every inch of the way is a bloody creeping advance for our boys.

In the Luneta, a large park in which the relatively new government building complex is located, the Japs have constructed a series of fortified bunkers. The massive concrete government buildings have themselves become forts. They will suffer bombardment and the eventual cruel fate of almost complete destruction before victory is possible. Whatever has been given up by the Jap defenders is nothing better than a pile of rubble and unfortunately many Filipinos have lost their lives in the role of front-line hostages. The city rocks with land mines set off in demolition and there is a continual pall of smoke attesting to the many fires.

Tragedy again struck Santo Tomas this early afternoon. An undiscovered Jap gun emplacement blazed away, without warning, at the Education Building which so far had been hit only once, that of my unhappy experience this morning. Now there was a sudden unexpected hail of steel and iron into the area of the front entrance, killing several and wounding many of the patients and staff-members alike. The huge Red Cross banner marking the hospital was totally ignored and the defenseless hospital became the target briefly, of a murderous and inhuman barrage. The gun was eventually silenced but not until after it had accomplished its lethal mission.

Later on in the afternoon, a continual line of refugees from all over the city had shown up at the front gates of the University. Most of them came from the southern sector, Filipinos who had escaped from behind the Jap lines, fording the Pasig River in many cases. Many of them were wounded or in a poor physical condition from starvation. Room was made for them in the former hospital which still housed a few of our Internees. Their tales of barbarism far surpassed the stories of our own hardships during this last week. The atrocities committed by the suicide-minded Jap soldiers filled us with pity and fury. They came in rags, rich and poor alike, their possessions gone save what they could carry. Families had been separated. Some had been forced to watch their children mowed down by machine gun fire or torn to bits by grenades. Japs, marching by houses in the southern residential area, had wantonly tossed live grenades in open windows, laughing when the loud explosion was followed by screams of pain and fires which destroyed the frail construction of the home.

Today, February 10th, peace seemed a long way off indeed!

We spent the night again in the Main Building for safety's sake. "Bloody Saturday" was thankfully behind us and Sunday morning we attended Mass for the first time, in the seminary chapel. The fences were down and we met many of those anonymous friends among the seminarians outside of the church and they greeted us like long-lost family! Most of them were young Filipinos, in their twenties, and these had been the brave people who had occasionally tossed food over the fence whenever the Jap guards' backs were turned. There would have been even more of this clandestine help save for the fact that they, while nominally not prisoners, were prohibited from leaving their quarters save for exceptional family reasons and furthermore were not permitted to carry anything out of the building.

Some friends stopped us as we left the vicinity of the chapel and told us of the death of two good friends, one from beri-beri and the other from a burst appendix and peritonitis and whose body did not respond to medication because of its emaciated condition.

We are hearing more of the unbelievably cruel stories of the atrocities committed by the Jap soldiers in the city. Children have been murdered even as they were held in their mother's arms. The rape and pillaging by small unorganized groups of soldiers added to the sufferings of these unfortunates who were only trying to escape a war in which they were neither participants nor instigators. The civilian population of Manila who were forced to welcome the Jap invaders in their occupation of the city, now was paying the price! The refugee crowd clamors at the gate, many on their knees, thanking the Lord for their deliverance while others just stood, silent with only the blank stare of shock, so eloquently expressing their need.

A communique has been received from General MacArthur! It is posted in the main entrance and we are informed that Manila is now in our hands! He could have added but the war is still in the laps of the Internees! It is true that the shelling has just about ceased and the joy of walking about the campus is still tinged with caution. We always keep shelter within reach as we move about to greet old friends and neighbors.

The most thrilling event of the day was the raising and unfurling of "Old Glory." The ceremony took place at 10 a.m.

at the flagpole in front of the Main Building and everyone who could walk or crawl made it to the plaza. My eyes and, I'm sure, those of the people around us, filled with tears as our precious flag was "still there" as it billowed in the breeze. What a sight!

We now settle down to the tedium of waiting. The days go by with the last pockets of Jap resistance being cleared out, leaving behind the dust of destruction and waste. Manila is a rubble heap. There is very little standing and from the top floor our eyes witness a never-to-be-forgotten scene. Manila has perished! The "Pearl of the Orient" is no more!

Father "Johnny," one of the seminarians from across the fence who had taken a fancy to our little boys, back in the early days when communication was still possible, paid us a visit. He came to our shanty and told us that he had been to see his family somewhere in Rizal Province. His younger brother had been killed by shrapnel, only a few days before. He said, "My family's grief is great, but they carry on. We have to think of the living!"

He brings us a startling bit of news. According to a dispatch intercepted by the U.S. Armed Forces, all males between the ages of 15 and 50 were to be taken from Santo Tomas on February 4 by the Jap military. Their ultimate fate had to be certain death as front-line hostages. The dispatch mentioned orders to destroy Manila, evidence now that the Imperial Japanese Army had a well-planned and deliberate campaign of retribution, days before our rescue was executed. We will never know what might have been our fate if our legendary rescue had not been successful or if it had not been timely. It is a chilling thought indeed!

Father Johnny is courageous in the face of personal tragedy. He spends his days at the hospitals, thinking only of the living and how he can be of service to them. He is with the wounded and dying Filipino civilians, consoling them, helping with their care, running messages among separated families, exhausting himself, leaving no room to dwell on the death of his brother. There are many such heroes even now in those first post-war days. Most everyone has found a job to do and the spirit of cooperation and brotherhood has never been more in evidence.

I finally told Eleanor of my brush with death. She was horrified but grateful to our Maker that I was spared. Further news from outside told us that all four bridges had been destroyed but that our engineers were in the process of erecting a "Bailey" bridge to replace the Jones bridge and there would soon be a resumption of traffic between north and south Manila. The massive U.S. Post Office, recently constructed, was a blackened mass of rubble. Jap snipers were still firing desultory shots from the ruins. Again from the top floor I could see the city's burning wreckage but I found it difficult to pick out the main thoroughfares such as the Escolta and Avenida Bizal. The Far Eastern hotel was one of the very few buildings still standing but on close inspection, it turned out to be completely gutted, a complete ruin. The inside was a blank, charred maze of twisted steel, wire, and fragments of mortar and cement. This was the scene of our last social gathering before the holocaust!

The Japs now hold positions in the Marikina Hills, not far from our old residential section of San Juan. The thunder of our artillery can now be heard in that direction and, coupled with air support, we are fast winning the battle!

About this time one of our old pre-war friends had come into camp. She was a Spanish girl, married to an American, and because of her nationality had been permitted to live outside of the camp. She had a six-year old daughter and had cared for Donny in the early days of our imprisonment. Some friends had come to her home and warned her that the Japs were intending to burn all the homes in her district, so she joined a party of her Spanish friends and, guided by a Filipino guerrilla, made her way to a nearby rice paddy. From there they had to crawl most of the way to the river where the opposite bank was secured by our troops.

As they dove into the waist-high field of maturing rice crop, several shots rang out in rapid succession. They had been discovered! There was no choice but to make a run for it and as they had a fair start on their pursuers, and by dodging every which way, they managed to escape being hit. When they sighted the river, they realized with dismay that a wide stretch of open land separated them from its banks. There was great likelihood that the area was well covered by Jap gun emplacements, but in their eagerness to reach safety, a few of the group took off and made a mad dash for the river. The staccato beat of shots kept time to falling bodies, mercilessly mowed down as they dashed toward freedom.

Women who had pulled their children with them in their haste, now lay moaning on the ground, mortally wounded. Their children, pulled to the earth for protection cried out in bewilderment at the sudden turn of events. Some crumpled up and were stilled forever, dying in the arms of their wounded mothers and fathers. The panic was now general, everyone breaking from cover and madly dashing across the vulnerable open space toward the river. Only a few survived!

Our friend, her story told, looked at us in stunned sorrow. Those people had been her friends, her relatives, and they had died as she watched! The handful of people who had reached the river yet alive, threw themselves into the foul water, grateful for the protection it offered. They waded through knee-deep muck until they were hidden from the enemy by a turn in the bank. There they met the welcome sight of an American soldier with his jeep, apparently on a reconnaissance tour. They clambered up the bank, threw themselves at the feet of the soldier, kissed his muddy shoes and deliriously hugged the jeep. He piled them in and brought them to Santo Tomas, as the nearest place of refuge and medical aid.

As we took our friend and her little daughter to our shanty, she said somewhat hysterically, "Imagine! They brought us here in a jeep! Yes, really a jeep! Imagine coming here in a jeep!"

She needed the comfort of her American husband and I set out to find him. I was lucky and shortly able to give him the exciting news that his wife and little girl were safe and sound and now resting in our shanty. He could hardly contain his happiness and dashed madly ahead to great them. Nora and Fred Hart, it will be a long time before I forget that scene!

Although Nora Hart had lived outside of camp for most of the war, she was as thin and undernourished as the rest of us. Things had not been easy for anyone in Manila and there were particular difficulties facing the daily existence of an alien, even friendly or neutral. But this was behind her now and she was reunited with her husband and her child safe and sound.

On a certain St. Valentine's Day, not so many years ago, there was a massacre. It made headlines in all the newspapers because it took place in Chicago and was the culmination of a gang war! Although there was no particular cause for national mourning, the story was the biggest newspaper event for several days.

Today, February 15, 1945, the massacre of Filipinos continues, unabated and although the newspapers today headline military events, this inhumanity of man to man will survive in memory long after victory has been won. The atrocities continue behind Jap lines, out in the provinces and with no cause nor plan apparent. Like Pearl Harbor, these days too will live long in infamy!

Among the horror stories came rumors of the fate of the people at the Philippine General hospital. It was said that they had all been machine-gunned, but there was no substance to the story. The many relatives and friends of those who were patients at the P.G.H. were beside themselves with anxiety but there was nothing, no news yet. Every war correspondent who was seen around camp was besieged with questions, but there just was no word.

Father Johnny passed by the shanty. He had been out all morning attending the patients at San Lazaro Hospital, not far from Santo Tomas. He says that wounded Filipinos are arriving in such numbers that the dying, for whom all hope has been given up, are being transferred to the mortuary while yet alive, to make room for the needier cases piling up outside. There is need for ten times the number of doctors, attendants, and beds. The present condition of the hospital is beyond belief! He told us of his aunt, who along with several friends had sought refuge in the Vienna Bakery, on the other side of the Pasig, at the Ayala bridge, then held by the Japs. They managed to barricade themselves with comparative security in the large brick building. The Japs seemed aware of their presence but did nothing for a couple of days. Their food and water ran out and as the Japs slowly gave ground across the bridge, the position became precarious. Finally the Japs set fire to the building's front while setting up a couple of machine gun posts near the rear exit. Those inside decided their only chance was to rush the rear door and take their lives in the hands. The signal was given and they burst out only to be met with withering fire from the Japs. As they came through, everyone was hit and the bodies fell in a heap in front of the door. By the rarest of luck, Father Johnny's aunt, although wounded, fell beneath some of the others, so that she was literally on the bottom of the pile. One or two of the others had not been hit but were now standing with their backs to the wall. The Japs rushed over, bayonets swinging and proceeded to knife those who had not been hit, and were standing, dazed and hoping for mercy. Taking no chances that anyone was still alive, they proceeded to plunge their bayonets into the pile of bodies indiscriminately. By the rarest of good fortune, Fr. Johnny's aunt was still conscious although slightly wounded by one of the bullets. She felt the thump of the bayonets as they were thrust into the bodies on top of her. She lay absolutely still as the thumps continued, missing her until one bayonet blade came through the body on top of her, penetrated her side and severed her breast. She still did not lose consciousness although in shock and great pain.

    The Japs finally backed off so that she was able to make some effort to stem the flow of blood from her wounds after what must have seemed to be hours of agonized waiting, there was complete silence and the courageous woman managed to crawl from beneath the mounds of dead bodies and made her way to the river nearby.

    She does not know how and no one will ever know how she managed to reach the house of her relatives, still alive and able to tell her incredible story. Father Johnny saw to it that she reached San Lazaro, but it is expected that she will not survive.

Along side of this parade of tragedies among the Filipino population our own recent hardships fade into insignificance. Someday the chronicles of perseverance and survival of the Filipino people will be compiled, hopefully soon, so that the bitter lessons learned once, will not be easily forgotten. The never-ending line of blood-stained weary refugees continues day after day. Camp hospital facilities have long since been exhausted and the eastern end of the campus has become tent city with clusters of first aid centers. As far as we can see from the roof, most of southern Manila is in ashes. Homes, churches, convents, schools, have shared a common fate. We are told that the Japs burned the Concordia Orphanage with almost a total loss of life. Only a handful of the children escaped. The Japs supposedly poured gasoline over the inflammable parts of the building, at the same time covering the doors with machine guns, much like the story of the Vienna Bakery. Those children who failed to make their escape died with their faces lifted in prayer, side by side with the brave nuns who would not leave their charges.

The Japs have retired behind the thick walls of Intramuros, the old Walled City. One company of American soldiers upon reaching the entrance nearest the old Jones Bridge, now down in the river, found a horrible sight. The naked bodies of some young Filipina women were impaled upon the walls and gates. They had been trussed up and forced upon the sharp stakes which had been embedded in the fortress-like walls and gate since the Spanish occupation. The Americans learned that thousands of Filipinos had been taken into the Walled City as hostages, facing the same fate as might have befallen us.

XXVI

As we sit with companions of our last three years, we muddle over the fates which brought us to our misery. Was the motivation for Japan's attack on Pearl Harbor and Luzon completely unprovoked? We knew from news accounts that the straw which broke the camel's back, was the embargo on shipments of scrap steel and iron to Japan. But our conclusions irrevocably found no justification for the barbaric attacks without warning, not only on our military but more importantly on the civilian population. The invitation of neutral countries under the guise of establishing an economic bloc propagandized as "The Greater East Asia Co-Prosperity Sphere" was a transparent drive to expand the Japanese Empire.

Now half of the far eastern world is in ruins. Only eighty years ago the Japanese monarch stepped out of the dark ages into the light of modern civilization. It seems to us that in eight decades they have only acquired a thin veneer, holding to their feudal customs, believing religiously that suicide is the only avenging of dishonor and that dying is an act of heroism, according to their codes, will ensure reincarnation as a warrior, rather than as an animal. The Japanese have failed to assimilate or even tolerate western culture. The old guard rules with the philosophy of Bushido and Samurai, in which life has less meaning than death.

Their so-called "fight to the death" defense of Manila has left the once beautiful city in ruins. The Japs have torn down and destroyed the capital city of a nation of more than twenty-five million people who have been alienated from them for generations to come. Why did they not leave in peace, leaving their Filipino neighbors with the belief that they were in truth, a good friend, a brother in the "Greater East Asia Co-Prosperity Sphere" indeed as well as in word? But now who would believe them? They have committed suicide as individuals and as a nation right here in Manila these last two devastating weeks and the vaunted East Asian solidarity has been shattered beyond repair!

We continue to hear horror stories which can neither be affirmed nor denied since they are at least third hand. Nevertheless they are in such great detail, that we are easily convinced of their veracity. We are told of a native woman carrying a year old baby being stopped by a Jap soldier clad only in his hat and a G-string, who grabbed her, attempted to rip off her dress. She and the baby screamed and in annoyance he placed the muzzle of his pistol in the baby's mouth and pulled the trigger. Having killed the baby and grievously wounded the mother, witnesses said, he just ran off.

The German population of Manila, former Axis partners of the Japs, fared poorly at their hands. In one instance several German men were lined up against a wall with every third man chosen and shot until there were but three left. These were then ceremoniously beheaded with an officer's Samurai sword for no other apparent reason save that they were not orientals and particularly not Japanese. As soon as word of the callous massacre of the German men was made known, the remaining German citizens sought refuge at the gates of Santo Tomas and were promptly interned by the American army.

A third story, repeated here only to illustrate the animal savagery of a defeated, retreating army, will stand as one of the indictments against the old militarism of the Imperial Japanese nation.

Since the American charge against northern Manila, La Salle College, a small Jesuit school, had become a refuge for many Filipino civilians. On February 7th, in addition to the staff of brothers and priests who taught there, some seventy men, women, and children were sheltered within its sturdy walls. During the afternoon, the brother-in-charge and a prominent Filipino attorney were taken out of the building by a small detail of Jap soldiers. They have not been heard from. The others were warned to stay away from the doors and windows and to remain silent at all times.

After five days of waiting while the war went on at full blast in the surrounded area, a Jap officer and about twenty soldiers appeared at the front door, breaking it in and deploying themselves around the front hall. The officer ordered all of the civilians to assemble before the soldiers. As soon as he was assured of the presence of everyone, with no further preliminary, he gave orders to his soldiers who immediately responded by fixing their bayonets. Another order was given and the soldiers charged the standing group of people. There was a brief frenzied slashing of bayonets as the people screamed and milled about in blind panic. Some attempted to defend themselves and some ran toward the nearest stairwell only to be shot by the officer who stood by with his pistol cocked! The bloodied bayonets killed and wounded men, women, and children until the entire hall floor was a river of red flowing around heaps of dead and dying bodies. By the stair was another mound of those who had been shot, but beneath was one body of a wounded American Jesuit Father, so far not seriously hurt. Still conscious, he lay still as the death around and over him. He watched the Japs finally leave after wantonly sticking their bayonets randomly into bodies.

After a long watchful interval, he finally and painfully pulled himself from beneath the stack of bodies above. He searched and was overjoyed to find a few of the refugees still alive and some just barely so. He anointed as many of the dead as his waning strength allowed and did the same for the few mortally wounded but still alive. One of the other injured civilians said, "They'll be coming back! What can we do?"

The priest knew of an attic compartment where they might be safe until a rescue could be effected. So he helped those who could move up the stairway to the next floor and then to an attic which was entered through a trap door. They could still keep an eye on the lower floor down the stairwell.

One time the Japs did re-enter the building some of the soldiers spitting on the dead bodies. Satisfied as to their inhuman deed, they left and the sound of battle continued outside.

Four days passed when late in the afternoon of February 16th, American soldiers reached the grounds of the college, appearing just in time to rescue the eleven people, wounded but still alive. They had hidden four long days and nights, without food or any help for their wounds. Ironically, among the dead was the son of Benigno Aquino, one of the more prominent collaborators of the Japanese regime.

The news regarding the American patients at the Philippine General Hospital was not reassuring. The slow and systematic destruction of the Jap strongholds in south Manila has brought our forces to the vicinity of the hospital only to find that the Japs have turned it into a stronghold of defense. Our counter-fire deliberately is aimed not at the building but at the surrounding walls and property. The Japs fire from the building as well as from pill-boxes elsewhere nearby. This will be in the nature of a long siege and since there are so many Internees hospitalized, we will all be watching and praying that they are delivered safely.

The attack against Corregidor is being pushed. It is difficult to remember that only three eternal years ago the present occupants were the attackers who, after a long siege, forced the heroic Lt. General Jonathan "Skinny" Wainwright to finally surrender. The re-capture of Corregidor will only be a matter of days in this go-round.

XXVII

We have written everyone at home to tell them that we are alive and well. Some incoming "stateside" mail has already reached camp but as late as this morning we had not been among those favored recipients. After lunch I went to the Main Building to take another look at the posted list and found to my joy that there was mail for us. When I reached the desk, I found that someone, presumably Eleanor, had already picked up the mail, so I hurried back to our shanty as I was more than anxious to hear how it was with the folks back home!

Just a short distance away I saw Eleanor with a letter in her hand, standing in the doorway. Something was wrong! I could tell from the anguished look she gave me as I approached and I knew that I was in for some kind of shock! With tears glistening on her cheeks, she said, "It's...it's your Dad!"

I stopped in a state of shock as she went on to say, "He died more than two years ago! Mom's letter says that he had a cerebral hemorrhage. Here is Mom's letter."

I stood there on the next to the top step, not really absorbing what she had said, and standing there facing her with only a blank stare. She reached out, still holding the letter which I did not offer to take, took my head in her arms, and said, "My God! He was not that old!"

As I slowly gained comprehension of the news, I said, "He never knew whether we were alive or dead, nor for that matter, what really happened to us!" We knew that there had been no official confirmation of the imprisonment of the American civilians until well after the date of his death and even then, we were never sure that such news carried names of those who were captured. And to think that we only learned of his death which had occurred in January 1943, two years after the fact!

My dad had not been in ill health although he was inclined to be hypertensive, but controlled with medication. He was but sixty-two years of age and would have had a lot to look forward to with the safe return of our family, especially his two grandsons whom he loved dearly. There were undoubtedly many attempts to communicate this news to us since both he and my in-laws were in frequent contact, as we later learned. I read my mother-in-law's letter many times over, but there were still many questions in my mind as to the circumstances surrounding his death and burial that would have to wait.

How about our brothers? Eleanor had three, the last, Eddie, too young to be involved in this war. Where were Fred, the older, and Raymond, the younger brother, at this moment? We knew that they had volunteered themselves into the army and must have seen action, possibly in our area, according to Mom's letter. My brother Ed, who was fourteen months my junior, had volunteered for army service along with Eleanor's brother Fred and they could possibly be in the same outfit.

Thank God that Eleanor's mom and dad were both in good health and according to their letter doing their part to help the war effort at home. The wartime emergency measures were mentioned briefly by Mom and it was apparent that we had not been forgotten for a single instant by relatives and friends alike. All of them had besieged the Red Cross, the State Department, and the War Department at one time or another, for some news of us and what was happening with our rescue effort. No news of any kind specifically concerning us and our fate was available until 1943, after my father's death.

The next day we received another letter from Eleanor's folks. This one told how they received a short message from us in 1943. The message was one permitted by the Japs who imposed restrictions on what could be said. For example, we were allowed to say that we were "In good health and receiving adequate food and general care" the words being prescribed by our captors. We could add a one-sentence personal message which in our case read, "Donny is walking, Roger is in kindergarten and we are well and happy and tell the Sweeneys." I remembered that in World War I, German propaganda was given the lie by Americans who countered with "Tell it to Sweeney!" I hoped that the readers of our message would understand that all was far from well despite our apparently encouraging words.

Our message was eventually relayed to Tokyo and through the help of the Red Cross, arrangements were made to broadcast our words over Tokyo radio. Shortwave hams all over the free world picked up the messages and by letter, telegram, or cable sent them on to the addressees. So it was that my father-in-law to whom the message was addressed received over a long period of time, varied communications from all over the world, despite errors in spelling his name or in the deletion of part of the address or mistakes in street or numbers. It was a minor miracle but it did advise them that we were still alive, at least.

There was good news and bad news by mail, for practically every one of the Internees. Some were saddened by the news of a death in the family while others were overjoyed to find the folks back home still in good health. Employers of many were quick to communicate their pleasure at the good news of our rescue, advising them at the same time that their earnings had continued to accumulate during their incarceration and would be available upon their return home or to their local employment as the case might be. My own employer must certainly have sent word even though it failed to reach me at Santo Tomas.

This latter dearth of news from Parke Davis and Company left the decision of whether or not to remain in Manila entirely in my hands. My family's health and welfare was my most major concern and after a physical examination by the army doctors, I was in no condition to go back to work, at least for awhile. In the three weeks since our rescue, I had gained about twenty pounds and was beginning to recoup my energy, but I was told that I had a long road ahead, as did Eleanor, before we could be pronounced normal in health again. The children seemed to be a little better off and we were assured that there would be no lasting ill effects on their growth.

A questionnaire was handed to us and we were asked to state our plans for the immediate future. After much soul-searching, we agreed that after three long years of hardship and privation we would not be separated. Furthermore, Manila, for some time to come, would be no place for Eleanor and the boys. Therefore I indicated our desire to get back to the United States, as a family, as soon as safe transportation could be obtained. Perhaps the interests of my employer would not best be served by my action but the pressures of our actual circumstances, health and otherwise, made any other decision unthinkable.

We watched with keen interest the progress of the liberating army since our departure would now occur only when Manila and Southern Luzon were reasonably secure. Bataan province had been sealed off by the 38th Division and there had been a successful airborne landing on Corregidor according to the morning bulletin of February 20th. Even more happy and exciting was the news that the Philippine General Hospital had been rescued and all American patients were safe and sound! The closest action now centered around the old Walled City where our advance had to be measured in inches and with heavy casualties. The fighting was hand-to-hand as every hold in the ancient walls seemed to contain hara-kiri minded Jap defenders. Every housetop, cellar, sewer, and rat-hole, now barricaded and fortified, spelled potential death to our advancing soldiers.

Anxious to get a first hand impression of what was left of Manila, I begged a ride with a young army lieutenant, with whom we had become quite friendly. He was from Brooklyn and a fellow New Yorker since that was the city of my birth. As we drove through the gates for the first time in so many months, I was exhilarated by the feeling of freedom. This joy was almost immediately replaced with the horror of desolation and destruction all around us. We entered an incredible world of ruin and confusion. The few streets from which rubble had been cleared were dirty and dusty, crowded with bewildered, ragged people with staring empty eyes. Their wandering seemed aimless as they trudged the streets, slowly, with their few possessions wrapped in pitiful dirty bundles under their arms or over their shoulders. Here and there were small relief centers, temporarily set up by the Red Cross, overworked and understaffed and with little ability to cope with the urgent needs of the population who sought comfort. The long lines moved with agonizing slowness and grew faster than the number of people who had been served.

The unmistakable stench of death hung like a pall over the ruined buildings. Though I could see no sign of them, they were there, the dead, part of the rubble now, buried until the cleanup task could be gotten under way.

We followed the ragged canyon which was former busy Dasmariñas Street, our jeep picking its way among the craters and ruins of the pavement. Sentries were posted here and there to warn army vehicles of possible hidden mines or unexploded shells. We had to beware of walls, empty reminders of former businesses which might come tumbling down at any moment. We entered the main street in the financial district where formerly the major banks and brokerage houses had carried on their trade. It was a sea, ankle deep in "Mickey Mouse" Jap military bank notes. I saw denominations of ten, hundred, and thousand peso notes, nothing more than worthless paper at this moment.

Fire had played its part in wiping out the rickety Chinese barrios, where more than a million people were now left homeless. They faced the situation with a certain amount of stoicism as they salvaged what they could, even to the extent of setting up makeshift tables upon which they set their meager wares to sell or exchange for food or clothing. Unbelievably, some were already flourishing as their stocks contained a wide variety of army rations, American cigarettes, a dubious bottle of "whisky" or rum and other sundries.

The main thoroughfares, Azcárraga, Rizal, and Quezon were a continuous rumble of dusty military convoys, jeeps, tanks, and rehabilitated civilian vehicles. Gasoline was available only to the military so far and only horse-drawn makeshift buses moved civilians. Armed American soldiers were all over town and it seemed that they were usually engaged in handing out some of their rations to hungry children. Considerable commerce was being done in alcoholic beverages. These unauthorized dealings had already taken their toll in poisoning several of our G.I.s, but the demand was already far greater than the supply, and increasing! The present price was U.S. $25 for raw alcohol, colored and flavored to resemble whiskey. Even the labels were bogus with misspelled words and ink which would run at the slightest touch of moisture. Those who spent money for the relaxing effect of alcohol were almost knowingly bent on self-destruction.

Completely worn out and quite frustrated with my view of the city and its half-hearted efforts to restore law and order, we returned to camp to report our findings. I could see no possibility of a quick rebirth of Manila's former civic pride. From the looks of all the buying, selling, trading, and black marketeering going on, commerce at the retail level would have no trouble getting back on its feet. However it seems inevitable that once hostilities have ceased the Philippines' reconstruction period will be burdened with speculation and inflation, two more good reasons for us to go home, rather than stay.

Today the final chapter of the lives of the four men who had been taken from camp during Christmas week, 1944, were finally and grimly written. A small wooden box was carried into camp this morning. It contained the remains of those men, among them Cliff Larsen and Carroll Grinell. According to the testimony of a Filipino who had witnessed their execution and followed their bodies to the grave site, they had been shot or beheaded early in January, their bodies dumped into a large pit containing the remains of others, Filipino guerrillas who had suffered the same fate. They had been identified by odd bits of clothing, empty eye-glass rims and teeth, by relatives who had been brought to the grave by Army personnel.

We will never know the reason why they were brought to their cruel fate. Each one was a man of unquestioned character, involved as in the case of Grinnell and Duggleby, with Internee welfare as their Executive Committee representatives, or as in Cliff Larsen's case, an innocent bystander, perhaps a case of mistaken identity. The entire camp population mourned their deaths and all of Emily Larsen's friends gave her what comfort was possible. All four men were buried in camp, in terrain hallowed by our memories. We chose the shady peace of "The Fathers' Garden," a small retreat surrounded by high hedges and used by the Internees for religious serves when weather permitted. It was located next to the seminary on the side of the Main Building and it was hoped that it would be a sanctuary for many years to come. There rest the mortal remains of our own heroes!

February 22 was a red-letter day for us and also one which would be marked in history. The news announced that the Fifth Marine Corps had effected a landing on the Japanese-owned Iwo Jima. Tokyo had been bombed by B-29s for the first time! Our great thrill came with the arrival, unexpectedly, of Eleanor's two brothers, Fred and Ray, who literally dropped in on us from out of the sky! Fred, the older, flew in his "Piper Cub" from his job as an artillery spotter in the northern Luzon combat zone. Ray, an infantry sergeant in the same division, arranged to fly to Manila where he and Fred met and sought us out.

Although we learned from the earlier letters from Eleanor's family that both lads were "somewhere in the Pacific area," we had no idea that they had reached Luzon. We had first believed that Ray must still be at home since his original medical draft classification was 4-F. We found later that he had enlisted immediately after Pearl Harbor, joined his brother's outfit and had been in successive Pacific operations from New Guinea northward.

With my usual burden of four or five buckets, I left the shanty to pick up our noonday meal. A few yards along the path I passed two G.I.s, husky-looking, tanned specimens, fully armed and vaguely familiar. They passed me with hardly a glance and as I turned, out of curiosity, to watch where they were going, I saw Eleanor come to the door of the shanty. They looked up, saw her, and shouted their sister's name and broke into a run! Then the light dawned and I knew who they must be.

What a reunion! Everyone hugging and kissing, crying and laughing at the same time. Even our two little boys who had only the vaguest recollection of such things as "uncles" were caught up in the whirlwind of the moment. As we caught our breaths, Ray said, "Tom, was that really you we passed on the path? God, I never would have recognized you! You look awful!"

Of course, I looked some seventy or so pounds lighter than when they had last seen me but I didn't think I was all that bad. So I said, "Well you guys have changed a lot, too…and for the better I might add!"

Fred held Eleanor out at arm's length and Ray did the same for me. "Ray, I can't believe this is our sister! She's so skinny she looks like a little kid!"

Roger and Donny now sported a G.I. combat cap and were more interested in the equipment Fred and Ray were carrying rather than the conversations going on about them. Both brothers were full of news and they told us that they had a single aim in the war and that was to personally rescue us from our late captors. They told us that the last word heard from my brother Ed was that he had been transferred to the European theater and was probably deep in the campaign to beat the Germans to their knees.

Army life seemed to agree with Fred and Ray. They both had put on some solid weight and were tanned and healthy-looking. When I commented on this, they told me that the color was part Atabrine, the antimalarial drug which they had to take routinely, and part much exposure to tropical sun. Fred had miraculously escaped enemy fire in his small 'plane but Ray had been wounded and received the Purple Heart, deservedly. He seemed reluctant to talk about his experiences and in particular the present campaign in the northern provinces. Fred was a bit more philosophical and recounted some of the brushes he had with death.

Our shanty area, "Shantytown," was blacked out as was all of the rear campus as sniper fire was still heard from time to time. As we sat talking over old times, Eleanor said, "I've got a great idea! Let's all sit down and write a letter to Mom and Dad, each one writing a paragraph, at least, about this wonderful day!"

Everyone agreed enthusiastically and we pulled our little wicker table under the flickering light from the kerosene lantern hanging from the rafters and sat down to transcribe our thoughts. As we discussed what each one was going to say or should say in these special circumstances, there was a sudden whine of a bullet followed almost simultaneously with a "smack" where it must have hit. The shot had come through our roof although we had no idea from which direction. Both Fred and Ray reacted and shouted "Hit the deck!"

And we did, all six bodies spread flat out on the split bamboo floor. I had closed the flaps of the shanty but some sniper outside of the walls must have spotted an errant glimmer of light and wantonly fired at us. Naturally our next thought was to get to the safety of the Main Building where we still maintained our "safe" quarters. Fred ordered us to keep low and one by one quietly crawl out of the shanty after he doused the light. Roger and Donny took this as some kind of a game so we had no problem with them. Fred and Ray took one boy each under their arms, once we had crawled down the steps to the path below. We scurried on in the darkness and made the Main Building safely.

There was so much to talk about, despite the fact that neither of the brothers had been home since the beginning of the Pacific campaign. They found some place to bunk along with the military contingent guarding the camp. The next morning we were up bright and early, ready to begin where we had left off. They took photos of us, the shanty, and the camp in general and we hope that they will someday be seen by us to remind us again of the last three interminable years. As all good things come to an end, Fred and Ray had to leave early that afternoon, flying back north to get into the action again at the risk of their lives. We parted with prayers for their safety and fervent hopes that we would all be together again soon! There was no way that they could assure us of another unexpected and happy visit. Their campaigns came first!

Eleanor, Tom, Donny and Roger.
Sentries had patrolled this path in front of their hut.
February 19, 1945

Eleanor, Donny, and Roger
February 19, 1945

Tom on his way to get water.

Donny and Roger at Santo Tomas, 1945

On the reverse of this photo is written:
"Roger, Pam, & Donny on their way for their mid-morning milk ration. Donny's wearing the Jap R.C. armband. Each is holding a ration ticket. 2/19/45"

Donny and Roger and some of their Santo Tomas playmates. Donny is holding a Red Cross armband. February 19, 1945

Tom, Roger, and Donny in 1945

The note on the back of this photo reads,
"Santo Tomas Univ. - Manila. Ray & I two rough guys, eh?
At least we have on our fighting togs.
Love you and miss you, Sweets   Fred   Feb 19, 1945"

Left to right, Fred Hoffmann, Roger Lewis, Eleanor Hoffmann Lewis, Ray Hoffmann, Donny Lewis at Santo Tomas in 1945.

The newly-rescued family with Eleanor's brothers.

After visiting Santo Tomas, Eleanor's brother Fred wrote the following letter to his wife.

> Philippine Islands-
> Monday, Feb. 19, 1945
> My Very Dearest Una-
>
>   I owe you a very long letter tonight because I did not write at all last night. I think you will forgive me, under the circumstances, for it was a very happy occasion and there was so much to talk about. Know now what that occasion was? Well, here's the story, minus a lot of gruesome details:
>
>   Ray and I just got back from Manilla. Being fortunate enough to be able to fly, it took us a little less than two hours to make it each way. We arrived at Santo Tomas University yesterday morning, about 10 o'clock, and after ten minutes of inquiry and directions we were walking down a path in the Shantytown section of the camp, Ray looking into the row of shanties on one side and I on the other. All of a sudden Ray let out a yell and started running. I tore along behind him and both of us cried out Eleanor's name.
>
>   I'll never forget, as long as I live, the moment when we dashed into their shanty and held Eleanor and Tom to us, nor the moment shortly thereafter when we held the children in our arms. They were out at the time we arrived, getting little cans full of drinking water. As you can well imagine, there was plenty of confusion for quite a while, with all of us talking and asking questions at the same time but eventually we calmed down and each talked and asked our questions in turn.
>
>   The Red Cross had only given them my name and they knew I'd get to see them as quickly as possible, so they were doubly delighted when both Ray and I walked in. The light of supreme happiness which suffused their faces was more than full compensation for all of the discomfort we've had in the Army. It wasn't long before all of the people of shantytown knew that Eleanor's two brothers were there and a lot of them came over to meet us, all of them with so many questions to ask. It wasn't until late in the evening that we really had them to ourselves.
>
>   Thank God, all of them are well and are regaining their weight and strength as quickly as possible. They are still thin and weak, and that just shows how badly off they were when our troops got there. Eleanor, Roger and Donny were easy to recognize, but Tom's face was so thin that we hardly knew him for a moment or two.

Tom weighed 118 lbs, Eleanor 96 lbs, Roger 34 lbs, and Donny just 29 lbs when our troops arrived two weeks ago. Some thoughtful soul had provided a scale for the internees so they can note their improvement, so we had all four of them weigh themselves last night. Tom gained 18 lbs, Eleanor gained 8, Roger gained 6 ½, (that's the first time he's ever weighed over 40 lbs), and Donny gained 7 lbs. Those are notable gains, but they still have a long way to go. They are being fed extremely well with good fattening foods and believe me, Sweets, it was a pleasure to watch them eat heartily.

Practically all that the Japs gave them during the past year were small amounts of watery rice and corn meal or sweet potato tops or bitter mango beans, and in order to exist they were reduced to eating weeds as a sort of substitute for spinach, and banana leaves and roots. It is amazing to me how any of them lived through it. The only thing that saved them was the fact that they just lived from day to day, always with the hope that tomorrow would bring the Americans. Sis said that none of them should have been able to stand it if they had known they would be in that camp for over three years and had to go through what they did.

As it was, they were very near to giving up hopes, even though they knew our troops were on Leyte. On Jan. 1st Eleanor made a calendar for Jan. & Feb;, the first time they had done so, and the last time they expected to be able to, as they felt that they couldn't live beyond the end of February if they weren't rescued by then. Eleanor used to cry every time she looked at the children, so emaciated were they. The last month was the worst period of all.

They were even more fortunate than they realized, for, on Feb. 2nd, our Army HQ intercepted the following orders from Tokyo:

Feb. 4-All male internees between the ages of 15-50 were to be removed from the camp (presumably to be used as hostages at the front). All women and children in the camp were to be liquidated.

Feb. 5-All persons remaining in the camp to be liquidated.

Feb. 6-All Filipinos to be locked in their homes, those homes to be burned.

Feb. 7-The remainder of the city to be razed to the ground as planned.

That's why the 1st Cavalry and 37th Divisions made the mad dash of 25 miles into Manila early during the night of the 3rd. The first troops in surrounded the camp and a tank crashed through the main gate. All of the internees were hoarse the next morning from cheering and shouting, except for those who got such big lumps in their throats, from the realization that they were in safe hands, that they couldn't speak at all. The troops gave the internees every scrap of food they had with them, and then many of them went without food themselves for about 36 hours. Our boys were horrified and enraged at the condition of the children.

I gave Eleanor your address and she will write to you. Ray and I brought lots of pictures with us and a great deal of them were of you. She is so very anxious to meet you, Darling, and wanted to know all about you, where and how we met, etc., how long it has been since we were together last. She too hopes it wouldn't be long before we are reunited again and forever. I told her that you intended to write and she'll be so delighted to hear from you.

Gosh, Darling, wait until you see Roger and Donny. They are such grand children. Their experience has made them far older than their years and they can hold a far more serious conversation than many adults can. Their accounts of what they went through were enough to instill a deep hatred of the Japs within us and at the same time fill us with admiration for their pluck. They stood the long ordeal very well as far as their nerves are concerned. They are not at all bothered or concerned by the sound of the heavy shelling of the not so distant walled city, but some of the other poor kids scream every time a gun goes off or a shell explodes.

I'll have to continue the story in my following letters, Sweets, as it is very late now and I'm tired. I've twice been interrupted, while writing this, by air alerts. The moon is coming out nice and bright now, so we can expect them to come over pretty often whether or not they drop bombs. They didn't drop any tonight, thank goodness. At least we're not all crowded into a comparatively small area as we were in the Moluccas, and I doubt that they'd drop any where we are. We're away from the more important installations here.

When I got back to my tent this evening I found something which made my happiness even more complete—a huge jackpot of six long sweet letters from you, those of Jan 30th and Feb 1st through the 5th. My morale has never been as high as it is tonight, since I had to leave you, and it will only be surpassed upon the day we find ourselves together again. I hope it won't be very long before that glorious day arrives, Sweetheart, because I miss you and need you so very much. It will be wonderful when we are all together for a big family reunion. I hope that yours and my folks can all be there for it.

One thing we did before we left Santo Tomas was to write what we had longed to do, a joint letter to Mom and Dad. They will be delighted to receive that documentary proof of our visit and the realization of Ray's and my personal goal in this war. Believe me, Darling, it was tough to have to leave them! We wished we could stay with them until they were repatriated, and they expect to be within one month, but, as it was, we stayed on a day over our pass. The war couldn't wait for us.

I'll bid you a sweet Goodnight now, Darling, and hop into bed. Ray's been sound asleep for some time now. He's staying with me tonight. I wish he didn't have to go back to the front as it's a tough fight up there. Please say some extra prayers for his safety. I love you so very desperately, Muggins, and I always will. Please take good care of you for me and I'll do the same. I adore you, Mrs. H. You're perfect!

Your devoted husband,
Fred

XXVIII

Three days after the visit of Eleanor's brothers, we celebrated "Old Home Week" once again. My first cousin, Rusty MacDaniels, a former New York State Trooper, now an MP Sergeant with the paratroopers, came looking for us. Like Eleanor's brothers, he had pursued a goal of finding us when, following induction, he was sent to the Pacific theater of war. He had been part of the airborne invasion of the Lingayen Gulf area and once that territory was secured, made his way to Manila and Santo Tomas.

Rusty was a big man, well over six feet and built like a football tackle, so that next to him, Eleanor and I were strikingly undernourished and underfed midgets! He was so shocked by our appearance and that of Roger and Donny, he simply said, "I've gotta go and get something for you which they obviously can't give you here!"

I said, "Rusty, the army is doing all it can and we're getting along just fine. It's going to take a while before we look reasonably human again. Don't worry, man!"

Unconvinced he went off in a hurry back to his unit which must have been fairly close to the northern limits of Manila. Early next morning as I was walking with Roger and Donny in front of the Main Building, here comes Rusty driving a jeep which was loaded down with cartons and bags. He spotted me right away and called over to meet him in the rear of the building at the entrance to Shantytown.

When I reached the Jeep I could see that his load consisted of cartons of six pound tins of luncheon meat, corned beef, margarine, stew, and other foods. The bags contained cigarettes, chocolate and enough provisions of sorts to take care of a small army for at least a week!

Of course we could not use any of the gorgeous assortment although we were deeply indebted for his kind intentions. The camp kitchen was now taking care of us and our needs in good fashion. Rusty, for his part, was quite philosophical over his rejection. He said, "Well, I can't really take this stuff the way back to where it came from, so I'll try and trade it for rum or whiskey which'll do our outfit a lot better than the food!"

I was a bit shocked over the blasé attitude he expressed, but kept my thoughts to myself in appreciation for the good intent of his raid on the supply depot, wherever it might have been! There was consolation in the thought that he and his buddies had been in the thick of battle for some time and were certainly deserving of something akin to "R & R" after securing an important part of the war-torn countryside!

These visits of close family members made us happy and thoughtful as we realized that their efforts, in part, meant our release from imprisonment, and of far greater importance, victory for the United States over its arch enemy, Japan!

Inside Santo Tomas, our desire to leave this war-torn city gave all of us extra strength to assist the army in its task of registration, rehabilitation and return of most of us to continental United States. The proper and equitable handling of repatriation was a monumental job requiring much patience and understanding of the needs of each civilian family and individual. Plans were underway to evacuate families with small children once all of the critically ill and wounded had been cared for. Manila Harbor was still saturated with mines and the San Barnardino Straits through which our rescue vessels would have had to pass was unsafe. Therefore it was decided to fly the evacuees from any available airfield near Santo Tomas, to Leyte, where trans-ocean shipping was now coming and going. Naturally in view of security needs, no word as to the exact time and place of departure would be given until the very moment it would take place.

Out in the countryside which had been freed of enemy troops, President Osmeña was busy rallying his people to the cause of reconstruction. With the promise of Independence a near reality, the people responded, as he said, "With unshaken spirit, fortified by the sympathetic understanding of the American people, Filipinos face now with grim determination their immediate objectives which are, first the prosecution of the struggle against the enemy on Philippine soil, and second the rehabilitation of the country and the relief of thousands of families without shelter and in rags and the threat of starvation which hangs over the rest of the nation!"

We are finally rejoicing at the news that the camp at Los Baños has been liberated! A daring raid by paratroopers from the 11th Airborne Division had landed twenty-five miles behind the Jap lines, right at the area in which the camp was located. They proceeded to destroy the entire Jap garrison of 243 men with the loss of but two paratroopers. The Internees were hurriedly led out of camp to Tugima de Bay, a nearby lake, where amphibious craft whisked them across the lake to the safety of our own lines.

The cooperation of Filipino guerrillas in the area was responsible for a heroic rearguard action as well as the destruction of communication facilities of the Japs. The raid was carried out with clock-like precision and was a timely demonstration of the commando tactics in which our paratroopers had so well been trained.

This widely cheered news was followed by another happy communique announcing that the troops of the 37th Infantry Division and the First Cavalry had overwhelmed the enemy's final position in South Manila and completed the annihilation of the trapped garrison, successfully rescuing the three thousand civilians caught in Intraluros, the Walled City. A large number of Catholic priests and nuns were among those rescued. All had suffered unbelievable indignities and some lost their lives!

The war is over in Manila!

The morning of February 28th, I heard Sergio Osmeña speak. Accompanied by General Douglas MacArthur, he had entered Santo Tomas where we gathered in a solid body of more than three thousand souls, American, British and other nationalities who had spent those many months behind the walls, to greet both and cheer them. Osmeña, an old man, was not a politician and served only as the "caretaker" head-of-state and perhaps for that reason his words will not go down in history. The man spoke of loyalty to the United States, the need for a continuing close working relationship, until the

Commonwealth was completely back on its feet. He spoke of the coming wave of power politics, the fiery rhetoric, the clamor for Independence which was coming. He asked for patience and cooperation of his people and above all for an orderly transition from the chaos of war to the peaceful prosperity which would come with Independence. The wave of nationalism which was already being tied in with the clamor for Independence by August had to be tempered with reality. The war was far from over, except for Manila, and its demands for successful prosecution would suggest that Independence wait perhaps, until July 4th, 1946!

In early March we were treated to a second visit of Eleanor's brothers. Fred recounted an exciting experience he had since his last visit. On one of his "spotting" assignments, he had been fired on from a Jap mortar position, the shell missing his plane on its upward trajectory but blowing off the tail of the Piper Cub on its way down, narrowly missing "filling his fanny with splinters!" To him, it was all in the day's work as he managed to land his craft in a rice paddy not far from his outfit.

As it was apparent that we would soon be on our way, our parting was full of messages from the boys to their mother and dad, and fervent wishes for their continued safety from us. We hated to see them go. Our shanty has been our home for so long a time that we saw no reason to try to improve its durability at this late stage. It had served its purpose well and was the place we would remember as "home" for a long time to come. We were now having visits from old friends who had been my business associates before the war and one day Jose and Luis TeeHanKee, the drug wholesalers who had done so much for us when I was serving as an outside "buyer" for the camp, came in. What a pleasure to know that these valued friends had survived and were now busy reestablishing their business at the old place on Rizal Avenue. We owed them so much! Their gifts of vitamins and other medicines had done much to keep us alive. How could we ever repay them?

Although I had yet to hear from my company, I felt safe in assuring them that all-necessary credit would be granted their business and that we would get supplies to them as fast as I could get word to Detroit, where Parke Davis is located. When they were saying goodbye, perhaps for the last time, I looked around the shanty to see if there was anything, anything at all, of value to me, which I could give them. My eyes lit on my old Martin ukulele, companion of so many years, now cracked a bit and taped up with adhesive to hold it together. I said, "Joe, you remember my playing this uke at one of our pre-war parties. I want you to have it! I can take it with me, but it is all I have to offer you as a token of appreciation for what you did for us!"

He must have understood that it had a good deal of meaning for me for he said, "Luis and I will never forget you and your sweet wife. I promise you that I will not let you down. I'll take lessons and some day I may play like you. Thank you so very much!"

Luis' parting remarks made me think that he could see our future better than I could. "Tom, we hope you will come back and bring your family, but even if you do not come back, we will understand!"

As they walked away, I had a vision of my first visit to the TeeHanKees, where I found the two young men, busily building a pharmaceutical wholesale business in a trade which was dominated by other Cantonese. They were aggressive, honest, industrious in contrast to the Filipinos, who maintained their equity in the trade, despite their natural laziness and indifference, by being "nationals." The American drug houses preferred doing business with wholesalers who could move their products and the TeeHanKees were among the most promising until the war came to the Philippines. I had recommended an extension of their credit in order to help them build inventory and we were rewarded with a sizable increase in their business in the six months before the war. I promised myself that I would do my best to help them when I got back in the saddle.

The exodus has begun! The first group of repatriates, the service nurses who had been captured on Bataan and Corregidor, have been flown out of Manila and, we hope, will promptly be winging their way across the Pacific to a glorious welcome in California! The second group, those seriously ill, are also on their way and we have heard that a third group is being formed from a list of families with small children and we are praying that we will be among those selected. There has been no advance notice given any of the departing groups so far, and we are beginning to bite our fingernails!

Monday March 12, 7:30 p.m, and there is a call over the loud speaker system for Tom Lewis to report to the Administration Office! Although it is already night all of the camp offices are humming with activity. No one rests, especially since the lifting of the blackout regulations has permitted work to continue without interruption, for the benefit of all of the anxious Internees. I ran all the way to the old Main Building where the office was located. The officer-in-charge smiled at my breathlessness and said, "Your number came up! Have your family packed and ready to leave at 7 a.m. tomorrow morning! You had better go right away to the Army Clothing Issue Section with your wife and children to be outfitted for the trip! You will be permitted to take a maximum of fifty pounds of belongings per person."

"Okay! You bet!" and I was off!

From that moment on we moved in a frenzy of preparation. We stood on various lines, children falling asleep on their feet, so that we would receive suitable clothing for the colder season which would greet us in California, where we certainly must be going. Staggering along with other families with young children like us, we managed to be completely outfitted by two o'clock in the morning. There was still time for a short sleep back in the shanty where we made our way. This would be our last night in Shantytown and we had no regrets!

Eleanor and I couldn't sleep and we talked until almost 5 a.m. when it was time to get the boys up and dressed for a bite of breakfast. The convoy of trucks was due to leave camp at 7 a.m. sharp!

Needless to say, everyone who was scheduled to go was ready and waiting in the main plaza at the appointed hour. There had been no time to say good bye to our friends, the

Grimes, the Kneedlers, Duckworths, Sperings, Emily Larson with whom we had shared so much, but we knew in our hearts that somehow, somewhere we would all get together again. Many of those who were still awaiting their transfer orders were on hand to wave and cheer us on our way but in the early darkness before dawn there was sort of an organized confusion which precluded anything more than a perfunctory "See you later!"

The truck convoy rolled in at 7 a.m. sharp and loading began from the list of the repatriates. We had been told nothing of our next destination and we simply placed our faith in God and the Army as the procession of trucks rolled out onto España. Eleanor and I held hands with the boys as the faces of those we were leaving behind rushed by. It was a moment of sadness immediately thrust aside by the excitement of moving away from Santo Tomas and heading for home!

Dawn had broken and in the daylight we had our first glimpse of one another in our new clothes. Eleanor looked cute in her Women's Army Corps uniform, size 3, still a bit large for her re-developing figure. Roger had been dressed in his best remaining shirt and shorts, socks and sneakers as the Red Cross and the army had very little clothing for small children. Someone had given Donny a sweater which was two or three sizes too big for him, but it was warm and covered the rest of his tattered garments so that he looked reasonably respectable. I was comfortable in a G.I. shirt and trousers and hoped that at our first stop after Manila, we would all fare a little better clothing-wise. The other families who were along in the truck were similarly attired and none of us complained in view of our more important travel prospects.

As the trucks made their way through the city, crowds of Filipinos gathered along the streets, waving and wishing us a happy and safe trip. We saw them now, free of the oppressive Japanese occupation, anxious to rebuild their country and start a new life. We were leaving not as conquerors, nor as vanquished, but as citizens like themselves, victims of the cruel war, facing similar problems to theirs. We would work together, our nations, to bring back prosperity and dignity to these people.

As we turned into Quezon Boulevard, we looked back at the disappearing tower of the University of Santo Tomas, our prison camp for the last 1162 days. The very last sight was of the stone cross atop the tower, a symbol of our faith in God who was with us all of the way!

Manila is a sea of devastation. Nowhere is there a building which has not been ravaged. The skyline of this formerly beautiful city is now nothing more than a vista of rubble reminding me of a devastated forest after a terrible fire. Our eyes cannot comprehend what we are seeing and tears come easily as we see one after another of places we knew before the war.

The convoy turns slowly into the largest airfield we have ever seen. As far as the eye can reach, planes are landing and taking off, fighters, bombers, freighters, and transports of every description. Along the edges of the field, we see the wreckage of Japanese planes of all sizes. The "fried egg" which had dominated the skies over Manila for so long a time was now scrambled all over the lot.

The weather looked ominous and sure enough after a wait of about two hours, we were told that our departure would be delayed until the next day! What a break! Our spirits sank and our disappointment was great as we returned to camp for another day.

Our return was greeted with sympathy and we were fortunate indeed to find our shanty intact, mattresses and all. We had given away or sold our remaining furnishings and belongings, but the new owners had not yet taken possession which was our good fortune.

Good use was made of our time back in camp. We were now able to say proper goodbyes to our neighbors and friends, take note of their addresses back in the States and confirm promises to get together again at the first opportunity.

Once again we went through the excitement of an early morning departure and were back at the airfield at 9 a.m.

March 14th for take-off! There were several C-47s, the military version of the D-3, awaiting and we were expeditiously loaded for take-off in a matter of minutes. And then, we were in the air! We learned that our immediate destination was Tacloban on the island of Leyte, the port where General MacArthur had made his first landing in the Philippines!

Our flight consisted of several planes, guarded by P-51 fighters. The weather was clear and once along the way we were given a thrill by the sighting of one Jap plane which took off in the opposite direction as soon as it spotted us. After three hours of riding the bucket seats of the C-47, we sighted Tacloban. As seen from the air, the town was a sea of khaki tents, military equipment, mud and more mud! We landed at a temporary field, were loaded into trucks and taken to a large tent area. We paid scant attention to the discomfort of our surroundings, being exhausted by the day's events. The welcome given us by the military was warm and helpful and we were made to feel at home as far as possible, in a large, hospital-type tent, along with other Santo Tomas families.

Our stay included a thorough check-up by army doctors and a session with army intelligence as the first step in our "processing." More clothing was made available to us by the Red Cross, most of which was outerwear to protect us from the colder temperatures of the West Coast. Again we learned little of our specific departure plans although it was evident that our return across the Pacific would be by ship.

We were besieged by reporters and feature writers who wanted the story of "Santo Tomas." My own diary, scribbled as it was on scraps of paper and held together "by the Grace of God" was sought after by a couple of news service correspondents, but to me it was too precious to let out of my hands, even for a moment. Nevertheless they got their stories. There was little reluctance on the part of those ex-Internees to tell of the suffering and privation of those many months.

An announcement was made that we would be leaving on Friday, March 16th. A modern transport was being readied for our journey and we would soon be on our way across the

Pacific. Naturally we wanted to have a look at the ship and our stroll down to the port revealed a whole new world of military transportation.

For the first time we saw the various landing craft which had been developed in the war. There were Landing Craft Tanks (LCTs), troop carriers with bows which lowered into the beach to disgorge troops and their equipment and numerous other odd-looking craft, each of which had the capability of running their cargo right up on the beaches. Our ship was pointed out to us and we were told that it was a new ship on its maiden run and that after the war it would be converted into a cruise vessel, luxurious and fast. It was manned by the U. S. Coast Guard and temporarily named the U.S.S. *Admiral Capps*.

Next morning we took leave of our new-found military friends and were loaded along with trucks carrying our belongings, into an LCT. He plowed our way across the bay to where the 25,000 ton two-stacker awaited its precious cargo. Her decks were already crowded with troops and other civilians who had already boarded. For the first time in a long while families were broken up, with the men being assigned to quarters in the holds below decks, while women and children were given more private accommodations in quarters set aside for officers, comparatively pleasant and above decks.

My bunk was located in Hold "3," D-deck, forward and not far removed from the bilges, or so it seemed to me. The bunk was a wire-framed affair with a mattress, all folding up to provide walking room when not in use. I decided that I would spend as little time as possible down there during the trip! Eleanor and the boys had a small cabin to themselves and we stowed all of our sparse belongings with her.

There were some three hundred Santo Tomasites on board and my next door bunk-mate was an elderly man who had barely survived the last days of his imprisonment. He was still quite emaciated and needed assistance to get in and out of his bunk. Matters were not helped by the lack of cool air from the air conditioning unit which was supposed to function below decks. It was hot in port!

Once aboard ship we expected to sail momentarily, but for the next four days we sat and suffered. Meals were excellent and the happiest hours of the day, but time really hung heavily and our impatience grew with each passing hour. Finally at 2:00 p.m., Tuesday, March 20th, the bugle sounded over the ship's P.A. system and we knew we were about to get under way when the welcome tune of "California, Here I Come" sounded! Yippee!

The *Admiral Capps* majestically took her place in the long convoy line and we sailed slowly out of Tacloban Harbor, headed for the South Pacific and safety, homeward bound at long last!

TO OUR LIBERATED PASSENGERS

GREETINGS FROM THE CAPTAIN

I would like to take this opportunity to welcome you aboard ship. The officers and crew are happy and consider it a privilege to have you on board for the journey back to the homeland.

It will be our aim to make your voyage as pleasant and safe as possible under wartime travel conditions.

We hope that life aboard ship will be beneficial to you and aid you in recuperating from the hardships and suffering you have endured at the hands of the cruel enemy.

Be assured that everything possible for your health and comfort will be done.

But I am sure you will agree with me that safety is of the first order of importance aboard ship, and for that reason I shall ask you to give full cooperation in carrying out Darken Ship Regulations, emergency drills etc. even if it does mean the sacrifice of small comforts and privileges at the time.

Here is wishing you a safe and pleasant voyage home.

N.S. HAUGEN, Captain USCG
Commanding Officer

***

FROM TROOP HEADQUARTERS

MESS DECK- All troops and civilians eating on the Mess Deck are requested to leave the Mess Deck immediately on completion of their meals in order to expedite the feeding of those troops who have not been fed.

***

TROOP OFFICERS' WARD ROOM - It is requested that passengers be on time for their meal hours. Any complaints or criticisms are welcome and will be received at the Troop Offices.

***

BATTLE FOR IWO JIMA ENDS, BLOODIEST IN MARINE HISTORY; SUPER-FORTS BLAST KOBE

The battle for Iwo Jima, the bloodiest, toughest and costliest in the history of the Marine Corps, is ended. Admiral Nimitz announced that PACIFIC organized resistance THEATER ceased at 6 p.m. Friday, when units of the Third and Fifth Marine divisions overran the last Japanese holdout at Kitano, northern tip of the island. The conquest of Iwo cost almost 20,000 casualties among the Third, Fourth and Fifth divisions. Four thousand, one hundred and eighty-nine Marines lost their lives. A very considerable number of wounded have turned to action, however. The and the Navy paid tribute to the gallant Marines. "It makes one proud to be an American, thinking what those brave men have done," said Lt. Gen. Richardson, commanding Armed Forces in the Pacific. Admiral Nimitz congratulated the Marines and all supporting forces. The conquest of the island is already paying dividends. Thirty super-fortresses have landed on Iwo Jima air strips already. Many of them, out of fuel or damaged after strikes on Japan, would have been forced to make crash landings at sea had Iwo Jima not been available. Twenty-one thousand Japanese died.

***

2500 TONS DROPPED ON KOBE TARGETS

More than 300 super-fortresses, operating from Marianas bases, dropped 2500 tons of incendiary bombs over a 5-mile target area in the heart of Kobe, Japan's fifth largest city, early Friday. It was a record tonnage. The bombs were poured on shipbuilding, ship repair centers and the industrial section of the city. The super-forts swept over the targets at low altitude, dropping bombs in an area

Next morning I turned over in my bunk to reach across and awaken the old gentleman, my neighbor, who was still apparently fast asleep. He didn't respond and with creeping horror, I realized that he wasn't breathing. I jumped out of my bunk and called for a corpsman. He was pronounced dead of natural causes, having passed away some time during the night and arrangements were made to bury him at sea. How sad! Having made it all the way through to his rescue, he died before he could have reached his homeland and his relatives.

As an ex-sailor, I was keenly interested in our course, the location of any landfalls and also the incredibly beautiful night sky of the South Pacific. We crossed the Equator a couple of days out of Tacloban and there was the usual ceremony of initiation in the domain of "Neptunus Rex." Our convoy moved slowly through placid seas, protected on its flanks by several Destroyer Escort ships. They hovered around the edges of the convoy, speeding up stragglers and nervously trying to keep the transports within reasonable bounds. We were assured that there was little danger from attack except for the possibility of Jap submarines based at Yap or the Palaus. These islands lay to the east of us so that we were forced to cross to the southeast, well below the Equator, in order to keep out of their range.

We were heading for the Admiralty Islands where we would take on fuel and supplies and then continue on, northeastward toward Hawaii. At night I was fascinated with the Southern Cross which rose higher and higher as we headed south. In other circumstances, I thought, how romantic! Just Eleanor and me, staring over the rail at the slowly moving indigo sea, while myriad stars shone brightly above in the pitch-black sky, while in reality, she was in her cabin, tending to the boys, tucking them in for the night and usually too tired to do anything but fall into bed! And so it went for the most part.

Our first port of call, Manus in the Admiraltys, was of only casual interest to us since we were not permitted ashore. It was a typical South Sea Island scene, with palm trees swaying in the breeze, but the harbor was a beehive of military activity with tankers and tugs plowing up the peaceful waters. We watched with interest but were glad when the ship finally weighed anchor.

On this leg, we re-crossed the Equator, no longer "Pollywogs" since we were now seasoned members of King Neptune's reign. At night the Southern Cross finally dipped into the sea and before long the stars of the northern hemisphere rose into the firmament. The days crawled by as we slowly sailed north-eastward, alert to the possibility of a sub attack. We were now east of the Jap held bases at Yap and the Palaus but not out of range so that the convoy could be broken up. Our speed was that of the slowest vessel and I had to guess our speed at no more than ten or twelve knots. The crew of the *Admiral Capps* was most attentive to our comfort and one young chap, a Coast Guard Petty Officer named Gig Young told us of his budding career in motion pictures and of his particular interest in the Internees of Santo Tomas, since his fiancee was among those rescued. Since she was on board, their romance bloomed under the starry, tropical skies.

After more days of endless horizons and deep blue sea, we made our first landfall since the Admiralty Islands. The mountaintop which rose as a tiny brown speck in the distance must have been Haleakala, the ten thousand-foot volcano on Maui. As the chain of islands materialized, someone identified Koko Head on Oahu and excitement rose as we were able to pick out Diamond Head, Honolulu and Pearl Harbor in turn. Then came the frustrating news that we would not be permitted to go ashore as the purpose of our call was to pick up government representatives who would sail on with us, to carry out "processing" and expedite our clearance. Members of the Federal Bureau of Investigation, Immigration, and Customs quickly set up shop shortly after we had anchored in outer Pearl Harbor and three hundred ex-Internees got ready to get in line once again.

We remained in port long enough to experience one unexpected thrill. The heroic aircraft carrier *Franklin* was towed into the harbor not far from our anchorage. We were informed that she had been the target of Kamikaze attacks barely surviving despite one-half of its structure being completely gutted and destroyed by bombs. The twisted and now rusting metal was mute testimony to her gallant fight and to the remainder of the crew which had kept her afloat. Our last look at her was underscored by the tattered flag still flying from her ruined stern.

XXIX

We bade our convoy farewell and as the beautiful Hawaiian shoreline faded into the setting sun, our ship under full power sailed away toward home! We were now on the last leg of the long journey and within a day or so we would feel the colder April winds in our faces. Our voyage had been quite smooth and we had been blessed with good weather. We all forgot our impatience in the activities of "processing," and in our case, had no difficulty with any of the officials. After the first day out, Eleanor, the boys and I were left to our own devices.

As we neared the California coast we received several "briefings." We were told that our arrival was "top secret" as a protective measure against an unlikely enemy attack on our presently un-escorted ship. This meant that no relatives or friends could possibly be aware of our arrival other than that we were on our way and somewhere in the broad Pacific. We were told that we would land at San Francisco, news which pleased us greatly, since my many cousins lived in or near there.

April 8th, 1945 dawned with a heavy off-shore mist blotting out the horizon completely. This was our arrival day and everyone who could walk was on deck at the crack of dawn. There was a sudden stopping of the ship's engines and we asked each other, "Now what?" It was 7 a.m. and in the brief delay we made out the small vessel which had come alongside to deliver the pilot. Our forward progress began again and we crowded forward, now more anxious than ever for that first look at the California coast.

As though it were the lifting of the curtain for a pageant, the mist suddenly dissipated and the rugged highlands of the coastal range revealed themselves in the rising sun. The dramatic splendor of the moment made this a scene which will never be forgotten. There was a spontaneous cheer and we turned to each other with hugs, kisses, and handshakes. No one was anxious to leave the ship's rail even though breakfast had not yet been eaten by anyone. Finally the last "Come and get it" was heard and we made a dash for some sustenance which would be gobbled up in the shortest time on record.

The ship's bell tolled 8:00 as we approached the Golden Gate Bridge and Donny, our little one, his eyes riveted on the Presidio asked, "Is that the new concentration camp we're going to?" We explained that it was a military camp where only soldiers lived and that it protected the harbor and had nothing to do with where he was going to spend the next few years of his life. So far, his life had been limited by fences, walls and sentries, so no wonder his lack of understanding of the word "freedom."

A flotilla of small craft approached us from all sides as we slowed to a stop. This gave the lie to our alleged "top secret" arrival. We now hoped to find a familiar face in the welcoming crowd. Some of the vessels tied into the ship and a gangway was lowered to allow some officials and newspaper people to come aboard. There was a band playing on one of the larger boats and some screams of recognition came from both passengers and those in the boats. Obviously this was a welcoming party which had taken some planning as the fire boats were shooting their streams of water into the air to add to the festivities.

The tugs went about their business of positioning themselves to guide *Admiral Capps* into its berth. Meanwhile reporters were interviewing anyone who would stand still long enough to be photographed and talked to. One young man from a radio station had gotten hold of Roger and after a few leading questions was sitting open-mouthed while he listened to a seven-year old's description of prison-camp life. Another reporter had gotten our names, addresses, details of our local relatives and promised that the information would be broad cast at noon. This was one way of assuring ourselves that someone would be aware of our arrival.

We are all in somewhat of a daze, between the excitement of our long-anticipated arrival and the confusion of the interviews. We see the faces of our friends and companions of the voyage, glowing with happiness, everyone just waiting to be told what to do next. It is difficult to think for ones-self and the adjustment to "freedom" will not come easily. We have been told to have our "bags" on deck, and be ready to disembark as the ship bumps against its dock. Again some long lines with everyone eagerly waiting to set foot on our home soil. Then the gangplank is in place and the line starts to move. The four of us in a tight knot step gingerly down the way and are quickly on solid United States' ground! What a glorious moment! I bent down and patted the cement floor as though it was the sole reason for my being there, alive and well.

Eleanor took my arm and said, "I thought you were going to kiss that dirty floor!"

Roger and Donny had yet to realize just what our return would mean to them. They were so young when it all began and their memory of "home and family" was practically non-existent. They shared our excitement just from the aura of happiness that Eleanor and I showed. We knew that unpleasant memories of starvation and regimentation would quickly fade from their minds and we prayed that the last three years would leave no other scars, mental or physical.

Our passage through customs was rapid thanks to the on-board "processing" of those departments. We were assigned to a Red Cross desk for further disposition since we seemed to have no one waiting for us at the pier. Everyone is smiling and warmly greeting us as we pass from one desk to another. A suite at the Hotel Maurice has been made available to us for whatever the length of our stay in San Francisco and that was an unanswered question at this moment. We have been given certificates for clothing since all we have is on our backs. Tickets for meals at the hotel were also provided and we are told that if we are unable to turn up means of transporting ourselves back home, that would be taken care of at a later date. Meanwhile, our fairy godmother was to be the American Red Cross for which we were deeply grateful.

After providing the Red Cross with our vital statistics, we were shown to a bus which was to deliver us and others of our group to our various hotels. As soon as enough of us were aboard, the bus moved out into cheering crowds gathered around the pier and across the Embarcadero.

At 1:00 p.m. we arrived at the Hotel Maurice where we were warmly greeted and conducted to our suite, two bedrooms and two baths, what luxury! The view was breathtaking as we could see the harbor, the Golden Gate Bridge and a sweeping panorama of the city all at the same time. I offered the bellman a tip from my meager supply of dollars and he firmly but politely refused. He said, "Not only is this on the house, but you'll find that the whole city feels the same way. You're the first civilian prisoners to come this way since the war began and we're tickled to have you back, safe and sound!"

I'm certain that we were tired and hungry and showed it, for shortly after he left, there was a knock on the door for another bellman with a cart loaded down with food! He quickly wheeled it in and said, "Compliments of the hotel and all of us. Enjoy it!"

After he had departed, I looked at Eleanor and said, "Let's dig in!"

"I don't feel so well. I think I'm running a temperature. You go ahead and eat." Eleanor appeared to be a bit feverish and despite our appreciation for our first sample of American home cooking, she seemed unable to bring herself to eat.

We had a small supply of aspirin and she agreed to take a couple and to lie down for a rest while we ate. About that time the phone rang and the voice of my cousin Rita Mae said without preamble, "Thank God! You're back, safe and sound! We tracked you through the Red Cross. No one would tell us anything about your arrival until we heard about it over the radio!"

While she recovered her breath, I told her about our arrival, where we were and that Eleanor was not feeling well. She went on to tell me that some reporter had described his interview with our children and so she knew that we were among the repatriates who had arrived this morning.

I asked her to come over to the hotel with her mother early the next day as we would need the rest of today just to rest and gather our thoughts. She and her mother were living across the bay and despite their anxiety to see us, she agreed to wait until tomorrow.

Our noon meal over, I found Eleanor somewhat improved and we decided that a small prayer of thanksgiving should not wait any longer. And so Donny, Roger, Mother and Dad, with arms wrapped around each other said simply, "Thank You God for bringing us all back home safely!" We realized that our present outfits marked us as refugees of some sort or someone's poor relations, so we agreed to take our certificates down to the Emporium and get into something more suitable. We were certainly marked with our bits and pieces of uniforms, and the oversized sweaters and trousers which the boys were sporting. So we went downstairs, found a waiting taxi and were whisked away to Market Street and the beautiful Emporium, one of San Francisco's finest stores. Again payment for the trip was refused and people began to gather and stare at us as we got out of the cab and made our way to the imposing front entrance of the store. We were quite self-conscious and tried our best for a degree of nonchalance as we entered the store, where we were almost immediately welcomed by a well-dressed man, obviously one of the floorwalkers, who introduced himself and said, "You must be among the folks who arrived from the Philippines this morning."

I established our identity, showed him our certificates and he graciously told us that we were most welcome and that it would be a honor to serve us. He motioned to a couple of nearby clerks and said that each of us would be in their charge while we made our selection of all needed wearing apparel. So for the next couple of hours, we were treated royally, selecting a complete outfit from each of the appropriate departments, even enjoying the immediate attention of tailors and seamstresses while we waited our fittings. We discarded our makeshift clothing happily, having no further use for any of it.

As we enjoyed these unaccustomed attentions, we were asked so many questions that we found ourselves literally out of voice when we gathered to take our leave. All of our clerks were now old friends and their solicitations put us in debt to them. When we finally took our leave there was a sincere exchange of promises to write and "keep in touch." At the front door we looked at each other, incredibly dressed in unfamiliar and elegant raiment for the first time in three and a half years, and all four of us wound up, in an orgy of giggles. This was indeed a far cry from the shorts, undershirts and bakias which had been our daily uniform for so long!

Everyone with whom we had come in contact treated us with kindness and a deference due only to heroes. We knew that we were not heroes! We were merely survivors! Our presence was due to the Grace of God, faith in our country and, for our part, also the will to live! We were very tired now and we finally made our way back to the hotel, grateful for its privacy and comfort.

On arrival, I was handed a telegram by the desk clerk. It was a message which read, "Consider yourself on leave of absence without pay until you are able to resume work." That was all! No personal signature. No explanation, no other word to soften the message. As the offices of my company in Detroit had already closed for the day, I had no alternative but to wait until the next day to phone and get some clarification. I was furious and completely dumbfounded since in my opinion, I was still an employee of some importance, their key man in the Philippine market and deserving of more consideration than this unhappy message implied!

We had so much to be thankful for otherwise, that we soon closed our minds to the disturbing message, prepared to have dinner in our suite and get to bed early for a good night's rest. After a most enjoyable meal, thanks to a very considerate room service, the boys were tucked into their beds and fell asleep almost as their heads touched the pillows. Eleanor and I sat down with sighs of contentment and opened the drapes wide in order to fill our eyes with the fairyland out there before us. But not for long! The exciting prospect of our own bed, in our own private bedroom was too much! It had been more than three years since the interruption of our normal married life.

Early next morning I made my collect call to the main office in Detroit. After some delay, my boss's voice came on with a most cordial welcome and no indication that he had any knowledge of yesterday's telegram. Nevertheless, as he talked I could not help thinking that it would have been a simple matter for the company's San Francisco office to have become aware of our arrival and to have given us sufficient assistance so that we would not have found it necessary to become wards of the American Red Cross. When I mentioned our penniless plight he advised me to accept the Red Cross' offer of transportation to Detroit where he assured me that we would be met and given an appropriate welcome. The Red Cross would be reimbursed for the expense of our transportation and the company would see that we were delivered to our home base in New York later. He further assured me that my salary had been accrued and would be available to me in the near future. Since I did not have a strong position from which to argue, I did not mention the telegram nor my reservations concerning their failure to meet us upon our arrival, intending to confront him in person with my feelings. At this point there was nothing further to talk about so I promised that I would keep in touch so that they would know of our exact place and time of arrival in Detroit, probably within the next week.

My cousin and her mother arrived at the hotel in mid-morning and picked us up for a tour of the city and a family reunion across the bay in Oakland. San Francisco is always a delight! We enjoyed every stop and even the boys were never bored. Later on in the afternoon, we visited the Oliveira homestead, and were lovingly greeted by cousins who had been only vague names in exchanges of letters. They were all sincerely interested in our experiences and with this kind of audience each of us rose to the occasion. Even Donny provided some excitement when he told of our diving for a muddy ditch as a phosphorous bomb struck near the seminary and not far from our shanty. He made it clear that he enjoyed the mud bath much more than we did!

After the reunion, Rita Mae insisted that we be their guests at the International Settlement, one of the more prominent restaurants of the city. Somehow the word got around after we were seated at our dinner table, and people came by to say how glad they were for our safe return. We were quite self-conscious and found some difficulty in consuming our delicious meal with all of the interruptions.

Back at the hotel we found a message from the Red Cross advising us that transportation to Detroit had been arranged and we would be leaving day after tomorrow. We again became anxious to be on the way and most of the next day was spent in a walking tour of downtown San Francisco. Our tickets were delivered to the front desk, and we luckily drew a compartment which would comfortably accommodate the four of us. Our train was the "Super Chief" of the Santa Fe Lines and when we were ready to board the next day, we found a long, long train of Pullmans and Day Coaches, loading with men and women in uniform with only a handful of civilians all of whom seemed to be our old friends and companions from Santo Tomas.

Everyone was in high spirits at the prospect of "going home!" The train slowly moved out of the station and we were once again on our way. Our compartment was at the end of a Pullman car and despite finding ourselves a bit crowded, there were no complaints from anyone. As the train moved across the California panorama, the boys busied themselves traipsing up and down the aisles making new friends, especially among the uniformed people. We had no problems with baby-sitting. As a matter of fact, it became evident that the two boys were in danger of being spoiled by the attentions given them.

Next day we pulled in to Gallup, New Mexico for an hour's layover. It was eleven o'clock, the morning of April 11th and as we prepared to get off the train and stretch our legs, someone passed by with the shocking news that President Roosevelt had passed away. Serving his fourth term as our nation's leader, in peace and then in war, everyone took his death as a personal loss. Many of us who had clung to his image as our Chief of State who had promised to redeem the Philippines, and we, consequently, cried bitter tears, knowing that he would not be present at that imminently glorious day when victory in Europe and the Pacific would be achieved. The world would mourn his passing!

We became quite friendly with a couple of ex-Internees whose berths were just outside of our compartment. Almost from the outset of the trip he raved about a steak that he and his wife would eat in Kansas City where we had a forty-five minute stopover about 6 p.m. the second night out. I warned him that there was hardly time to accomplish their desire. He reminded me that for the last three years they both had dreamed about the day when they could get back to Kansas City to enjoy "the world's greatest steak"! He added that the steak house was right across from the Santa Fe station and they neither wanted to miss their train nor the steak dinner, and in this case, the last came first!

They were to go on to Chicago where they had formerly made their home and I kiddingly said that if they were so bent on carrying out their crazy idea, I would personally see that their baggage would be held for them at the Chicago rail terminal.

As we pulled into the Kansas City station, the two of them were standing by the Pullman door, ready to fly! The train finally came to a halt, the door opened and they jumped off, running for the station exit. That was to be the last sight of them ever, for us. I kept my promise and turned over their few bags to the stationmaster from whom, I assume, they made their recovery.

It took each of us, Eleanor, the two boys and me, almost a week to accept the fact that our lives had changed. We were out of the war zone, back in security of our homeland which had changed considerably in four years. Our adjustment would not be easy, but as it turned out, I was given an assignment by my employer which permitted me to recover soundness of mind as well as body.

After emotional reunions with families in New York and New Jersey, we were able to rent a house in Englewood for the summer. Meanwhile we hunted for a permanent home near to Eleanor's folks, and convenient to my new job assignment in New York. Although pressed by my company to return to the Philippines, they were forced to accept our decision not to go back. My return to Manila would have meant leaving Eleanor and the boys at home for a year or more. This I would not do and as for their coming with me, the chaotic post-war conditions would have made their life unsafe and uncomfortable, to say the least. We had gone through so much together that any lengthy separation was unthinkable to either of us, or to the boys who would soon be going to school.

My job now was to serve as a Pharmaceutical Representative responsible for all business with New York City and State hospitals. My contacts would be the Medical Directors, Administrators and Purchasing Agents of these institutions as well as the corresponding people in the municipal and state government offices. I was also given a plum in being assigned the territory of Bermuda for two six week periods per year, once in the spring and once in the fall. As a final gesture, I was also asked to cover Newfoundland for a similar six-week period in the summer, all of this ostensibly to help me get my health back. As it turned out, these special considerations by the Company paid off with substantial sales growth in each of the markets, and a complete recovery for me.

XXX

As time went on, we met groups of former Internees, either for social get-togethers or for the more serious business of putting together a united effort to obtain some government assistance to take care of our many medical expenses and losses of homes and possessions. After the conclusion of the war, there were Japanese assets to be tapped for this purpose and we sought help from the Congress with eventual moderate success.

Each of us had our own individual concept of what we had experienced. I felt that the three years both took away and gave us something to remember for the rest of our lives. First of all, we were not heroes, we were survivors. The real heroes were the folks back home who went through the agonies of not knowing what had happened to us. My father was one of these. He died not ever knowing!

The heroism of our rescue would never be forgotten by us, nor would the faithful and mostly fruitless efforts made by our camp committees before the Japanese Commandant and his staff. These were real heroes, especially the latter who risked their lives everytime they spoke up for us. Those who died because of their insistence on our rights and those who died for no reason, Carroll Grinnell, A. F. Duggleby and Cliff Larson, for instance, and many more whose names will be remembered by their fellow Internees forever, these are real heroes!

It is over now. Can it happen again? Will there be hostages taken to guarantee payment of ransom? Will our citizens be captured by the enemy in some foreign land and if so, how shall we react? Does the difference between a "Police Action" and a full-scale war dictate the promptness with which civilian Americans, living in a foreign country, may be rescued? Treaties between nations as well as International Law need to speak to the mutual protection of the world's civilian population living in foreign lands. Let us hope that at some future time, they will!

Roger and Donny and their 'toys'— empty shell cases. Roger is wearing his uncle's helmet liner. March 9, 1945

The note on the back of this photo reads, "Santo Tomas Univ, Manila. Tom is showing off his new-found strength from Army chow.   3/9/45"

Donny Lewis at the shanty, 1945

The happy ending to an amazing story of survival as a family.

"Protective Custody"

Viewing the destruction of downtown Manila.

Internment camp at Santo Tomas University, Manila
(US military photo)
Main Building and surrounding shanties, constructed by internees.

Roger and Don, 2013
Always friends!

Tom and Eleanor, 1981

In the center is the matriarch Eleanor, at ninety, surrounded by her family. Don and Roger are front right.

www.ingramcontent.com/pod-product-compliance
Lightning Source LLC
Chambersburg PA
CBHW070531010526
44118CB00012B/1102